✳

DR GAVIN PEEBLES was Senior Research Fellow in the Contemporary China Centre of the Research School of Pacific Studies at the Australian National University when he wrote this book. He graduated with degrees in Economics from the University College of Wales, Aberystwyth and the University of Liverpool. His main teaching and research interests lie in the field of Comparative Economic Studies and he has published articles on aspects of the economies of China, the Soviet Union, Eastern Europe and Hong Kong. He is the author of *Hong Kong's Economy: An Introductory Macroeconomic Analysis* and *Money in the People's Republic of China: A Comparative Perspective* (Allen & Unwin, 1991).

✳

A Short History
of Socialist Money

By the same author

Money in the People's Republic of China
A Comparative Perspective

A Short History of Socialist Money

Gavin Peebles

ALLEN & UNWIN
Sydney London Boston

© Gavin Peebles, 1991

First published in 1991
Allen & Unwin Pty Ltd
8 Napier Street, North Sydney, NSW 2059

UK distribution:
University College London Press
Gower Street, London WC1E 6BT

US distribution:
Paul and Company Publishing Consortium Inc.
141 Old Bedford Road, Concord MA 01742

National Library of Australia
Cataloguing-in-Publication entry:

Peebles, Gavin, 1947–
    A short history of socialist money.

    Bibliography.
    Includes index.
    ISBN 1 86373 113 X.
    ISBN 1 86373 071 0 (pbk.).

    1. Money. 2. Socialism. I. Title.

332.4

Set in 10.5/11.5 Sabon by Adtype Graphics Pty Ltd, Sydney
Printed by SRM Production Services Sdn Bhd, Malaysia

Contents

Figures and tables

Acknowledgements

This book was written between October 1990 and January 1991 while I was Senior Research Fellow in the Contemporary China Centre of the Research School of Pacific Studies of the Australian National University. I am grateful to the university for so employing me and to the centre for obtaining a few sources that were not available to me otherwise. Konstantin Probst informed me of the location of some relevant books, Dr C.H. Chai (of the University of Hong Kong) had earlier told me of Davis and Charemza (1989b), and ANU colleagues Christopher Buckley, You Ji, Keith Forster and Cao Yong drew my attention to Tsang (1990), Chen Wenlin (1989), Delfs and Bowring (1990), and Nordhaus (1990) and Wolf (1990), respectively, for which I am grateful. Also, Keith Forster again for bringing *Zhongguo Shangye Waijing Tongj Ziliao 1952–1988* (1990) to my attention. As for other sources, I was blessed with many instances of serendipity when a useful reference seemed to appear all of its own accord just when I needed it.

I am grateful to my colleagues at the centre for the occasional help with a language problem when I was working full time on China and to Irina Somina for helping me to repolish my rusty spoken Russian and giving me her impressions of economic conditions in the Soviet Union.

I would also like to thank Prentice Hall for permission to reproduce a figure from Haitani (1986: 139) as Figure 3.1 in this book and Cambridge University Press to quote a long passage from *The Cambridge Encyclopedia of Russia and the Soviet Union* in chapter 5 below.

Finally, and for the second time in three months, I would like to thank Anna Beth McCormack and Bernadette Foley for their work editing and redesigning my typescript.

Gavin Peebles
Canberra
22 January, 1991

Introduction and author's notes

I decided to write this book in October 1990. I had just finished a larger work on the monetary history of the People's Republic of China (Peebles, 1991). Events in China had become less interesting than they had been a few years earlier, whereas events in the Soviet Union and Eastern Europe were becoming much more interesting for an economist interested in monetary developments. These events constituted financial crisis and almost complete financial collapse. A few months before this I had been reading recent articles that failed to predict these events and did in fact suggest that these events would be very unlikely. I had read an article of March 1990 arguing that there was no problem of sustained repressed inflation in East Germany. At the same time we knew that East Germany was to abandon its own currency and adopt that of West Germany. It was hard to reconcile this with the arguments of that article. I recalled that there had been an earlier article arguing that East Germany did in fact suffer from the most serious repressed inflation of the Eastern European planned economies. A few months earlier I had read an article published at the end of 1989 that argued that East Germany was in the vanguard of financial development among the planned economies. The author did not mean that East Germany would be the first to abandon its currency; the author meant that, as it was the richest, it was understandable that people held so much money and that monetary holdings in the other planned economies would increase without there being any problems. This article also argued that monetary holdings in the Soviet Union were not excessive, an interpretation I accepted in 1981. Now we are reading Soviet economists complaining about the excessive amounts of money in the economy and debating radical policies to deal with the problem. I recalled an article published some ten years ago, but written earlier, that predicted imminent financial crisis in the Soviet Union, and others that argued that there was no such crisis or even potential for crisis. The recent articles, which presumably had more information available for their analysis, were wrong; the earlier ones (or some of them) were correct well before the actual events. This seemed an interesting contrast to investigate.

These experiences prompted me to write this book as a brief summary of the monetary experiences of several planned economies and as a survey of the different interpretations of these events by Western economists. By the term 'socialist money' I simply mean the monetary system found in planned economies that profess or professed to be socialist or communist. The countries studied are the Soviet Union, East Germany, Czechoslovakia, Poland, Hungary and the People's Republic of China. Until the mid or late 1980s they all operated similar economic and monetary systems. The European countries are abandoning these systems; China has largely retained them. Explaining this contrast is an interesting issue in itself.

The approach I have taken is simple and empirical. I have not presented detailed discussions of the nature of monetary and financial institutions in these economies. Such an approach would not tell us how they behave and would give the false impression of greater control over monetary aggregates than in fact there has been. Anyway, the old institutions are well covered in the literature but they are being abandoned. We do not yet know the exact nature of the systems that will emerge in their place in the different countries. I have tried to discuss these monetary events within a consistent framework that reveals the essentials of the problem. I have ignored one extreme found in certain writings on these matters of 'gathering a handful of time series from a data bank and running them through a regression meat grinder' (Cagan, 1989: 118). Meat grinders are useful if you like that sort of thing, but the results do depend on how the grinders work and are used and on what is put into them. That approach would ignore the institutional differences between these economies and the Western economies where the theories (if any) that underlie the regression analysis were developed. I have also ignored the methodology of detailed institutional description with the odd piece of data thrown in to illustrate a point. In such, still common, studies very often these figures are put in no context at all and so the reader gains no understanding of their significance. I have tried to present the evidence clearly and in an understandable manner in a consistent framework intended to highlight the differences between socialist money and that found in market economies.

I hope that this book will be of interest to the general reader interested in any of the following topics: monetary history, the planned economies, comparative economic systems or all three, as I am. It is a small book on a huge topic. To be able to write it I have had to rely on many larger books on narrower topics and many journal articles from a number of countries. Specialists will see the influences on it. I have not identified the writers who I think were responsible for introducing the useful terms that have become standard in this field (for example, active and passive money, the monobank, internal exports, monetary overhang), and I hope that their inventors will forgive me for this omission. Although this book is intended for a general audience, I hope that specialists in the various fields surveyed here will appreciate the consistent comparative perspective I have used.

There has been a controversial debate about the interpretation of the macroeconomic and monetary developments in these countries. This book represents one side of this debate. Events have judged between the different viewpoints. I could thus be accused of cynically benefiting from hindsight in selecting one viewpoint and not applying alternate theories. This is correct, but this is the way we make progress; we abandon the approaches and resulting theories that are refuted and provisionally accept those that are not. Unfortunately, the correct predictions of crisis were not based on any easily usable theory, whereas the methodology that suggested that there was a low probability of crisis is, to a great extent, standard Western economic theory.

The structure of the book is as follows.

Chapter 1 presents a brief overview of the nature of disagreement about money in planned economies, indicates the problems we have in analysing such events and clarifies the terms used in the analysis.

Chapter 2 discusses the origins of the currencies of the six countries under study. It also discusses the theory underlying their value and contrasts this theory with that of a market economy. It then discusses various features of these economies, their implications for any monetary study, the nature of their recent inflation and growth experiences, and the relationship between them.

Chapter 3 discusses the nature of the monetary institutions in these economies. It shows an example of the money supply process in detail. Unfortunately, the data are not sufficient to show this empirically for all the countries under study. It discusses the main instruments of monetary planning, the principles underlying recent banking reforms, controllability of the money supply during reform and the implications of private foreign-exchange markets and transactions for the analysis.

Chapter 4 attempts to explain the patterns of monetary growth and price increases presented in chapter 2. It does this by simplifying the actual institutional structure of these economies into a model of the narrow money-supply process and of how planners can try to influence the rate of narrow monetary growth. It draws implications for the likely degree of monetary growth in different countries of these reactions and identifies the actual relationship between money incomes, money stock, liquidity and the price level. It examines this issue empirically for all the countries under study for the last eighteen or so years.

Chapter 5 reviews the different methodologies and different conclusions of various writers on the subject of chronic excess demand in the planned economies during the last ten years.

Chapter 6 offers some conclusions of the whole short study.

The principal abbreviations I have used are:

USSR	Union of Soviet Socialist Republics (the Soviet Union)
GDR	German Democratic Republic (East Germany). Although ceasing to exist in October 1990, it was a separate country for the period under study here. Other European countries are referred to by their usual English short form (for example Poland) and not by their full official titles.
PRC	People's Republic of China (China)
CPE	centrally planned economy
STE	Soviet-type economy
S	Saving (a flow)
SD	Savings deposits (a stock)
HM	Household money (savings deposits plus cash)
M	Money (various definitions at different places)
APS	Average propensity to save
MPS	Marginal propensity to save
P	Prices or a price index
Q	Real output
Y	Nominal income ($= PQ$)
V	Income velocity of circulation of money ($= Y/M$)
GNP	Gross national product
GDP	Gross domestic product

NMP	Net material product (socialist national income)
MIP	money incomes of the population
PPI	Purchasing power imbalance
ln	natural logarithm
DW	Durbin–Watson statistic
d.f.	degrees of freedom
R^2	coefficient of determination
r	Pearson product–moment coefficient of correlation
n.a.	not available
IMF	International Monetary Fund
MNBPB	*Moscow Narodny Bank Press Bulletin*
ESE	*Economic Survey of Europe in 1989-1990*
ZGTJNJ89	*Zhongguo Tongji Nianjian 1989* (Statistical Yearbook of China 1989); similarly for the 1990 edition.

Other abbreviations will be explained in the text.

All statistical calculations were performed using Microfit (formerly Datafit) (Oxford Electronic Publishing, 1987).

I have used *Hanyu pinyin* to transliterate all Chinese names and titles of publications except where a name is given in another form or where a Chinese word has entered English in a different transliteration. I have transliterated Russian using no standard method but hope that it is clear and intelligible. Diacritics have not been universally used, especially when they fall on consonants.

One billion is 1000 million (a US billion), equivalent to a milliard in European languages and *shi yi* in Chinese.

1 Subject and method

This book is a short, empirical, institutional and theoretical review of the monetary developments in six planned economies. The countries studied here are the Soviet Union, East Germany, Czechoslovakia, Poland, Hungary and the People's Republic of China. These countries shared similar economic institutions, and their monetary systems were the same in all essentials, copied from that created in the Soviet Union by the beginning of the 1930s. The main focus of this book will be on events since the Second World War, and only passing reference will be made to events in the Soviet Union before this time.

1.1 AIMS OF THIS STUDY

This book unashamedly makes use of hindsight in examining the monetary histories of these countries and making judgements on the relevance of various approaches to these countries. As we have seen, the late 1980s brought major changes to the monetary affairs of some of these countries. It is fair to say that East Germany and the Soviet Union have experienced financial crises. Poland has experienced hyperinflation, and Hungary has seen rising inflation rates towards the end of the 1980s. China saw high, unstable and rising open inflation rates during the 1980s, popular protest against inflation and corruption being made possible by some of the economic reforms.

By financial crisis I mean the situation when the government adopts policies to abandon the traditional Soviet monetary system or when it adopts policies that the traditional system was designed to make unnecessary. This definition clearly applies to East Germany; it abandoned its own currency in July 1990 without foreign invasion or conquest and is now part of a united Germany. In the Soviet Union plans have been announced to abandon the administrative command system and reform to some sort of a market economy. Massive retail price rises are being contemplated, and even a confiscatory monetary reform is being discussed. The last stage of the two-year four-stage Gorbachev reform programme adopted in October 1990 (more moderate than Boris Yeltsin's 500-day programme) calls for full convertibility of the rouble. Individual Soviet republics demanded the right to issue their own currencies. This is not likely to be allowed to happen but it shows the extent of dissatisfaction with the centralised Soviet system and its monobank.[1] Such currency independence may come about spontaneously of course. Poland and Czechoslovakia plan to make their currencies convertible from the beginning of 1991 and Hungary sometime later. All these proposed reforms are not part of the traditional system, and that is why we can say that there is a financial crisis in the Soviet Union. The European countries have dealt with financial crisis by abandoning the system that caused it. China dealt with its problems by retaining the modified system that emerged during the 1980s. It used restrictive monetary and fiscal policies in late 1988 and retreated from its ambitious reform programme slightly and reimposed price control in 1989 and after.

There is a large and growing controversial body of literature concerning the monetary and macroeconomic analysis of planned economies, which goes back more than ten years. Much of the debate is about the correct methodology to use in studying the monetary developments in these countries. Two schools of thought have been distinguished, and disagreement between them concerning method and conclusions has been marked. Chapter 5 will discuss this literature in detail, concentrating on the different methodologies used by different contributors. Here it is necessary to review the main points of contention.

It has traditionally been the view that planned economies suffer from chronic excess demand for consumer goods. The Hungarian economist János Kornai has described them as shortage economies (Kornai, 1980) and this term is frequently used (Birman, 1983; Hare, 1989; Brabant, 1990). The argument is that excess demand on the consumer goods market is not the result of mistaken policies or supply shocks that cause temporary shortages but is the result of the very nature of the planning system itself. The consequences of this excess demand are said to be plain to see in such phenomena as the commonly observed queues for goods, the necessity of bribing shop staff for scarce goods (buying them 'on the left', *navelo*, in the Soviet Union or going 'to the back door', *zou houmen*, in China), and rapidly growing household savings deposits and cash holdings. These growing holdings of financial assets are seen as forced savings as people just cannot find the goods they wish to buy.

This chronic–excess–demand hypothesis is offered as an explanation of these phenomena and underlies early predictions of financial crisis in the Soviet Union. In a number of neglected works (Birman, 1980a; 1980b; 1981; 1983) and in Birman and Clarke (1985) Igor Birman predicted that there would be a financial crisis in the Soviet Union. His prediction can be dated as having been first made in at least 1977, so the events he predicted cannot just be explained as the result of later developments under Mikhail Gorbachev when things did get worse. Birman and Clarke (1985) have listed four possible options for dealing with the monetary problems identified by Birman. At least three of them (radical reforms in agriculture, reducing defence spending and increasing retail prices) are part of current Soviet policy. Many of the writers who have claimed that planned economies suffer from permanent excess demand (for example, Kornai, 1980; Birman, 1980a; Winiecki, 1988; Podkaminer, 1989— although they may not all agree on the applicability of the concept of aggregate excess demand) are citizens or former citizens of the countries under study and have been very critical of the attitudes and methods used by Western students of these economies.

The chronic–excess–demand hypothesis has never been formulated very rigorously, and this has made it unpalatable to a number of Western economists. From the late 1970s Richard Portes and a number colleagues have argued that the chronic–excess–demand hypothesis cannot be verified simply by listing various pieces of anecdotal evidence but must be subjected to rigorous econometric testing. This they have done in a number of papers (see Portes and Winter 1980; and the papers cited in Portes, 1989). Their approach has been to use disequilibrium macroeconometrics to test the chronic–excess–demand hypothesis for four Eastern European countries (East Germany, Czechoslovakia, Hungary and Poland). Their comparative work has never gone beyond 1975, although they have continued with work on Poland. They have never studied the Soviet Union, although Portes (1982) has expressed his views that the excess demand hypothesis cannot be accepted for that country. Their conclusion is that there is no evidence that excess demand was the dominant regime in these four countries and that, although there is more evidence of excess demand in East Germany, this evidence is not sufficiently pervasive to invalidate the rejection of the chronic–excess–demand hypotheses (Portes and Winter, 1980). Van der Lijn

(1990) has applied their methodology to East Germany up until 1985 and rejected the hypothesis of excess demand, ascribing shortages and the other excess demand phenomena to temporary excess demands and irrational relative prices.

In the useful terms of Wanless (1985), their claims can be called the new view of planned economy macroeconomics. Its implication is that what excess demands exist are only temporary phenomena caused by supply shocks or mistakes in planning. A policy conclusion is that no radical changes are required to the planning or monetary systems. The phenomena that are said to support the chronic-excess–demand hypothesis are explained on different grounds. For example, queues are said to be the consequences of the underdeveloped retail-trade network and the selling practices of these countries. Portes (1982: 363; 1989: 43), among others, drawing on studies of retailing in these countries, uses this argument. Queues are also said to be the result of irrational relative prices and shortages of specific goods, not the result of overall macroeconomic excess demand. The policy implication is to adjust relative prices and improve the planning of consumer goods supplies. The rapidly growing volume of household financial assets is said to be the natural result of rising incomes, and such assets are interpreted as household desired holdings (Farrell, 1989).

In contrast, the traditional view that there is chronic excess demand has differed on the nature of the policies required to deal with permanent shortages. Davis and Charemza (1989a: 18) summarise them as the requirement that the budget constraints of firms should be tightened, their behaviour should be changed and planners should not plan using physical norms. There are two possible ways of doing these things. One method would be to retain the existing system of socialist ownership and introduce market discipline into various sectors of the economy, with more reliance on incentives, more market co-ordination with uncontrolled prices, the creation of competition for the state sector and the establishment of an independent banking system. To some extent this is what the Chinese economic reforms tried to do. The other, more extreme solution is to abandon the existing system of ownership and command planning entirely. This is what East Germany has done in its own unique way and may be the solution to be achieved by the Soviet Union. Kornai (1990) now advocates 'shifting from a socialist system' for Hungary. The other countries all have plans for rapid privatisation of their economies.

Birman (1983; 1988) became more apocalyptic in his prediction of

Soviet economic and political collapse. He cites evidence of the falling effectiveness of monetary incentives and falling productivity, and he predicted collapse, which he defines as falling output, and the fall of the communist regime. Although his later works do not discuss the monetary factors underlying these phenomena, it is clear that they are seen as the main cause of all these problems relating to productivity and growth.

The controversy between the traditional school (mainly represented by Kornai's theory of the shortage economy but better represented by Birman's neglected works) and the new view of Portes and associates has produced two summary discussions of the state of disagreement about late 1988. The volume edited by Davis and Charemza (1989b) contains some very interesting papers relating to these issues. It allows Portes (1989) to reply to his critics and state exactly what he and his colleagues were claiming. Brabant (1990) also surveys this debate. Unfortunately, the timing of these publications meant that they could not ask simple questions such as: Why did East Germany give up its own currency? Why is the Soviet Union contemplating massive price rises and creating a convertible currency? Who predicted these events, who did not, and how? These are the important issues.

This book will not be a test of the various theories. I do not think that this is necessary, as events have judged between them. The chronic–excess–demand hypothesis, and particularly Birman's prediction of financial crisis in the Soviet Union that was based on it, have been shown to be correct. This book could thus be accused of cynically benefiting from hindsight to simplify the issue and of ignoring the detailed aspects of certain contributions to the debate. It does benefit in this way, but, of course, that is exactly how we progress. Refuted theories are discarded, and those not discarded are retained and applied until they are succeeded by better theories. Only hindsight can be used to judge between theories. I think that events have shown that the chronic–excess–demand hypothesis was a better description of the situation in the planned economies than anything else available. Therefore the approach of this book will be to explain events in these countries in the framework of this hypothesis, using its presuppositions and only parenthetically pointing out alternate explanations.

The approach taken is simple and mainly empirical. It is tempting to say that the approach is to let the facts speak for themselves and that, with the benefit of hindsight they are eloquent in support of the chronic–excess–demand hypothesis. I have not just done this, however, but have tried to explain events using this approach, showing why there were different degrees of monetary growth in these countries, what the money supply process was, why prices increased, the nature of the relationship between money and prices, the value basis of these currencies and so on. I conclude with a review of the different approaches to these questions and of the debate, or sometimes lack of it, between different writers.[2]

This is not an issue made irrelevant by the abandonment of the traditional monetary system in East Germany and the Soviet Union. It has general methodological lessons for all types of comparative economic studies, in particular for the choice of approach for writing the monetary history of these countries, and for studying current events in such countries as China.

1.2 PROBLEMS IN THE ANALYSIS

There are many well-known difficulties in writing about the planned economies.

The first problem relates to the reliability of data. Many writers who uphold the traditional view regard official statistics from the planned economies as distorted, misleading or faked. Birman (1988) warns against accepting them. Vanous argues that output statistics for the Soviet Union were deliberately distorted under Gorbachev, but Treml (1989) points out his methodological errors in arriving at this conclusion. Winiecki (1988: 51) argues that East Germany's statistics are the most distorted; he really means that they were subject to 'doctoring' (p. 68, fn. 16). Planned economy data must be used with caution. Even Birman (1980a; 1980b; 1981) had to rely on official data for his basic information, but his interpretation of them is very different from that of such organisations as the Central Intelligence Agency (CIA) of the United States. Li Chengrui (1984) defends the general reliability of Chinese data, even for the ten years of chaos of the Cultural Revolution—data that suddenly appeared in the early 1980s after twenty years of no statistical yearbooks. This body of data has been enthusiastically accepted by econometricians studying China (Chow, 1987; Portes and Santorum, 1987; Santorum, 1989; Feltenstein and Farhadian, 1987; Feltenstein, Lebow and van Wijnbergen, 1990; Chen Chien-Hsun 1989). The general trends shown by the data are probably correct. Cautious acceptance seems to be the general attitude.

Certain statistical studies of the planned economies report statistical results to the third or even fourth decimal place. This presents a false and unscientific impression of precision that the underlying data just cannot support. I was tempted to report all statistics to the nearest whole number, but this is perhaps going a bit too far.

Data availability is another problem. For the Soviet Union, for example, no official data of currency in circulation are available for the postwar period, and it is said that such data have been a state secret since 1936 (Wiles, 1982: 145; Grossman, 1989: 32, fn. 4). This means that Portes and Winter could not apply their model to the Soviet Union. For the Soviet Union I have had to rely on Western estimates of currency and some recent Soviet statements. China publishes a whole table of money incomes and expenditures of the population as well as the consolidated balance sheet of the banking system. Both data sets allow us to see why household money holdings change, viewed from two different perspectives. Although there are problems with the household income and expenditure data (Peebles, 1987), they are extremely useful and have been used here. Currency and savings deposit data are available for China right back to 1952. During the 1980s China, Poland and Hungary joined the International Monetary Fund (IMF), and this organisation published their monetary data for recent years using IMF definitions. I have not made much use of these data in the subsequent statistical work but have referred to them for comparisons with other sources. One exception is that I have used the series 'currency outside banks' for Hungary for a few years as these data are not available to me from other sources. For other countries I have relied on Western compilations taken from official national statistical yearbooks.

The differences in the availability of data have meant that studies of different countries have taken very different forms. This can be illustrated by the nature of studies of China and the Soviet Union. In the early 1980s China began to publish long runs of macroeconomic data in its statistical yearbooks and, soon after this, monetary data. These data have been used in several econometric studies referred to above and by Chinese econometricians. Yet at the same time there are recent works that continue to use the old-style China-studies approach that developed when there were no statistical publications. This approach required the combing of newspapers, radio broadcasts and so on to produce valuable quantitative information, which was often only an isolated figure for a single year. Even today one can read studies of the 1980s that ignore the statistical yearbooks and quote isolated figures the significance of which the reader is supposed to appreciate. Combing Chinese newspapers is no longer necessary to provide relevant data. On the other hand, when studying the Soviet Union, where much macroeconomic and especially monetary data are not published, reference to isolated statements in newspapers and journals is necessary. There have been some interesting recent statements on such things as the extent of monetary growth, the size of household money incomes and the stock of currency in newspaper reports on the economy and in speeches. These concepts are basic to this book but were hardly ever talked of in the Soviet Union when Soviet writers denied that there was any problem of inflation. It is necessary to use such figures. Given the lack of data for the Soviet Union, there are hardly any statistical studies of macroeconomic developments by Western scholars for this country—certainly, not to the extent to which they are appearing for China. Monetary and macroeconomic work on the Soviet Union is, from necessity, very patchy.

The upholders of the chronic–excess–demand hypothesis have another feature in common: many of them consistently deny the applicability of Western economic concepts and models to planned economies. Birman (1980b), for example, rejects the relevance of such a simple concept as the marginal propensity to save for understanding saving behaviour in the Soviet Union. Birman and Clarke (1985: 498) even argue that it can bear no interpretation there. Winiecki (1988: 55) argues that aggregate demand cannot be measured in economies with soft budget constraints and so no attempt should be made to measure the unmeasurable. I do not accept this argument. The soft budget constraint just means that over time firms will be subsidised, so they can continue paying wages out of unrepayable bank loans. Households, however, have finite stocks of monetary assets and fixed current incomes, so their budget constraints are hard in any time period. How we identify their demand for consumer goods, and what determines it, is a problem. Many authors talk about planners' responses to excess demand on the consumer goods market. To examine these views we need an operational measure of excess demand and an assumption about planners' preferences and how they are likely and able to react to excess demand. A simple operational measure of excess demand will be proposed in chapter 4 and used to identify planners' responses and their consequences for monetary growth.

As Farrell (1989: 2) points out, financial crises occur in market economies because of a shortage of money in the face of an increased search for liquidity. The repressed inflation hypothesis argues that the crises in the planned economies were caused by an excess of money, not a shortage. This again pinpoints a difference between planned economies and the market economy system. It brings to my mind the words of Stalin (1930), who, when listing the differences between the features of the market economies (unemployment, supply exceeding demand, and so on), kept repeating 'With us, it's the other way around'.[3] This is a good maxim for studying the planned economies and a warning that Western concepts and tools of analysis are not easily applied there.

Another feature of the upholders of the chronic–excess–demand hypothesis is their belief in the ability of planned economies to sustain disequilibrium in a number of markets for many years. For example, Kornai authored the book *Anti-Equilibrium* (1971: especially ch. 19). Birman obviously felt that whatever piecemeal reforms were adopted were insufficient to deal with the disequilibrium excess–demand problem; he therefore predicted a series of major reforms to the system, before he started predicting collapse. The view that disequilibrium can persist is uncongenial to many Western economists. The traditional view was that there is excess demand in the producer goods sector because of the imposition of taut plans on enterprises, the investment hunger of enterprises and the hoarding of materials without punishment for cost overruns. Despite the existence of institutions and planning tools supposed to prevent these factors from creating excess monetary demand for consumer goods, it was argued, such excess demand does occur. Because there is extensive retail price control, this excess demand is reflected in undesired household monetary accumulation (forced saving). This in turn diminishes the marginal value of money, creating disincentives for labour, an implication of which is the necessity of applying strict labour discipline in these economies (Howard, 1979a). Kornai (1980; 1982) describes these disequilibria phenomena, and Winiecki (1988), for example, elaborates them.

If one believes in pervasive disequilibrium and sees phenomena of it every day, one does not worry too much about whether these assumptions accord with orthodox Western economic theory based on maximising behaviour and static equilibrium solutions. The traditional view did not have much of a theoretical foundation and was largely based on induction from close observation of the planned economies and from listening to what people in them said and complained about. Kornai's (1982) theoretical model, an attempt to model regularities of behaviour in planned economies, does not have money in it. Winiecki (1985; 1988) criticises the lack of reality in the models of the new view, whose believers used more rigorous models of household and planners' behaviour derived from models of market economies under rationing. The traditional view, with the exception of Kornai, generally tended to present the evidence and an interpretation of it and did not worry too much about the lack of generally accepted theory. Critics of the excess–demand hypothesis tried to fit the evidence into standard Western models (for example, Pickersgill, 1976 and 1980b, estimating household savings functions; and Farrell, 1989, using an implicit money demand function).

1.3 A CLARIFICATION OF TERMS

One consequence of the differences between market and planned economy institutions is that familiar terms are often used in different ways in the study of the planned economies. Take the word 'inflation' as an example. A standard economics-textbook definition is that 'Inflation occurs when the general level of prices and costs is rising', and this is shown by 'a rise in the general level of prices as measured by price indexes which are averages of consumer or producer prices' (Samuelson and Nordhaus, 1985: 226). Believers in chronic–excess demand revert to earlier, less specific definitions of inflation. These are seen as relevant to the planned economies as there is widespread price control, which, together with the possible doctoring of consumer price indexes, means that in many countries published price indexes either do not rise at all (East Germany) or show rises less than those actually occurring (Soviet Union).

Arnold (1937: 231–2) provides an early definition of inflation applicable to the young Soviet Union:

> *Inflation is a condition caused by an increase of purchasing power that is not accompanied by a corresponding increase in the volume of goods and services available for distribution.* It may be added further that this condition may result in a fall of the value of money and, therefore in a higher price level in countries in which 'free' prices prevail, and in a shortage of commodities (which may or may not be accompanied by a fall of the value of money) in countries in which prices are controlled or regulated. (Italics in original)

Modern writers preserve the same distinction when writing of planned economies. A Soviet writer, Grinberg (1990), refers to the quantitative and qualitative aspects of inflation in socialist countries. The first occurs when the price level does rise and money loses its value. The second occurs when there are constant prices but shortages due to excess demand, and money again loses its value as the goods just cannot be obtained.

Various terms are used to describe the true nature of inflation, sometimes with different meanings by different authors, but generally the following terms are used. 'Repressed inflation' or 'suppressed inflation' is said to exist when there is excess effective demand at the existing level of prices.[4] This situation refers to flow variables and is sometimes called 'excess demand' or the 'inflationary gap'. It is described as 'repressed' inflation because price control represses any movements in prices. 'Hidden inflation' is sometimes used to describe the fact that although prices have actually risen they are not reflected in the official price index. For example, a new 'better' product with a higher price may be introduced and cause the old one to disappear, but in fact the new product is essentially the same and the statisticians do not take its higher price into account or regard it as offset by the claimed quality improvement. 'Open inflation' is used to describe the extent of price rises actually reflected in the official index. Nuti (1986: 38; 1989: 102) tries to standardise terms, disliking the term 'repressed inflation' as applied to the situation of excess demand. As a once-and-for-all price increase could eliminate the inflationary gap, he does not think that the term 'inflation' should be applied; it should only be implied if the inflationary gap is increasing over time. Cassel (1990) refers to inflation in planned economies as 'cash balance inflation', stressing that it shows up not as increases in price indexes (open inflation) but as increases in unwanted cash balances (forced saving). The relationship between excess demand, open inflation and cash balance inflation will be investigated empirically in chapter 4.

Another common term is 'monetary overhang', which refers to the holding of excess liquid assets and to a stock variable. The image is that of a large money stock hanging over a limited supply of consumer goods or consumer stocks in the state retail-trade network. It is controversial as how to measure monetary holdings in real terms in planned economies. It is felt that deflating by a price index is insufficient to show changes in the real money stock. For reasons advanced in chapter 2, money stocks are often related to retail sales flows in order to assess real monetary holdings.

To clarify usage I define certain terms as follows. 'Saving' is the activity of retaining part of current income instead of consuming it all. It is a flow variable. 'Savings', with a terminal 's', is the stock of financial wealth accumulated by means of saving. In the countries under study this is the stock of financial assets held by households. It consists of cash, savings deposits at savings banks or other state banks, plus household holdings of government bonds. As this latter item is quantitatively unimportant, the empirical measure of financial savings used below is currency plus savings deposits.

Note that this measure can also be defined as the narrow measure of the money supply, and either currency itself or currency plus savings deposits has often been taken as the definition of money in empirical studies of these economies. This money stock changes because households do not consume all their income. In macroeconomic models of market economies it is often assumed that there can be an exogenous change in the money supply without prior changes in other variables such as personal incomes; then the impact of the change in the money stock on the economy is analysed. There is no point in applying such models to the planned economies, as there could not be such a change in the narrow money supply without there first being a change in the relationship between household nominal incomes and expenditures or a change in household saving. In planned economies household incomes, saving and narrow monetary change are connected in a way they cannot be in a market economy.

The 'average propensity to save' is the proportion of income not consumed, S/Y. It is sometimes referred to as the 'saving(s) ratio'. Saving includes the accumulation of savings deposits and cash. As she had no data of household currency accumulation in the Soviet Union for her empirical estimates of savings functions, Pickersgill (1976; 1980b) defines saving as the accumulation of only savings deposits. She says that this is a problem of the time series data, not the analysis (Pickersgill, 1980a: 583). Other studies have taken this narrow concept of saving in planned economies, identifying saving with the accumulation of savings deposits only (for example, Feltenstein, Lebow and van Wijnbergen, 1990, for China). However, saving should be identified as the accumulation of both cash and savings deposits and it is reasonable to assume that the proportions allocated to either asset reflect household choices even though the total amount of income remaining unspent may not.

The 'marginal propensity to save' is the increase in saving (the flow) divided by the increase in income, $\Delta S/\Delta Y$. Some writers present a completely erroneous measure, $S/\Delta Y$, and say that it shows the proportion of the increase in income that is not being spent. If this measure is shown to be increasing in a planned economy it is then said that this shows increasing difficulty for consumers in spending their increasing incomes. In fact it shows nothing of the sort and is a meaningless indicator. Consider what the measure would be if people saved 5 per cent of their income, income was 100 monetary units and income rose only 1 unit. This measure would be $5.05/1$ and cannot be interpreted as showing that 505 per cent of the increase in income could not be spent. People would continue to save even if their incomes did not rise at all. As Asselain (1981: 21–2) points out, when criticising such computations for the Soviet Union by a J. Pavleski, they are not the marginal propensity to save and are meaningless. Keizer (1971: 81) presents similarly meaningless calculations for the Soviet Union. They have crept into China studies (Li and Xia, 1986: 97) and have even been translated into English with no qualifications (Xia and Li, 1987: 95–6). However, the fact that such mistakes can be easily spotted in the works of some who uphold the excess demand hypothesis does not invalidate other evidence they may cite.

I use the word 'data' to mean published quantitative information about economic variables and reserve the word 'statistics' for measures that describe aspects of the data. These measures may be ratios calculated from the data, average annual growth rates or such test statistics as the t-statistic of a coefficient in a regression result.

Socialist countries use the material product approach to calculating their national output. They followed the views of Adam Smith, Karl Marx and other classical economists on the distinction between productive labour (which produces material objects) and non-productive labour (which produces non-material services). This means that their national income data include only the output of the branches of material production and omit many non-material services. Transporting coal is a material service that would therefore be included, whereas such important services as education, health care, defence and administration, which do not produce material goods directly, are therefore omitted from the national income accounts. The national income data used here are official data of net material product (*NMP*). Occasional reference is made to a Western estimate of gross national product (*GNP*). The Chinese national-income concept used here is *guomin shouru* (national income). This is a net concept in which double counting of production has been avoided; it is not a gross measure of output that has double (or more) counting of the gross value of some outputs. Some students of China cite these gross output data. Caution is advised in interpreting them.

It is now generally felt that in all the six countries under study official output statistics have overestimated actual growth rates, as they are deflated by an unsuitable deflator that underestimates the true extent of inflation (Winiecki, 1985: 47–8). Winiecki is thus claiming that Nove's 'law of equal cheating' is not applicable after all. This 'law' was the observation that, if levels of output are overestimated consistently by the same proportion, published growth rates will still be an accurate reflection of the true rate of growth of the lower level of output.

13

On the other hand, official output statistics in our six countries often underestimate the extent of private economic activity in the 'second economy', so actual past growth rates could be lower than indicated but incomes and the standard of living could be higher. Jackson (1990: 35–6) warns us that the current figures showing rapidly falling output in Eastern Europe (especially in industrial production) overstate the true extent of the fall in total output and the standard of living. Official output would have been overstated for 1989 (the base for his calculations), and no allowance is made for the rapid growth in private activity during the reform of these economies.

The next chapter discusses the origins of the currencies of our six countries, general features of their economies, and their recent inflation and output growth experiences.

2 The currencies: nature and quantities

This chapter examines the general characteristics of the currencies of the countries under study (Soviet Union, East Germany, Czechoslovakia, Poland, Hungary, People's Republic of China), describes the main institutional features and economic events in these countries, and concludes with an assessment of the changes in the quantity of money in each country. No theory is advanced to explain the features described here.

2.1 THE CURRENCIES: MONETARY REFORMS AND CURRENCY REVALUATIONS

This sections identifies the currencies under study and the timing of monetary reforms and currency revaluations.

A currency reform occurs when the government replaces one currency with another, often retaining the name of the former currency. In a monetary reform the rate of exchange between the old and new currencies is such that the real stock of money is reduced. In other words, a monetary reform confiscates part of the existing stock of currency held by people. These monetary reforms occurred in the countries under study after the Second World War and were mainly aimed at confiscating what were thought of as the illegitimately earned gains of wartime speculators and traders. The reforms in the Eastern European economies were modelled on that of the Soviet Union of December 1947. A monetary reform not only reveals who has cash and confiscates it but also can be used to reduce household real money holdings below their desired levels. This may make cash holders more prepared to convert leisure into income and income into monetary assets than formerly. In plain words, they may work harder for the government and save more of their income than other-wise. This effectively transfers resources to the government, which it can then use for industrialization and socialist construction. This could be a motive for a disequilibrating confiscatory monetary reform in a socialist economy (Pesek, 1958). The motive when a communist party first takes over is very often to confiscate the liquid wealth of the bourgeoisie and the petty peasantry, as Lenin put it in 1918 (Arnold, 1937: 104).

A currency revaluation occurs when all nominal values such as wages and prices are changed. There is no attempt at confiscating any part of the monetary stock. A currency revaluation just entails delet-ing a given number of zeros from existing nominal units and issuing new notes in smaller denominations. Currency revaluations tend to occur after periods of severe inflation when nominal units have become unmanageably large. They occur in market economies as well as planned economies, particularly in Latin America. Although a currency revaluation does not try to confiscate existing currency holdings, it is very likely that real currency holdings will be observed to fall in such circumstances. Very often savings deposits are con-verted automatically, and so, on hearing of an imminent revaluation, people are likely to switch from cash to savings deposits to save them the trouble of tendering old notes for new. In addition, part of the old currency stock will have been lost or damaged and so will not be available for replacement. A fall in currency holdings at the time of a currency revaluation is not a sign that currency is being confiscated. In relation to currency revaluations the term 'heavy' is often applied to the new unit, as it buys more goods. The heavy franc introduced in France in 1960 is a good example of a currency revaluation in a market economy.

USSR

The currency of the Soviet Union is the *rouble*, divided into 100 *kopieki* (kopecks). A relatively stable currency was established through the monetary reform of 1924 during the period of the New Economic Policy, and the modern Soviet currency dates back to this period. This book will not discuss the prewar monetary history of the Soviet Union; readers are referred to Arnold (1937) and Griffith-Jones (1981: chs 2 and 3). Monetary reform was announced on 14 December 1947 with no forewarning, with a conversion rate for cash of 1 new rouble for 10 old. Savings deposits up to 3000 roubles were exchanged at par, and different confiscatory rates were applied to larger savings-deposit holdings (Garvy, 1977: 40; Kuschpèta, 1978:

42). This reform discriminated against peasants, who tended to hold cash, not savings deposits (Nove, 1982: 310). On the basis of a statement in a Soviet book, Harrison (1986: 205) states that by 22 December 1947 the stock of currency in circulation was 7.4 per cent of what it had been on 14 December. A currency revaluation, announced on 5 May 1960, took place on 1 January 1961 when 10 old roubles were replaced by 1 new 'heavy' rouble. All nominal units were changed in the same proportion (Bornstein, 1961).

GDR

The currency of East Germany was the *Mark,* usually known as the *Ostmark* (Eastern Mark); it was divided into 100 *Pfennig.* A 'Soviet-sponsored' monetary reform took place in June 1948 at the same time as one in West Germany. Only small amounts of savings deposits were converted at par (Gurley, 1953: 87–8). Gurley regards this not as a Soviet-type monetary reform but as a monetary reform required as the result of postwar inflation. Ames (1954) does not include it in a discussion of 'Soviet bloc currency conversions'. The reform predates the GDR, which was not established until 7 October 1949. In October 1957 there was a currency conversion. The East German Ostmark ceased to exist after 1 July 1990 when it was replaced by the D-mark. The basic conversion rate for all assets denominated in Ostmarks was 2 to 1, but an average of 4000 Ostmarks[1] could be converted at par. Different amounts could be converted at par according to the age of the owner, with those under 15 being allowed to exchange 2000 Ostmarks and those over 60 allowed 6000 Ostmarks. It was estimated that this made the average conversion rate for all personal savings and cash 1.5 to 1 and contributed to an overall 14 per cent increase in West Germany's broad money supply (*M3*) ('The new Germany' *The Economist* 30 June 1990, p. 10).

Czechoslovakia

The Czechoslovakian currency is the *koruna,* divided into 100 *haleru.* The National Front government instituted a currency and savings deposits freeze and price increases in November 1945. There was a confiscatory monetary reform under the communist government enacted in a law of 30 May 1953. The rate of exchange was 5 old *koruny* to 1 new. Small cash amounts were converted at this rate but larger amounts and savings deposits at different rates. It has been estimated that the reform amounted approximately to a 75 per cent confiscation (Pesek, 1958: 381; Michal, 1960: 140).

Poland

The Polish currency is the *zloty*, divided into 100 *grosze*. A new zloty became the country's sole legal tender after the reform of 28 February 1945 and replaced old zloty, German marks and Soviet roubles circulating in Poland. It was estimated at the time that about 60 per cent of the outstanding amount of money was confiscated (Podolski, 1973: 81). There was a second confiscatory monetary reform announced on 28 October 1950. Wages and prices were changed in the proportion of 100 to 3 and cash at the rate of 100 old zloty for 1 new. Small savings deposits were exchanged at the rate of 100 old zloty to 3 new, but large deposits were heavily penalised (Alton, 1955: 256–7; Podolski, 1973: 109–110).

Hungary

The Hungarian currency, the *forint*, divided into 100 *fillér*, was created on 1 August 1946 and replaced 400 000 quadrillion (1 million to the power four[2]) *pengo*, a necessity caused by the hyperinflation Hungary had suffered (Berend and Ranki, 1974: 190–1). This reform took place under a coalition government and before the communist takeover.

PRC

The name of the Chinese currency is the *Renminbi* (People's currency). Its basic unit is the *yuan*, divided into 10 *jiao* (*mao* in spoken modern Chinese), each jiao being divided into 10 *fen* and each fen into 10 *li*. The *Renminbi* was first issued on 1 December 1948 when the People's Bank of China was established. It thus predates the People's Republic of China. It replaced many currencies issued by communist and peasant banks as well as Kuomintang currencies issued at a wide variety of rates over the period 1945–48. Qian and Guo (1985: 238) provide a family tree showing the main conversions and the creation of the unified currency.

On 1 March 1955 there was a currency revaluation when a new *Renminbi* (with the same units) was introduced at a rate of 10 000 old *yuan* to 1 new. All nominal units were reduced at the same rate. This revaluation was necessary as the Kuomintang hyperinflation had left the basic unit valueless and as people had already grown accustomed to reckoning in units of 10 000 (which is a basic unit in Chinese counting). It also allowed the replacement of old notes with new better designed notes using languages other than those based on Chinese characters (such as Tibetan) and the provision of a set of differentiated notes for the illiterate to understand (Liu, 1980: 61–2).

In 1980 an alternative currency intended for the use of tourists and business visitors was introduced. This is the foreign exchange certificate (*waihui quan*), which has the same units as the *Renminbi* (see Sherer, 1981: 160, for the regulations governing its use). Many hotels and shops will accept only this currency, which must be obtained with foreign exchange. They will charge higher prices if *Renminbi* notes are offered. Special visitors and those who receive stipends in *Renminbi* are often issued with a card (known as the *baika*, 'white card', or more formally *youdaizheng*, literally, 'special treatment card'); by producing this card, holders can pay in *Renminbi*. This adds another complication to what should be the simple business of using the country's legal tender.

The above currencies have enough common features for them to be analysed usefully together using the same approach. Their basic common features are as follows. First, the monetary systems and basic nature of economic institutions of both the Eastern European countries and China were adopted from those of the Soviet Union. Although there are differences between their economies in certain important respects—such as the extent of collectivisation of agriculture, the extent of private trade allowed and the degree to which mandatory quantitative planning is used in the state sector—they are sufficiently similar to be regarded as planned or, better, administered economies. The monetary system they have adopted evolved over a period of at least a decade in the Soviet Union and was established by the beginning of the 1930s.

In the early years of Bolshevik rule and before the Soviet Union was established, civil war continued. The period from 1918 to 1921 has come to be known as the period of War Communism; different historians accord different stress to the 'war' and the 'communist' aspects of this description. Resources and labour were mobilised along military lines, and economic incentives, or what we would understand as economic behaviour, played a minor role in economic life. Wages were very often distributed in kind at the workplace. In this environment some writers thought that it would be possible to leap into full communism and abolish money entirely. Bukharin, in his early writings and before he embraced the New Economic Policy and the use of material incentives (Cohen, 1980: 160–212), argued that money would be abolished at some unspecified time. In their *ABC of Communism* of 1919, Bukharin and Preobrazhensky argued that eventually under communism there would be no money but that under socialism money was still needed for its role in the commodity economy. However, the first steps along the road to abolishing money were already being taken (Bukharin and Preobrazhensky, 1966: 333–5; Nove and Nuti, 1972: 34–40). From 1919 onwards many policies were seen as laying the foundation for the establishment of a moneyless economy (Arnold, 1937: 104–7). The main changes achieving this were seen as the use of moneyless accounting within the state production sector, the use of budget books and the payment of workers in kind. The budget books would be used to record each worker's contribution and hence show 'how much the State owes him'. (Bukharin and Preobrazhensky, 1966: 335).

When Bolshevik writers looked to Marx's writing for guidance they found very little of use in guiding the operation of a communist economy. It is now widely recognised that Marx's views on the role of money in a post-capitalist economy were naive in the extreme (Nove, 1983: 50–4; Buck, 1987: 181–3). He assumed away the problem of scarcity and hence the necessity of economic decision making and viewed money as a mere labour token. Workers would receive their labour token and present it at the state warehouses, where there would be an adequate supply of everything they might want. There would be no need for monetary circulation in such a society.[3] Interestingly, Frederick Engels (1884) criticised such views when they were proposed by Rodbertus as they ignored the problem of how to decide what quantities of all the different possible products should be produced. Although some prominent Bolsheviks such as Bukharin talked about the abolition of money, Lenin was more cautious, although he had in 1918 laid down the procedures required and the reasons for a confiscatory monetary reform (Arnold, 1937: 104).

The legacy of Marx's views and of those of the early Bolsheviks is that money in socialist economies is regarded as mainly a labour token.[4] It was called a 'Soviet token' (*sovznak*) in the early 1920s to differentiate it from pre-revolutionary money (Nove, 1982: 91–2). It is issued by the state in return for labour services or products (agricultural crops mainly) produced by their labour. In return the state supplies goods.

Of course, this labour token concept of money does not necessarily mean that wages and prices paid for procurements have to be based on the labour theory of value. The state is responsible for planning investment. This requires a deduction from the wage bill to finance investment and other non-consumption expenditures. Marx (1875) discussed this necessity in a communist society in a famous passage in the 'Critique of the Gotha programme'. Talking of the individual labourer, he writes that:

He receives a certificate from society that he has furnished such and such an amount of labour (after deducting his labour for the common funds) and with this certificate he draws from the social stock of means of consumption as much as costs the same amount of labour. The same amount of labour which he has given to society in one form he receives back in another.

Earlier in this passage he writes that: 'Accordingly, the individual producer receives back from society—after deductions have been made—exactly what he gives to it' (Marx, 1875: 323).

I wonder how many people have been struck by the complete illogicality of this proposition. If deductions are made, how can anyone receive back 'exactly what he gives'? This is no mere linguistic quibble. In 1990 a Soviet commentator was arguing for the privatisation of property without payment on the grounds that since the 1920s a large part of workers' wages had been deducted in order for the state to accumulate property and that this property should now be returned to its rightful owners (Zaichenko, 1990: 14). This view of socialist money and debt will be discussed further in section 6.1. Of course, no society can consume all it produces, but there are different ways of converting saving into accumulation.

By 1922 War Communism had been replaced by the New Economic Policy, which relied on private trade, material incentives, uncontrolled prices, taxes paid in money not in kind, and joint ventures with foreign firms to develop the economy. The commanding heights of the economy and the banking system remained nationalised, however. A stable currency was a necessity for such an economic policy to work. During the early 1920s there was hyperinflation, but a new currency was launched with the monetary reform of 1924 (Arnold, 1937: 200–43). The New Economic Policy was not to last, however. By the end of the 1920s Stalin was in control. Agriculture was collectivised, full scale nationalisation was achieved and command planning became the dominant method of economic co-ordination. On the basis of this Stalinist command system the Soviet Union began to industrialise through a series of five-year plans. Despite there being theoretical control over such things as the money supply, wages and prices, there was a considerable degree of open inflation over the period 1928–37 and retail rationing.

The Stalinist command system was imposed on the countries of Eastern Europe being studied here and was to an extent adopted in the People's Republic of China, although attitudes to the system there have fluctuated widely. Yugoslavia, not studied here, was the first country to abandon this system, and it tried to establish a form of market socialism based on self-management. Hungary and Czechoslovakia were in the vanguard of economic reform in an attempt to introduce market socialism with similar economic reforms (Batt, 1988). Czechoslovakian reforms that started in the early 1960s (Teichova, 1988: 149–59) were stopped in August 1968 by the invasion of Warsaw pact troops. After this Czechoslovakia became a fairly orthodox, centrally administered, planned economy.

In the 1950s China followed a policy of industrialisation based on planning with Soviet assistance. Mao Zedong's reckless policies in and after 1958, known as the Great Leap Forward, led to the withdrawal of Soviet support, the collapse of the economy, especially of agricultural output, and widespread famine during the period 1960–62. The Cultural Revolution period of roughly 1966–76 saw very little use of material incentives, and there was a virtual price and wage freeze during this period. During the early 1970s there were proposals to abolish money and rely on the direct distribution of goods to the population (Goodstadt, 1976). Output grew, but the standard of living hardly increased. At the end of 1978 a whole new development strategy was adopted, based on material incentives and higher prices for agricultural procurements. Agriculture was effectively decollectivised by about 1983, and compulsory agricultural procurements were abandoned by 1985. Ambitious reforms of the industrial sector were attempted from 1984, and there was a thorough reform of the banking and financial system. High rates of growth accompanied by high and increasing rates of open inflation in the 1980s led to the introduction of a severe austerity policy in late 1988. The inflation was slowed but growth rates fell dramatically. There was a virtual stop to the reform programme, especially price reform, as the leadership became preoccupied with the political consequences of the demonstrations and killings in Peking and other cities in the period from April to June 1989.

Until the dramatic events of 1989 and 1990 in East Germany and the Soviet Union the continuous implementation of economic reforms within the planned systems (Adam, 1989) had not changed the essence of the command system. State ownership continued to predominate, directive planning was used in the state industrial sector (except in Hungary), private trade was marginal, price controls were extensive, enterprises were given government subsidies, international trade was a virtual state monopoly, and the banking system was nationalised and never really independent.

The basic implication of these institutions of the Stalinist command system for monetary relations are as follows. Virtually all industry is state owned, so the state can set wages and try to control them closely. This is seemingly the perfect institutional arrangement for implementing anti-inflationary wages policy and has attracted the comment of Western economists (Wiles, 1973; Portes, 1977). Production within the state sector does not use money to ensure the production and transfer of a product. This is supposedly done by planners' commands. The state owns most of the retail trade network and so can set retail prices, seemingly the ideal conditions for implementing an anti-inflationary pricing policy. The state is responsible for supplying the bulk of retail goods to the population. This feature of the economy plays the dominant role in determining the value basis of these currencies. Although there were times when it was attempted to abolish the role of money in these economies (under War Communism in the Soviet Union and during the Cultural Revolution in China), money plays an important role in the household sector of these economies. Wages and transfer payments are received in money form. The government usually pays for agricultural produce it procures, although this is often done using compulsory quotas and state-determined prices. Retail supplies are bought using money, although at many times a ration card or ticket has to accompany the money to obtain certain goods at fixed prices. This reduces the currency of money. People accumulate financial assets in the form of cash, savings deposits and sometimes government bonds.

Despite the earlier virulent anti-money attitudes of extremists in China, the reforms of the 1980s saw money playing an important role in providing material incentives for workers in the form of bonuses. Unlike in the other economies, where there is more of a labour market and industrial workers are mobile between enterprises, material incentives are not really used in China to allocate labour. These incentives are used, however, to stimulate workers within the enterprises to which they have been allocated administratively. During the 1980s monetary rewards and punishments were being used in Chinese schools to discipline pupils. In East Germany monetary rewards are used in an attempt to stimulate population growth. Newly married young couples receive an interest–free credit to buy furniture and other things. As children are born, successively larger parts of the loan are written off (Buck, 1987: 200–1).

The above two examples show that incentives are expressed in the form of the offer of money. Money is used in buying and selling, as a means of distributing income and as a form of savings. At first glance money seems to perform roughly the same functions in the planned economies as in the market economies. To some extent this is true but there are many qualifying factors that change the nature of money in these economies. The three functions of money in an economy are to act as a measure of value, to be a means of exchange and to be a store of value. Let us take them in turn.

Although money does not play a major role in determining the structure of production and the allocation of resources in planned economies, prices are used, even in the state industrial sector. This is necessary to make possible the aggregation of the large variety of both inputs and outputs into total monetary units. This allows economic accounting to be applied to enterprises in order to assess and compare their efficiency. The original Soviet principle of economic accounting (*khozraschet*) has been adopted in all the other economies under study, including China. It may appear that money prices are being used to measure values, but this is not necessary true, as the prices applied to many products do not reflect their values at all. If there is a shortage of a commodity, its price has been set below the market price and its value is higher than the official price.

Money appears to act as means of exchange. For the population this is generally true. People receive money wages, which they exchange for retail goods from either the state sector or each other. However, because of shortages money alone does not act as the means of exchange. When rationing is imposed money itself is not sufficient to obtain retail supplies as another piece of government-issued paper (the ration card or ticket) has to be tendered. Money is supposed to be the instrument through which the private sector is induced to supply the state sector with inputs. On many occasions this is not achieved solely by the payment of money. As there are shortages of retail goods the government very often agrees to supply the goods themselves, or the goods at special prices, instead of money. In effect the government barters its retail supplies for required inputs. For example, this occurred in China at certain times during the 1980s when the government tried to procure agricultural produce. Instead of a simple monetary payment, the government had to offer desired consumer goods and required inputs such as fertilisers to induce farmers to 'sell' agricultural produce. At many times campaigns of voluntary labour are used to get workers and students to gather the harvest and supply labour inputs for other tasks. These examples show that at times money is not the sole means of exchange in these countries.

In certain countries the official state fiat currency is not the sole means of exchange, as there are special state shops that sell goods for foreign currencies or for special certificates issued to citizens in exchange for foreign currencies or as payments. Although they are intended for tourists and diplomats, certain such shops are a source of scarce and imported goods for the local population, who thus wish to obtain foreign currencies for use there. In East Germany there were the Intershops (taking foreign currencies) and *Genex* shops (taking certificates), in the Soviet Union the *Beryoska* shops, in Czechoslovakia the *Tuzex* shops and in China the Friendship (*Youyi*) stores. In Hungary, residents who received gifts of foreign currencies in the form of cheques from abroad (cash receipts were illegal) had to exchange them at the State Bank for domestic currency. Only Hungarian residents who earned foreign currency (through royalties, for example) could keep foreign currency accounts and draw on them to make purchases at Intertourist shops. Customers at Intertourist and Consumtourist shops (for diplomats) in Hungary had to show that they were foreigners. This means that foreign currencies could not be used for purchases there by Hungarians. This obviously reduced the demand for foreign currencies in Hungary and also had an effect on the black-market exchange rate (to be discussed in section 3.9). Such sales of domestic goods to residents for foreign exchange have been called 'internal exports' and are a further means by which the government obtains foreign currencies from its own citizens. Sometimes foreign currencies could be used directly for purchases, and sometimes they had to be surrendered for certificates denominated in domestic currencies that could be used only at these shops.[5] This was the case in the Soviet Union when Soviet citizens would be issued with alternative money denominated in roubles known simply as certificates (*sertificat*) for use in hard currency stores. They would obtain such certificates in return for surrendering foreign currency earnings (from royalties, for example) at the government's exchange rate, or as a result of privilege or as a direct payment for special work. For example, soldiers who fought in Afghanistan in the 1980s received such certificates. As far as I know this provision for Soviet citizens to use such shops was abolished under Gorbachev as a result of popular protest. Aslund (1989: 135) reports that such a decision was taken to abolish them from 1 July 1988. In Vanous's view, of all the countries studied here, 'the Polish government has long recognized the advantage of two-currency economy—one where goods are sold for zlotys at low prices and are frequently not available and one where goods are sold for dollars in hard-currency stores and are readily available' (1980: 34).

Cash is the principal means of transactions in these countries as personal cheques are virtually unknown. To various degrees in different countries, transfers from private savings deposits can be arranged to settle regular payments such as rent and utility charges. Despite this, cash is the main means of transacting. People are almost universally paid in cash at their workplace. The payments frequency differs across countries and may have an effect on the average amount of cash we observe being held. For example, workers in the Soviet Union are paid twice a month, whereas in China wage payments are made once a month. In China, agricultural procurements are mainly concentrated in the summer and in the second half of the year, and this has an effect on the seasonality of the amount of currency in circulation, which rises towards the end of the year (Peebles, 1991: ch. 6).

Although many incomes are received in monetary form, income in kind is common in these countries. This can take the form of farmers' own consumption of food produced on their private plots, or meals or even goods provided at the workplace. I know of no method to assess the extent to which income in kind plays a role in the different countries under study and how it may affect the need for currency. It is significant in rural China. In the 1970s, money income was hardly ever seen in the Chinese countryside (Oi, 1989: 37–8). Hungary is often viewed as one of the most market–oriented economies of those under study. In 1960, 23.3 per cent of all labour income was received in kind, and in 1980 the proportion was 10.8 per cent (*Vengerskaya Narodnaya Respublika*, (1983) p. 337). Monetisation of the Chinese economy during the 1980s undoubtedly increased the demand for currency for transactions purposes.

Money also seems to act as store of value. People can hold currency and obtain savings deposits in exchange for cash. Generally, there have been no other domestic financial assets for people to hold, with the exception of government bonds, which very often were forced on the population, and, during economic reform, shares in some co-operative or joint stock companies in China and elsewhere. There are restrictions on the ownership of foreign securities and bank balances. The former are only legal in Czechoslovakia and the latter only in Poland,[6] to the best of my knowledge, but this is a fluid field of law and radical reforms and convertible currencies may make this more possible. Cowitt (1986: 21) describes the monetary laws about ownership and exchange of currencies in Czechoslovakia, East Germany, Poland and the Soviet Union as constituting 'dictatorial control' and those in Hungary and China as being 'strict'.

Savings deposits have always provided a positive but low nominal rate of interest. For example, in the Soviet Union the rate of interest on private savings deposits has been 2 or 3 per cent, depending on the length of the deposit. These rates remained unchanged for many years. One of the first presidential decrees of Mikhail Gorbachev in October 1990, after he had been given power to rule by decree, was to increase interest rates. In addition, lottery bonds provided a chance to win money. In China the rate of interest on personal demand deposits was 0.18 per cent per month from January 1959 to April 1980 (Byrd, 1983: 154). Through the 1980s in China, a time of volatile and rising inflation rates, there were several increases in interest rates, until in September 1988, as part of a stringent anti-inflationary policy, certain personal deposits were indexed to the rate of inflation. Ownership, confidentiality and freedom of use of savings deposits have been protected by the various Chinese constitutions.

The controversy is whether the observed volumes of monetary assets are the desired ones. The fact that people are observed to store value in monetary form does not mean that all the money holdings are performing this function. If there are excessive amounts of monetary assets, people may have wished to store value in other forms such as housing, cars or equities, which are generally not available to them. These factors all tend to restrict and qualify the functions of money in planned economies.

All the currencies discussed above are, like most currencies, pure fiat currencies. They are issued by fiat of the government and have no backing in the form of gold, other precious metals, foreign exchange or government bonds. As Shubik (1987: 317) defines it, a fiat money is 'a form of credit where the issuing party is the state and the recourse of an individual creditor is negligible against the state, but by the law of the state the fiat money must be accepted in payment to extinguish other debts'.

Governments in market economies have a monopoly of currency issue and usually ensure that their intrinsically worthless paper money has value by two means: the government agrees to accept it in payment of taxes and decrees that it is legal tender and must be accepted to discharge any private debt. Of course, the bulk of the money stock in market economies is not currency but bank deposits created by what are usually privately owned profit-seeking commercial banks. These bank deposits are backed by fiat money, however. In the countries studied here these two options used in market economies to give the fiat currency value do not really exist. The burden of direct income tax on individuals is very low or non-existent, and there has been minimal reliance on private economic activity, with the consequence that private debts between individuals or between individuals and financial institutions are very limited.

Any government decree that makes the use or tendering of fiat currency legally necessary imbues it with value. The following is an example of a possible method that was *not* used in the People's Republic of China. In the early 1950s the communist government in China lost a chance to imbue its currency with value during the land reform programme of that time. Agriculture was still privately managed and commercial marketing was used; collectivisation had not yet been imposed. During the redistribution of land under this programme the government did not make compensation payments to either the previous owners or the government a requirement for receiving land. It thus lost an opportunity of making its fiat money a desirable commodity for peasants, who now had no interest in marketing their produce for cash; they could consume their output themselves. It might be argued that this oversight was the result of lack of understanding of monetary matters. However, in 1949 and 1950 the communist government had shown a quite sophisticated appreciation of monetary problems by indexing the value of savings deposits and government bonds to a price index as part of its anti-inflation policy.

The economies considered here do adopt the same method as each other to try to imbue their fiat currencies with value. This follows from the nature of the planning system. The state employs labour and procures produce from what private sector there is, using its fiat currency. The state also supplies retail commodities. This is the foundation for the value of the fiat currencies. The traditional Stalinist view has always been that the currency is backed by state-supplied retail goods put on the market at stable prices, not by gold or precious metals. This was clearly expressed in a speech by Stalin in 1953, when he said:

> The stability of Soviet money is assured above all through the enormous quantity of commodities over which the state disposes and *which are put into circulation at fixed prices*. Who among economists would deny that such a guarantee, which exists only in the USSR, is a more real safeguard of a stable currency than any gold reserve? (quoted from Varga, 1958: 221; italics in original)

This view is clearly expressed by Chinese writers also (such as Yi Hongren in Ma, 1982: 469-70). Yi states that the more important factor is that commodities (*shangpin*) can be sold at stable (*wending*) prices, thus guaranteeing the stability of the *Renminbi* over a long period (p. 470). The Eastern European countries adopted the Soviet system and hence had to guarantee their currencies in the same manner.

The theory underlying socialist money is that the individual *does* have recourse to the state for the discharge of the debt to him or her represented by the piece of paper called money issued by the state. The whole logic underlying this monetary system is that the currency has value as long as the state can supply all the goods people want in the correct assortment, at stable prices. The value of the currency is not determined by movements in the price level as it is in a market economy. In market economies we are used to assuming that whatever happens to the price level the goods will actually be in the shops in the quantities wanted (except when there are supply shocks or strikes leading to rationing of such things as petrol) and that the goods are available for those who do have the money to spend. In the planned economies it is not automatic that supplies will always be available in the quantities required. As remarked above, Engels (1884) fully appreciated the problem of co-ordinating the production decisions of independent producers in order to ensure that supplies would meet demands. Marx did not understand this problem of economic co-ordination. Central planners assume that it can be done by using material balance planning and then issuing orders to state-employed managers who will achieve what they are told to do.

Another common feature of all these currencies is that they are inconvertible: they are not freely traded on international currency markets. 'Socialist money is typically a domestic currency' (Varga, 1958: 231). Their exchanges rates are set administratively. There is usually a whole complex of exchange rates applied to different transactions and different classes of traders (see Wyczalkowski, 1966, and the country entries in *Pick's Currency Yearbook* and *World Currency Yearbook*). For details of the complicted nature of pricing and exchange rate systems used in trade between the members of the Council for Mutual Economic Assistance, see Brabant (1980; 1987). The state maintains a monopoly over trade in its currencies. Administrative means are used to decide who gets foreign currencies and at what price. State monopoly over foreign trade isolates domestic firms from international prices.

Some writers have seen this system as an important means of isolating domestic price level from changes in world prices (Wiles, 1973). The system is recognised by reforming economists in these economies as a cause of inefficient domestic production. An enthusiastic pro-market reformer would insist on a fully convertible currency so that domestic producers could discover where their international comparative advantage lay and thus specialise and export for the benefit of all. In China the government recognised the emerging private trade in foreign currencies by enterprises and institutionalised this activity from about 1986, by establishing a series of trade centres where currencies are traded under government supervision. In the Soviet Union, 1989 saw the first state-organised auction of foreign currencies organized by the Bank for Foreign Economic Affairs, where only state enterprises could bid for foreign exchange. It was a bit of mystery as to where the foreign exchange came from, and there was some speculation that the government drew on its reserves to supply the auction (*MNBPB* December 1989, p. 27). The late 1980s saw significant devaluations of most of these currencies. In Eastern European countries talk of making their currencies fully convertible started in the late 1980s. Some Soviet economists did not see this happening in their country until the beginning of the next century. By mid 1989 most of these countries had announced their intentions of making their currency convertible within a few years or, as in the case of Hungary's announcement in January 1989, as soon as practicable.

The logical basis for the value of these fiat currencies described above has led to the measurement of money supply in these countries by certain economists in terms of the relationship between money stocks and the annual flow of retail supplies (Fogaras 1978; Birman and Clarke, 1985; Winiecki, 1985 and 1988; Peebles, 1986a). Such a measure gives an idea of the extent of the state's indebtedness to the population. It is often interpreted as an indicator of the size of the monetary overhang, referred in the previous chapter. Although there is controversy among a few Western economists about the meaning of this simple measure, it is used by many writers both inside and outside these economies: for example, Shi (1981), Zeng (1983), and Li and Xia (1986) for China and Lokshin (1990: 74) for the Soviet Union. It has been enthusiastically embraced by the Secretariat of the Economic Commission of Europe of the United Nations in its *Economic Survey of Europe in 1989–1990* (pp. 120–8). Portes (1989: 39) calls this measure 'theoretically unjustifiable'. I see nothing wrong with it as an indicator of household real money holdings and a possible indicator of when planners might change their behaviour towards the supply of consumer goods. In fact, methodologies using such simple measures have been much more successful in predicting the actual monetary developments of these economies than more complicated methodologies that rejected them. This question will be investigated in chapter 5.

2.2 CHARACTERISTICS AND PERFORMANCE OF THE COUNTRIES UNDER STUDY

Table 2.1 gathers together some general data and statistics indicating certain relevant features of our six economies. The figures were assembled from a number of sources but are generally comparable. Their purpose is to show the differences in these economies and to suggest patterns in the relationship between income, growth and money.

One striking feature is the difference in size and level of income of these countries. There is no consensus among economists on the effect of a nation's size, whether it be its population, land area or whatever, on its economic performance. However, we might expect there to be some relationship between these aspects of size and the co-ordinating mechanism chosen. Among the six countries under study, China has a population 104 times that of Hungary and a landmass 103 times Hungary's, but its income per capita has been about one-fortieth of that of East Germany. We might think that small countries might be able to implement command planning quite easily. Hungary has a small, relatively homogeneous population, relatively good communications and a limited number of significant industrial enterprises. However, it was the small countries that first started to try to introduce market reforms, not the large Soviet Union (twice the size of China) or China. Size seems to have nothing to do with the willingness to introduce market reforms.

China has by far the largest proportion of its workforce in agriculture. The relevance of this for a monetary study is that the bulk of purchasing power issued by the state in any year will be to the rural population. This in turn means that changes in agricultural policy, not state wage policy, will have a significant impact on monetary purchasing power and monetary growth in that country.

Another related and important difference between these countries is whether the agricultural sector is collectivised, or not. If collectivised, there are important implications for the country's monetary system. First, collectivisation often means that the government uses compulsory procurements at state-determined prices to obtain inputs for state industry (for example, cotton) and food to feed the urban population. This means that the incomes of the rural sector can be controlled by the government to prevent high rural consumption, so that resources can be devoted to investment goods produced by the urban industrial workforce. This is the basis of the Stalinist model of industrialisation. A second implication is that most urban retail supplies are provided by the state at fixed, often subsidised prices and that there is very little free trade in agricultural products. This in turn means that the official retail price index is dominated by both industrial and agricultural goods provided by the state sector and so, as the prices of these goods remains largely unchanged despite the supply situation, the official retail price index remains unchanged for many years. Of course, these countries do permit some private production of agricultural produce for sale on free markets.

Among the countries under study, agriculture is collectivised in the Soviet Union, East Germany, Czechoslovakia and Hungary, and private farming is very much a small-scale sideline activity. Collective or state farm workers are given plots of land, which they cultivate, usually very intensively, for own consumption and for sale on local markets. These plots can produce a large proportion of the total output of the certain products for which they are suitable such as eggs, fruit, vegetables and meat, which are so often produced under contract for state institutional purchasers. Only in Poland is the agricultural sector privately owned and managed, with 78 per cent of all agricultural produce in 1985 coming from the small private farms that dominate this sector (Cochrane, 1988: 48).

China, as in many aspects of its economy, has swung widely between private farming and collectivisation. Generally, private farming survived from the land reform programme of the early 1950s to the mid 1950s and then there was full scale collectivisation when the rural people's communes were established in 1958. These lasted until the early 1980s. Under the commune system the government procured produce using quotas and fixed government prices. This kept rural incomes low and allowed a high accumulation rate. The policy was dramatically changed after December 1978. First, procurement prices were raised substantially. Then the communes were abandoned, and land was allocated on a leasehold basis to farmers, who contracted with the government to supply various products. After 1985, compulsory quotas were abandoned and the government had to obtain produce using voluntary contracts with farmers. After 1979, farmers were allowed to sell produce that exceeded their quotas on the many free markets, which were reopened.

This means that in those countries where free agricultural markets exist excess demand will be reflected in price rises there. Such markets and rising prices tend to redistribute cash from the urban population to the rural population and play no direct role in withdrawing cash from circulation.

As Table 2.1 shows, these countries have all been able to achieve

Table 2.1 Country characteristics

Measure/Year	USSR	GDR	Czechoslovakia	Poland	Hungary	PRC
Population (million)						
1988	286.7	16.6	15.5	37.9	10.7	1,109.6
GNP (US$ billion)						
1988 (approx.)	1,466[a]	209	118	69	28	316[b]
GNP per capita (US$)						
1988 (approx.)	5,000[a]	12,608	7,591	1,818	2,621	300[b]
% of workforce in agriculture (%)						
1980	20	11	13	29	18	74
Accumulation rate (%)						
1988	24.8	21.5	17.3	31.9	19.6	34.1
Personal savings rate (%)						
1989	7.2	5.0	2.5	7.7	4.0	12.3
Savings deposits/annual retail sales (%)						
1980	57.9	99.7	61.1	36.9	41.4	23.7
1985	68.0	110.0	73.4	33.0	46.9	39.6
1989 (approx.)	85	120	82	20	45	63
Inflation consumer prices (% p.a.)						
1971–75	0	–0.2	0.1	2.4	2.8	0.3
1976–80	0.6	0.1	2.0	6.8	6.3	2.8
1981–85	1.0	0	1.8	32.5	6.8	4.1
1986–89	2.1	0.5	0.6	69.7	11.5	15.7
1987	1.9	0	0.1	25.5	8.6	8.8
1988	2.3	0	0.2	59.0	15.7	20.7
1989	2.3	2.0	1.5	254.0	17.0	16.3
Growth in real output (% p.a.)						
1971–75	5.6	5.4	5.7	9.8	6.2	5.5
1976–80	4.3	4.1	3.6	1.2	2.8	6.1
1981–85	3.6	4.5	1.8	–0.8	1.3	10.0
1986	2.3	4.3	2.6	4.9	0.9	7.7
1987	1.6	3.6	2.1	1.9	4.1	10.2
1988	4.4	2.8	2.4	4.9	0.3	11.3
1989	2.4	2.0	1.3	n.a.	n.a.	3.3
Net indebtedness in convertible currencies (US$ billion)						
1989	36.4	11.0	3.1	36.5	19.5	n.a.

Notes: [a] USSR *GNP* data, 1990.
[b] PRC *GNP* data, 1986.

Sources: ESE (passim); Greenaway (1990: 578); *The Economist* 12 January 1991; *World Development Report 1988; Statistical Yearbook of China 1983; ZGTJN 89* and *ZGTJNJ90 (passim); International Financial Statistics* September 1990 (p. 166); *Comecon Data 1985* and *1987 (passim).*

high accumulation rates (that is, investment as a proportion of income).[7] In comparison, the accumulation rate in the industrial market economies is usually about 20 per cent and lower in such countries as the United Kingdom and the United States. It has long been argued that these high accumulation rates have not generated as much growth as they should have done. The planned economies are seen as having grown as result of intensive growth, which means just using more and more capital and labour and not increasing the productivity of these factors, which is extensive growth. One of the reasons for earlier economic reforms was to enable these economies to switch from an extensive growth strategy to an intensive one.

Although these economies have achieved high rates of investment, they have not relied on the household sector to generate the necessary savings. This has largely been done in the state sector, where, because of state ownership, profits are handed over to the state budget for the state to use in economic development. This factor is shown in the low personal saving rates in Table 2.1. Great caution should be used in interpreting these figures. Here, saving just means the accumulation of savings deposits. The ratios show the percentage of household incomes used to accumulate savings deposits. Great controversy arises from the different interpretation of trends in these ratios. In market economies households can save and accumulate financial assets in the form of currency, bank deposits, savings deposits, government bonds and shares in private companies. This last option, although not entirely absent from planned economies, especially in recent years, is not a major form for household financial asset holdings. The financial assets held by households in planned economies are largely the debts of the government or its banking system.

Because of the widespread attempt to provide social services, cheap housing, education and so on in these countries, we would expect the saving ratios in planned economies to be lower than those in most market economies, which in fact they have tended to be. It is usually argued that inflation expectations discourage saving. Yet, as Table 2.1 implies, in the high inflation countries of Poland and China the saving rate is high, but in inflationary Hungary it is low. Among the countries with low open inflation, the saving rate is low in Czechoslovakia and higher in the Soviet Union. The general trend in these ratios over the past few years has been for the ratio to increase in China, the Soviet Union and Poland, to fall in Hungary and Czechoslovakia, and to remain roughly constant in East Germany. Interpreting these phenomena will be reserved to chapter 4.

Equally controversial is the interpretation of household holdings of monetary stocks. Table 2.1 shows the ratio of household savings deposits to the value of annual retail sales. An attempt will be made to assess the extent of total real money holdings at the end of this chapter. There is a strong positive correlation between income per capita and the size of these real savings deposit holdings. In other words, the higher the income per capita, as in East Germany and Czechoslovakia, the higher the real savings deposits people hold; and the lower the average incomes, as in Poland, the less the real savings deposits people hold. China seems to be an exception: it has very low average incomes, but people hold more real savings than in Poland and Hungary. The interpretation of this phenomenon is extremely complex, and different interpretations lead to different views about the nature of money in planned economies. Some of these views will be discussed in chapter 5. In the countries with stable prices (the Soviet Union, East Germany and Czechoslovakia), this ratio tends to be relatively high. In the more inflationary countries it is lower. Only in highly inflationary Poland did it fall during the 1980s. This could be seen as the natural consequence of high inflation as people would not want to hold depreciating monetary assets. However, this is not the interpretation of this relationship, which will be discussed in chapter 4.

Table 2.1 shows the annual rates of inflation of consumer prices since 1971. It confirms the above groupings of countries according to the extent of their open inflationary experiences. In the Soviet Union, East Germany and Czechoslovakia open inflation rates were very low in the 1970s and 1980s, although in the former two countries they have been rising. East Germany's official price index shows hardly any increase since the early 1970s. In Poland, average annual inflation rates exceeded 30 per cent from the early 1980s, reaching 250 per cent in 1989. Hungary's open inflation rates also increased steadily in the 1980s, reaching 16 per cent in 1989. The same is true of China, although annual inflation rates varied considerably during the 1980s (Peebles, 1990a; 1990b). The cost of living of staff and workers rose nearly 21 per cent in 1988 and 16 per cent in 1989.

Table 2.1 also shows trends in the growth rate of real output in these economies. With the exception of China, these growth rates have all fallen since the early 1970s. The early 1980s saw real output falling in Hungary, Czechoslovakia, East Germany and Poland. In the former three countries this was just for one year (either 1980 or 1981), but in Poland real output fell in each of the years from 1979 to 1982 (*ESE*: 387). These features clearly differentiate the countries under study into two groups. In China there have been high and rising rates of growth of output together with high and rising rates of open inflation (Peebles, 1990a; 1990b). In the other five countries there was falling output growth and rising inflation, a phenomenon known in the West as stagflation (that is, stagnation and inflation).

Figure 2.1 shows movements in the ratio of savings deposits to annual retail sales in these countries for the period 1960–89. The ratios are based on estimates in Winiecki (1988: 63), calculations from data in *Comecon Data 1987*, estimates based on charts in *ESE* (p. 123) and calculations from *ZGTJNJ89* (pp. 597–9). The ratio will be called *Liquidity SD*, meaning liquidity measured using only savings deposits as the numerator. A further liquidity ratio, *Liquidity HM*, will be discussed shortly. It is apparent that there was rapid growth in *Liquidity SD* in East Germany, the Soviet Union and Czechoslovakia until the late 1970s or early 1980s. Thereupon the rate of growth fell slightly, but rapid growth resumed from the mid 1980s. This was apparent in East Germany and the Soviet Union during the 1980s, when *Liquidity SD* increased about 46 per cent and 20 per cent in each country respectively from 1980 to 1989.

In Hungary and Poland the growth rate of this liquidity ratio started to fall from the mid 1970s, and in Poland the ratio itself began to fall. Despite a sharp rise in 1981 in Poland the trend there has been downwards since the mid 1970s. Growth in the ratio was moderate in Hungary during the 1980s and began to fall after 1986.

In China the picture is somewhat different. There a was a sharp fall in the ratio in 1962, then growth until 1968, then a fall in 1969, whereupon the ratio stayed relatively constant until 1979. In 1979 the ratio started to rise very rapidly; the only setbacks to this steady rise occurred in 1985 and 1988.

Liquidity SD gives only a partial picture of household real monetary asset holdings as it includes only savings deposits. The data of Table 2.2 show *Liquidity HM*, which is the ratio of household money assets (that is, cash plus savings deposits) to annual retail sales, for selected years after 1960. Most of the data come from official sources, but cash data for the Soviet Union are estimates from Peebles (1981: 38). In addition to this liquidity ratio, the statistics in brackets are the proportion of total money assets held as cash. Several features are clear. The relative rankings of the countries according to *Liquidity SD* and *Liquidity HM* are the same. This is true despite the fact that cash holdings have generally grown more slowly than savings deposits. This is reflected in the falling proportion of total monetary assets held as cash. This ratio has fallen in all coun-

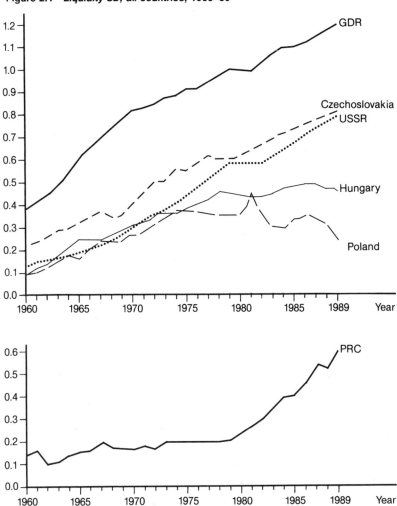

Figure 2.1 *Liquidity SD,* all countries, 1960–89

tries except Poland after 1975. Peebles (1981) shows that this falling ratio was also found in the Soviet Union. This implies that a study such as that of Howard (1979a), which assumes that the ratio of currency to savings deposits was constant, is based on unsound data. In Poland both measures of liquidity have fallen, but the fall in *Liquidity HM* has only been slight, which is reflected in the rise in the ratio of cash to total money after 1975. In China *Liquidity HM*

37

Table 2.2 *Liquidity HM* **and the ratio of cash to total household money**

Year	USSR	GDR	Czechoslovakia	Poland	Hungary	PRC
1960	18.2	49.0	28.5	18.9	22.6	25.3
	(24.1)	(21.0)	(27.3)	(61.9)	(59.9)	(42.4)
1970	48.8	92.9	38.9	38.7	50.9	26.3
	(38.5)	(12.9)	(21.9)	(33.8)	(30.6)	(41.0)
1975	46.0	104.3	43.0	54.5	62.0	28.5
	(27.1)	(11.9)	(19.3)	(31.8)	(29.9)	(37.0)
1980	n.a.	112.0	62.6	59.1	61.8	33.9
	"	(10.9)	(21.1)	(37.5)	(33.0)	(35.6)
1985	n.a.	122.1	91.6	53.7	69.3	58.6
	"	(9.8)	(19.9)	(38.5)	(32.0)	(32.5)
1988	105.4	n.a.	n.a.	n.a.	n.a.	73.8
	(19.1)	"	"	"	"	(30.8)

Sources: Soviet Union: 1960–85 retail sales and savings deposits from *Narodnoye Khozyaystvo SSSR* various issues, and cash estimates from Peebles (1981:63); 1988 from Lokshin (1990:74).
Hungary: 1960–75 calculated from Rudcenko (1979: 442); 1980, 1985 currency data from *International Financial Statistics Yearbook 1987* (p. 383), and other data from *Comecon Data 1987* (p. 294).
PRC: calculated from *ZGTJNJ89* (pp. 597–9).
Other countries: calculated from *Comecon Data 1987* (pp. 294, 410, 412).

has increased, but the ratio of cash to total money did not fall particularly during the 1980s. This means that cash holdings have grown almost as rapidly as savings deposits, the growth of which was very rapid after 1980.

2.3 CONCLUSIONS

The above analysis reveals some important features. East Germany, the Soviet Union and China have experienced rapid liquidity growth since the late 1970s. In the case of East Germany and the Soviet Union open inflation rates have been very low although showing signs of rising during the 1980s. In China inflation rates were high and erratic during the 1980s. In Poland and Hungary liquidity growth was restrained during the 1980s and open inflation has risen significantly, reaching hyperinflation rates in Poland in the late 1980s. The rate of increase of consumer prices in 1989 was recorded officially at about 254 per cent.[8] In all countries except China the 1980s saw falling rates of real growth. In China growth rates were high until after 1988.

Before discussing the reasons for these patterns of monetary development, it is necessary to discuss the institutional environment in which they occurred and the reasons for liquidity growth. This will be the aim of the next chapter.

3 Monetary institutions and the money supply

This chapter outlines the institutional structure within which the events described in the previous chapter took place. It also explains why the narrow measure of the money supply changes in these economies.

The basic monetary institutions of planned economies are quite well known: Atlas (1967), *Soviet Financial System* (1966), Garvy (1964; 1972; 1973; 1977), Kuschpèta (1978), Lavigne (1986), Zwass (1979); Buck (1987) and Vortmann (1989) for East Germany; Podolski (1973) for Poland; Liu Hongru (1980) and Huang Da et al. (1981) for China. Unfortunately, hard data on monetary flows are very scarce with the exception of China. The main distinguishing feature of these economies is that monetary flows are divided into two distinct circuits or spheres: a 'passive' one and an 'active' one.

Within the state planning sector, enterprises and all government units do not use cash in their transactions.[1] Their cash holdings are minimal as they must deposit all cash above a certain limit (which varies from country to country and according the proximity of a unit to a bank) in the unit's account. All units must hold accounts at an allocated branch of the government banking system, and their accounts are automatically debited and credited as transactions determined by the plan are made. This form of bank transfer money has been called 'passive' money: it passively follows a transaction and plays no role in initiating it by providing a material incentive for the supplier to supply the good. This system was first established on a wide basis in the state sector in the Soviet Union in the early 1930s. It is the one sphere of the economy where the desire of some Bolsheviks to see the elimination of money has been realised. Planning is supposed to allocate resources so that money flows passively according to the requirements of the physical plan. This reduces the significance of money in the state sector. 'Ownership of money does not give an absolute command over resources' (Garvy, 1972: 279). This monetary settlements system is found in all the planned economies. It was adopted in China, for example, in the early 1950s and is clearly described in Chinese monetary textbooks of the 1980s (for example, Huang et al., 1981: vol. 2, p. 501).

In contrast to the passive sphere there is a sphere of money circulation where cash is used. Money used here is usually called 'active' money. This sphere covers all cash payments from the combined state sector to the population in the form of wages, salaries, payments for agricultural procurements, transfer payments and payments from the financial system and all the return flows from the population in the form of retail purchases, taxes and other compulsory or voluntary payments, plus the accumulation of savings deposits.

Using two monetary circuits is supposed to help monetary planning.

> Separation of the two circuits not only facilitates control but also makes it easier to detect disequilibria, bottlenecks, and various shortfalls in the execution of economic plans. Because of the separation of the payments stream into two watertight compartments, and the considerable differences between the functions of balances in the two sectors, the concept of the total money supply has very limited analytical significance in the countries of Eastern Europe. (Garvy, 1972: 277).

For all the countries that use such a system it is very difficult to propose a satisfactory definition of the aggregate money supply. This is because of the different degrees of 'moneyness' of different deposits. In market economies different deposits have different degrees of liquidity because they have to be held at financial institutions for a given period before they can be converted into cash. They can then be converted into goods. This differentiates various monetary holdings by degree of liquidity. In the planned economies different monies are distinguished by the extent to which they can be converted into goods without other considerations like having planners' permission or showing a ration card.

For this reason nearly all empirical studies of money in planned economies take an empirical definition of money: what works as money is what we should call money. Most studies just examine developments in household money holdings, that is, their cash holdings or their holdings of cash plus savings deposits. This book will also take this approach and confine itself to these narrow measures of the money supply. It will not investigate the developments of broader aggregates that might include enterprise deposits. It has been suggested that such aggregates would have to be discounted if added to cash and other household monetary holdings to obtain a broader measure of the money supply (McKinnon, 1990). Another reason for ignoring broader monetary aggregates is that changes in the narrow measure of the money supply are likely to affect household behaviour in a way that changes in enterprise deposits would not. Enterprise behaviour is constrained by the planning system.

The theory behind the separation of monetary transactions is to allow planning of the growth of the narrow measure of the money supply so that it accords with household requirements. Transactions in the passive sphere are not supposed to result in unplanned spillovers of cash into the household sector. Garvy even goes so far as to say that the circuits are 'two watertight compartments' (1972: 277). The gap between total state payments to the household sector and total households' expenditures in any period equals the household sector's accumulation of narrow money. The theory is that there is control over wage payments in the state sector, the size of the workforce, the amount of payments for agricultural produce and so on. This is supposed to mean that planners can control the growth of household monetary incomes so that these incomes accord with the growth in the supply of retail goods, also supplied by planners. The issue is whether planners have been able to prevent the overflow from the non-cash circuit to the cash circuit in the form of excessive payments of wages and so on. This is a major empirical and theoretical issue in the study of these economies.

Given the nature of these institutions, the banking system does not have much control over the issue of currency. Planners determine wages, agricultural procurement prices and so on. The banking system must supply the cash when it is needed. If planners set prices in such a way that enterprises make losses, the banking system must cover their losses to allow them to stay in business and to keep on paying their workers, supplying the houses and pensions of retired workers, and even meeting enterprise tax obligations. It is felt that in these economies enterprises will always be able to get all the loans they need to stay in business. This phenomenon is know as the enterprise 'soft budget constraint' (Kornai, 1980; 1986). It is a concept widely used by analysts of money in planned economies.

The banking system is not independent and has to supply all the credit needed so that enterprises can meet physical plans, guarantee employment and so on. In addition, the banks have to supply the government with any funds it needs to cover its budget deficit. As we shall see, bank credit is the channel through which the narrow money supply changes: 'the money of the economy is based upon credit' (Fengővári, 1980: 277, describing Hungary). The banking systems in these countries cannot really follow an independent monetary policy. Their main purpose has been to ensure enough credit to realise the physical plan and to ensure that the household sector does not have excessive monetary balances. However, the tools necessary to do this do not lie in the hands of the banking system. As the banking system does not have much control over monetary payments it has to rely on a reactive monetary policy, coping with problems as they arise (Hsiao, 1971; Yeh, 1985; Garvy, 1972: 277–9 and 1977: 160–1). Many of these reactive policies are not available to the bankers: '[A]djustments needed to maintain such an equilibrium [in the cash sphere] are taken by the planning, not by the monetary, authorities' (Garvy, 1972: 278).

An example of the difficult position of the banks will clarify their awkward situation. It is based on the effects of the increased use of monetary incentives in China in the early years of economic reform. In 1979 the government increased the price it paid for agricultural produce procured under compulsory procurements. It also increased and extended the use of bonus prices for three main crops: grain, cotton, edible vegetable oils. The basic price for the quota amount was increased, and a higher bonus price was offered for all sales to the government in excess of the quota. The quota amount was fixed in absolute terms for a number of years. This meant that the demand curve facing farmers consisted of two horizontal lines: one at the quota price and another at the higher bonus price. These prices were the marginal revenues for the respective quantities. This meant that the average price the farmer would receive became a weighted average of each price, the weights being determined by the proportion sold at each price. As the amount of output the farmers sold to the government increased, the average price they received rose, thus reversing the usual inverse relationship between quantity and price. Farmers could not but benefit enormously. Their money incomes rose as both quantities sold and the average price received for these crops rose substantially over the period 1979–83 (Peebles, 1985). Grain procurement agencies made losses, as the retail price at which they sold grain in urban areas was lower than the rising procurement price. They thus had to be subsidised out of the budget by the government. This subsidisation leads to a net injection of cash into circulation. The banks had to keep supplying these agencies with credit so that they could meet the government's obligations to the farmers. The compulsory procurement system was abandoned in 1985. One earlier reaction to the problem was to increase retail prices — but not sufficiently to cover costs. In addition, wage subsidies were given to urban workers in compensation for the retail price increases.

This example illustrates how reform in one section of the economy prevents the banking system from controlling the issue of credit and hence from limiting the growth of the narrow money supply. As was remarked in the previous chapter, a large part of household money incomes in China goes to the rural population, and so these reforms caused a large increase in total money incomes.

3.2 MONETARY FLOWS: AN ILLUSTRATION

Monetary and financial data from planned economies are not sufficient to provide a full flow-of-funds analysis. One recent attempt illustrates the main features of these flows, and the way the information is presented allows us to see the presumptions in the mind of the analyst. The flows for the year 1977 in the Soviet Union are shown in Figure 3.1. The data used are from a number of sources, including Denton (1979) and official statistical works, supplemented by guesswork, and were compiled by Haitani (1986). Ames (1965: 175–9) had earlier shown the monetary flows in the Soviet economy graphically but put no numerical values on them. Haitani's numerical values are only approximate, but the compiler feels that they are close enough to reality to be of 'pedagogical value'.

Of the nine flows shown, seven take place within the state non-cash sector, and only two take place using cash. These latter two flows are the receipts of households and their expenditures. The diagram shows two main sources of household cash receipts: their receipts in the form of earnings from the state productive sector, and transfer payments from the government. Of course, unproductive labour also receives monetary income from the state sector (army personnel wages, salaries of bureaucrats and so on). The transfer payments include pensions, student grants, interest payments on households' savings, lottery winnings and so on. Any cash payment from the state to the household sector should be included in this flow. For example, in reconstructing such flows it is necessary to include such things as household receipts from the return of empty bottles and glass containers to state shops (Birman, 1981: 272–4).

Figure 3.1 Estimates of monetary flows in the Soviet Union, 1977

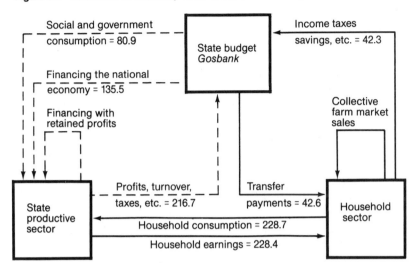

Figures in billions of roubles

— — ➤ Payments through bank accounts

———➤ Cash payments

Source: Reproduced from Haitani (1986: 139) with permission of the publishers.

In socialist monetary economics the total of all new cash receipts of the population is called money incomes of the population (MIP). This concept of money income differs from that used in Western economics as it includes transfer payments. It also excludes earnings from private economic activity that just involves the circulation of existing cash within the household sector. These payments are shown in Figure 3.1 as 'collective farm market sales' and do not have an estimate attached to them. Money incomes should also include the value of all private transactions within the household sector, such as the sale of second-hand goods, payments for private services such as tutoring and expenditures in private restaurants.

Figure 3.1 identifies household cash expenditures as two main flows. The first is household consumption from the state sector. The bulk of this item is the purchase of retail supplies, but it also includes payments for services and utilities (gas, electricity, rent), fees in public bath-houses and so on. The second flow is in the form of taxes and the accumulation of savings deposits; these are shown as receipts of the banking system.

Haitani's estimates imply that Soviet households received a total of 271 billion roubles in 1977, spent 228.7 billion on consumption (84 per cent of expenditure), and paid taxes and accumulated savings deposits to the extent of 42.3 billion. The actual extent of accumulation of savings deposits was 13.7 billion roubles in that year (*Narodnoye Khozyaystvo SSSR v 1980 godu* p. 408). Haitani's total incomes and expenditures balance exactly and show no accumulation of cash in this year. This is unrealistic. Peebles (1981: 63) estimates total money incomes in 1977 at 287.94 billion roubles, and total expenditures (including the increase in savings deposits) at 285.40 billion, leaving a gap of 2.54 billion, which was accumulated as cash. This put the saving rate at 4.8 per cent of total income and total monetary accumulation (increase in savings deposits, cash and lottery bonds) at 5.8 per cent of total monetary incomes. Birman (1981: 247) estimates total incomes in 1977 as 294.2 billion roubles, 2 per cent higher than Peebles's estimates but 9 per cent higher than Haitani's. Denton (1979: 785) estimates total personal money incomes as 276.8 billion roubles, 4 per cent lower than Peebles and 6 per cent lower than Birman. This shows the difficulty of estimating such flows on the basis of Soviet sources.

The terminology used to describe the state sectors and their flows is interesting. Haitani labels the state bank (*Gosbank*) as the state budget rather than identifying the custodian of the budget as the Ministry of Finance. His is a realistic approach as the state bank in this system (usually called the monobank by analysts) is not much more than the agent of the government in collecting taxes, disbursing grants to state enterprises and financing the government's budget.[2] The bulk of the budget's income is the profits and taxes from the state sector. State ownership means that virtually all profits are turned over to the budget. The part of enterprise profit that is retained can be used for financing investments, or for enterprise social-welfare funds and such things as building houses, or, sometimes, for paying bonuses.

Planners try to control enterprise use of retained funds through a number of administrative or fiscal devices. In addition to enterprise profit remissions and taxes to the budget there is the item 'turnover taxes' paid by the state retail–trade network. In the socialist system this is an important indirect means of raising income from consumers. In the Soviet Union it made up 31.1 per cent of all budget revenue in 1980 compared with 29.7 per cent in the form of remittance of profits, for example (*Narodnoye Khozyaystvo SSSR v 1980 godu* p. 523). This tax revenue allows the government to levy a very low direct income-tax burden on households (in China it has been virtually non-existent until recent years). This makes it look as though the household tax burden is low, but it is not. There is a large mark-up of the retail price over the wholesale price, which soaks up much of household expenditure

The bulk of budget expenditure goes on the national economy, that is, provides enterprises with funds for investment and renovation of equipment. This made up about 54 per cent of Soviet budget expenditures in 1977, for example. The other expenditures are for defence and for social consumption such as the provision of health care and education. The Soviet Union publishes a consolidated budget for the entire country every year in the statistical yearbook *Narodnoye Khozyaystvo SSSR* and in more detail in the *Budget Handbook*.

The whole process has been criticised by Birman (1981) for its complicated nature and for hiding certain income figures, which he identifies as the increase in cash in circulation. He finds it unbelievable that the budget shows a surplus for every year since 1944 and that defence expenditures are as low as the figures given in the official budget accounts. Birman's suspicions have been fully justified by the open acknowledgement in the Soviet Union of large and rising budget deficits that were concealed for many years. Birman (1990: 29–31) dates the first admission of a Soviet budget deficit to March 1988 and its official recognition to mid 1988. He wonders whether Gorbachev was told of the problem when he came to power in March 1985, as he introduced policies that exacerbated the problem, such as reducing vodka sales (a source of budget revenue).

The budget deficits have caused problems in managing the economy. As a Soviet writer puts it: 'As the existence of a budget deficit was carefully hidden, there is no clear view about its influence on the economy in the Soviet literature' (Kagalovsky, 1989: 450).

Haitani's rough estimates show exact balance between budget income and expenditure, which was certainly not the case. Because of this there is no way to show why household currency holdings changed in 1977. This will be done below. The relationship between the budget deficit and monetary growth in the Soviet Union in the 1980s will be discussed in section 3.8.

3.3 CONTROLLING CASH FLOWS: THE BALANCE OF MONEY INCOMES AND EXPENDITURES OF THE POPULATION

The basic tool developed in the Soviet Union to control the cash flows of the household sector is named the balance of money incomes and expenditure of the population (Varga, 1958; Borisov, 1966; Arouca, 1977; Kuschpèta, 1978: 168–72). It is the basis on which the cash plan of the banking system is constructed and has an equivalent in all the other planned economies (Rudcenko, 1979). The balance has two sections. Section A of the Soviet balance covers all money payments to the household sector from the combined state sector and the return flows from the population to the state sector. Section B of the balance covers all expenditures and transfers within the population. Only section A is relevant to explaining the change in household narrow money. Calculations such as those by Bush (1973: 100–1), which add private sector income to total money incomes to deal with the fact that most estimates of total money incomes that can be made using Soviet sources are less than expenditures, are incorrect. Any private income added to the income side should also be added to the expenditure side. Section B is supposed to help in accounting for regional transfers of money within the household sector, as these will produce a different geographical distribution of demand from the original distribution of purchasing power (Varga, 1958: 223–5).

Table 3.1 shows the main items of the balance for the Soviet Union. As far as I know the Soviet Union has never published any data of a complete balance. Estimates are available in Peebles (1981) for the period 1955–78, and Birman (1981) for the period 1960–78. Denton (1979) presents estimates of the composition of the income side for the period 1965–77 and selected years back to 1950. Rudcenko (1979) presents data for the four Eastern European countries for the period 1955–75. All these estimates were based on official data sources of the countries concerned.

The relative importance of various items on either side of the balance can be shown using independent estimates (that is, independent from my own previous estimates) by Denton for the same year as Haitani's flows, 1977. They are shown in Table 3.2 and refer solely to section A of the balance. Wages and salaries constituted the main source of money income. Monetary payments to collective farm members were low as part of their income was distributed in kind. Transfer payments made up a quite significant 15.4 per cent of total incomes. On the expenditure side the largest item was retail sales, which constituted the main channel through which purchasing

Table 3.1   Major items of the balance of money incomes and expenditures of the population, Soviet Union

Money incomes	Money expenditures
Section A (state and household sectors)	
Wages and salaries	Purchase of retail goods
Receipts from government and co-op	
enterprises and non-profit organisations	Payments for services, and utilities
	Taxes, voluntary payments (e.g. Party and
Money receipts of collective farms	trade union dues)
Individual receipts from selling agricultural	
produce to the government	Saving in form of increased savings deposits
Pensions, stipends etc.	Purchase of government bonds
Receipts from financial sector	
(e.g. interest payments)	
Other incomes	

Balance of section A = Increase in currency in circulation

Section B (within the household sector)	
Receipts from sales of goods and services	Payments for goods and services
Incomes from sales of farm products	Expenditures on sales of farm products
(collective farm market)	(collective farm market)

Balance of section B (by definition) = Zero (as incomes equal expenditures)

Source: Adapted from Garvy (1972: 301) and Kuschpèta (1978: 169).

power returned to the state sector. Deductions included personal income tax, which made up 7 per cent of incomes, the bachelor tax, local and state taxes, trade union and party dues and insurance premiums. The accumulation of savings deposits took 4.9 per cent of total incomes. The absolute amount of these three expenditure flows (retail sales, deductions, savings deposits) constituted 99.4 per cent of Denton's estimate for total incomes, not leaving much room for the accumulation of cash.

The above proportions have probably not changed very much since 1977. One item that may have increased in significance is the payment of interest on savings deposits as the stock of savings deposits has increased more rapidly than incomes and retail sales. The proportion of money incomes accumulating as savings deposits has increased. The average saving rate for the years 1986–89 was 5.9 per cent and in 1989 it was 7.2 per cent (*ESE* p. 126). An implication of these proportions is that, if planners wish to control the issue of cash in the form of purchasing power, wages and salaries and transfer payments are the major channels of issue. If planners wish to withdraw currency from circulation, state retail sales are the most important channel, followed by the increase in savings deposits. These facts explain the form of monetary planning in planned economies. In

Table 3.2 Structure of the balance, main items, Soviet Union, 1977

(selected items, percentage of total incomes)

Total money incomes	
Gross payments to wage and salary earners	71.6
Wages of collective farm members	6.3
Income from household sales of agricultural produce to the government	3.9
Transfer payments	15.4
Interest on savings deposits	0.8
Total expenditures	
Retail sales	83.3
Deductions (taxes, voluntary contributions)	10.9
Increase in savings deposits	4.9

Source: Calculated from Denton (1979: 785, 788) and supplemented with data from *Narodnoye Khozyaystvo SSSR v 1980 godu* (pp. 408, 421).

attempting to balance money incomes and expenditures in order to control the rate of growth of cash and savings deposits, there have been extensive attempts to control wages. Generally, wages in the state sector were determined centrally, and permission from banks was usually required for enterprises to draw on their bank accounts to issue cash as wages. In China, major enterprises had bank officials based in them to supervise cash payments to workers.

In theory, monetary planning is aimed at determining total money incomes, and hence currency issue, so that, given the expected increase in retail supplies in any year, households have just enough money to buy all the goods the state supplies and have enough unspent purchasing power to accumulate that amount of money which planners think is acceptable. This is often explained on the basis of an equation of exchange formulation, in which MV is identical to PQ. The required amount of money is therefore

$$M = (1/V)PQ$$

(Chai, 1981: 43–4 for China; Garvy, 1977: 161 for this 'inverted equation of exchange' in the Soviet Union; Kuschpèta, 1978: 164–6). It is recognised even in Hungary that the money supply and velocity do not determine the price level but are determined *by* it (Tarafás, 1985: 29; Tardos, 1985: 41). Planners are supposed to estimate some acceptable rate for velocity (V) and hence its inverse ($1/V$): the ratio of money (M) to total retail sales value (PQ).

The planned increase of whatever concept of M is being planned (usually currency) should equal the planned increase in the value of retail sales multiplied by the inverse of velocity. For example, in China, for a long time it was thought that a ratio of currency to retail sales of about 12 per cent was normal (Shi, 1982: 3). This ratio was based on historical experience of when the consumer goods market was in reasonable equilibrium. If monetary planners were told that retail supplies in current prices were planned to increase by 100 monetary units, they should plan so that the money stock increased by 12 units. This was supposed to be achieved by control over money income payments. When such control was inadequate, the planners would have to resort to policies on the state-monetary-receipts side of the balance. What these policies could be will be discussed in section 3.5. It is likely that monetary planners in the other planned economies had rough ratios of money to retail sales value that they regarded as acceptable.

3.4 EXPLAINING CHANGES IN THE NARROW MONEY SUPPLY: THE HOUSEHOLD PERSPECTIVE

The most complete figures of the ex post balance of incomes and expenditures available are those for China (*Statistical Yearbook of China 1986* pp. 442–4; *ZGTJNJ89* pp. 596–8). These figures allow us to account for changes in the narrow money supply, as this is just equal to the difference between total incomes and expenditures. It does not provide an explanation of these changes as it does not say why the particular items changed in any year. The form of the balance for China includes the incomes and expenditures of social organisations. The difference between incomes and expenditures is the annual increase in two forms of narrow money called cash in hand (*shoucun xianjin*) and savings deposits (*chuxu cunkuan*). Chinese sources refer to the stocks of monetary assets at the end of the year as 'remaining, or surplus, purchasing power' (*nian mo jieyu goumaili*), clearly showing their appreciation that narrow money comes into existence as unspent money incomes.

Table 3.3 provides some data for selected years in the 1980s. It is not absolutely clear whether the table refers solely to the section A concept of the Soviet balance, but the total figures do balance, except for 1979. This is a particularly interesting period as monetary growth became rapid and erratic from that year on. The coverage of the income series was changed in 1986.

Out of total expenditures in 1985, as an example, 76 per cent were realised through retail sales, only 1.9 per cent were paid in taxes, 9.7 per cent were accumulated as cash in hand and savings deposits, and 8.2 per cent were classified as 'other expenditures of the residents'. The item 'other' on both sides of the balance is larger than it should be and was probably put in to make the figures

Table 3.3 Money incomes, expenditures and narrow monetary growth in China, 1980-85

(billion yuan)

	1980	1981	1982	1983	1984	1985
Incomes						
State sector wages	62.80	66.04	70.89	74.81	87.58	106.48
Collectives' wages	20.70	24.00	26.00	29.48	37.75	47.15
Wages in other units	0	0	0	0	0.35	0.59
Incomes of professionals	4.26	4.10	4.18	4.43	4.76	6.14
Income of peasants from selling products	89.29	99.16	111.00	129.40	170.04	215.50
Peasants' service income	18.67	21.28	24.20	29.92	37.91	51.60
Government support	6.41	6.30	6.70	7.45	7.98	9.40
Net loans to agriculture and downpayments	3.65	1.14	2.08	2.64	12.72	2.10
Other incomes	31.18	34.11	37.03	42.29	56.27	87.42
Purchase of goods by foreigners	0.54	0.74	0.80	0.92	1.30	1.56
Purchases of goods by urban social groups	16.10	17.80	19.74	22.72	29.02	36.60
Total incomes	253.60	274.67	302.62	344.06	445.69	564.54
Expenditures						
Retail sales	214.00	235.00	257.00	284.94	337.64	430.50
Cultural expenditures	10.42	11.46	12.61	13.91	17.71	21.84
Taxes	4.86	4.89	5.51	5.91	8.62	10.66
Net decrease in agricultural loans and downpayments	0	0.05	0	0.07	0.01	0.20
Other expenditures	3.79	4.27	7.65	12.06	29.35	46.34
Total expenditures	233.07	255.67	282.77	316.89	393.33	509.54
Balance (Incomes minus expenditures)						
Increase in cash in hand	6.54	5.17	4.04	8.49	20.11	16.07
Increase in savings deposits	13.99	13.83	15.81	18.68	32.25	38.93
Increase in narrow money	20.53	19.00	19.85	27.17	52.36	55.00

Source: *Statistical Yearbook of China 1986* (pp. 442–4).

balance. On the incomes side only 27 per cent of incomes were in the form of wages in the state and collective sector whereas 47 per cent of incomes went to peasants for selling products or providing services. The incomes side includes some items that are expenditures, such as the purchase of consumer goods by urban social groups and by foreigners. This makes sense as these goods are not available for residents, whose monetary accumulation the table is supposed to explain. These expenditure items could be deducted from both sides to obtain the balance for residents only. Such a balance was published in *Zhongguo Maoyi Wujia Tongji Ziliao 1952–1983* (pp. 9–16).

This shows that planners do monitor residents' (*jumin*) monetary flows.

No theory will be offered here as to why residents' narrow money holdings grew at the rate they did in particular years. We can note that from the household perspective narrow monetary growth is determined in this balance. This way of looking at narrow monetary growth sees it as being issued as household purchasing power and then realised through purchases, taxes and increments in narrow money. This is why I have called this the household perspective on narrow monetary growth. The following must always be true:

$$W_G + W_E + AP + TP + O = VRS + DTAX$$
+ increase in cash + increase in savings deposits.

where

W_G	= wages from the government sector
W_E	= wages from state enterprises
AP	= the value of agricultural procurements
TP	= transfer payments
O	= other incomes from the state sector
VRS	= value of retail sales
$DTAX$	= direct taxes and levies on the population

So

increase in cash plus savings deposits = $W_G + W_E + AP + TP + O - VRS - DTAX$ (1)

Changes in the narrow money stock can be due to changes in any of these variables. It can be seen that most of them are out of the control of the banking system. If the monetary planners are trying to control the rate of growth of cash, attempts to influence households to hold savings deposits are a method for doing this, so interest rate policy can affect currency growth. Whether narrow monetary growth always accords with household demand for narrow money is a controversial issue.

Narrow money growth can be caused by changes on either side of the balance. There are bound to be self-adjusting links between both sides. For example, if output and retail supplies fell, employment and possibly wages would fall, thus reducing total incomes. However, the reduction in incomes might not be sufficient to prevent rapid narrow monetary growth. A good example of a period when supply side effects caused rapid monetary growth was in China in 1961. Real output fell 30 per cent and the value of retail sales fell 13 per cent;

and although total monetary incomes fell 10 per cent, total narrow money stock increased 14 per cent (Peebles 1991: ch. 2). In Poland in 1981 real output fell 12 per cent, and an estimate shows that real retail sales fell 4.4 per cent (*ESE* pp. 387, 390). Money incomes rose 31 per cent and the narrow money stock rose 36 per cent. Generally, the pattern is for both incomes and expenditures to increase, but not necessarily at the appropriate rates, thus causing monetary growth. However, these two extreme examples show us that rapid narrow monetary growth occurs at periods of what we can call 'purchasing power imbalance', that is, when developments in purchasing power are out of balance with developments in the availability of retail supplies. This insight will be developed in section 4.4.

The balance of money incomes and expenditure of the population is the basis on which the cash plan of the banking system is based. This planning tool shows all expected withdrawals of cash (for wages, procurements, transfer payments and so on) and expected cash receipts (retail sales receipts, savings deposits and so on). See Garvy (1972: 302–4; 1977: 44) for the cash plan in the Soviet Union and Ma (1981: 478–9) and Chai (1981: 43–4) for China. Montias (1962: 123–4) reconstructs the balance for Poland for 1956 and shows its link with the cash plan of the banking system.

For the Soviet Union, Aslund (1989: 85–6) presents estimates of the money incomes of the population (*MIP*) and official data of retail sales and saving deposits accumulations for 1980 and for the period 1985–87. The methods used to estimate the important monetary-incomes series are not particularly clearly described, nor is the presentation of the results. He describes the entire difference between money incomes and retail sales as the 'inflationary gap' and notes that in 1986 this was 8 billion roubles larger than in the previous year (p. 85). This estimate follows the statement that the population's incomes from the public sector grew 4.4 per cent, whereas retail sales in current prices 'stopped at an increase of 2.4 per cent', which is attributed to the anti-alcohol campaign. There is the germ of a theory in the order in which these pieces of evidence are written down. Peebles (1986b) and chapter 4 below offer such a theory.

3.5 TOOLS FOR ACHIEVING BALANCE

The methods planners may use to achieve balance between money incomes and expenditures are well known, although there has not been much systematic work to show which tools were used in different countries at different periods and with what consequences.

Equation 1 shows the reactions planners can take if money

incomes grow more rapidly than the potential expenditures shown on the right hand side. The implications for possible policies are well known in the literature. The following five possibilities are listed by Gregory and Stuart (1986: 186-9), together with an assessment of the extent to which they were used in the Soviet Union during the period 1928-40.

1 Institute a wage freeze. (This method was not used in the Soviet Union.)
2 Increase personal taxes. (This method was not used as the rates required would have been very high.)
3 Encourage personal saving. (Savings banks were established to encourage voluntary savings, but compulsory bond sales were also instituted.)
4 Increase state retail prices, which effectively increases the turn-over tax.[3] (This method was used over the long run.)
5 Allow repressed inflation, that is, not increase retail prices sufficiently to remove the inflationary gap; this requires rationing of what are considered essential goods. (This policy also occurred extensively.)

When discussing these policies in the context of China, Prybyla (1978: 139) adds these two obvious further reactive policies

6 Sell from state stockpiles of retail goods.
7 Adjust the structure of output and produce more consumer goods.

Prybyla feels that policies 1, 3, 5 and 6 are those that were used in China. Certainly there was rationing in China before he wrote, there were patriotic savings campaigns and forced bond sales (which also occurred in the late 1980s), and nominal wages were strictly controlled over the period 1967-77. In addition to 6 and 7, imported consumer goods could be used to supply the domestic market to absorb excess purchasing power. This is said to have happened in China in 1985 in response to the large increase in purchasing power in 1984 (Komiya, 1989). The effect of such policies on monetary growth will be shown in section 3.6.

Of these policies, selling from stocks and importing consumer goods can only be short term responses. If imbalances persisted, taxes would have to be raised every year, which would be unpopular. Repressed inflation and rationing could be used over the long run. This of course is the chronic–excess–demand hypothesis. How planners cope with imbalances in each country will be investigated in section 4.6. One reasonable assumption for the purposes of the subsequent analysis is that, if certain policies have been used in the past without major adverse consequences, we can assume that they will be used again when similar problems emerge.

3.6 EXPLAINING CHANGES IN THE NARROW MONEY SUPPLY: THE BANKERS' PERSPECTIVE

The above way of viewing the narrow money supply process looked at the actual flows of cash onto and from the consumer goods market, that is, from the perspective of the incomes and expenditures of the population. Another perspective is that of the banking system, where the bankers see who withdraws money in the form of cash from the banks and why and who deposits it. The difference between withdrawals and deposits will explain the change in narrow money, especially currency in circulation. In addition to people and organisations withdrawing existing cash, banks will create new cash by granting loans. In planned economies the bulk of loans goes to government enterprises and the government; very little goes to households or private businesses.

For market economies monetary economists identify three channels through which the money supply changes. These channels have counterparts in planned economies, but their relative importance and the nature of the causes differ. In a market economy change in the money supply equals

1. public-sector borrowing requirements *minus* the sale of public sector debt to the private sector, *plus*
2. net bank lending to the private sector, *plus*
3. net foreign exchange operations

The money supply that a Western economist would be concerned with explaining consists mainly of bank deposits, not just cash. In market economies privately owned commercial banks can create money. They do this by lending to their customers or by buying financial assets such as government bonds from them. When banks do this they just credit their customers' accounts; and when the latter draw on their accounts by writing cheques and giving them to someone else to deposit in their accounts the money supply increases. The banks are restrained in the amount of deposits they can create in this way by the need to have enough cash to meet the demand for cash withdrawals. In market economies it is private banks that create money and determine the growth of the money supply. The government has to influence their lending behaviour by indirect means, although many governments have in the past used direct means such as quotas on loans.

If the government runs a deficit, it can finance it in three ways: it can sell debt to its own citizens, it can sell debt to foreigners, or it can borrow from the banks. The first two methods do not have any impact on the money supply as they just redistribute existing money to the government, but when the government has to borrow from the banking system the money supply rises. In modern economies this happens virtually automatically. Assume that the government increases all pensions it pays and does not borrow to finance this extra expenditure. Assume that the government sends a cheque drawn on the relevant bank account to all recipients. They receive the cheque, deposit in their accounts and the money supply increases. They can convert all the deposit into cash if they wish. The banks present the cheques to the government, which credits the accounts the banks have with the central bank. The money supply has risen, and the banks have more funds that they can draw on if people want cash. Generally, the central bank is always willing to act as 'lender of last resort' to ensure that banks always have sufficient cash funds to meet withdrawals. This example shows how money is created as a result of government deficit spending. The government could borrow more directly by selling government bonds to the banks, which credit the government's account; the money supply increases when the government spends the money.

When the government increases the grant that leads to the increase in the money supply, the first effect is to increase the incomes of part of the community; that is, there is a flow of newly created purchasing power. The secondary effect of this policy is to increase the monetary stock. Western economists differ in the extent to which they emphasise the first-round effect in the form of the increased flow of incomes or the second-round effect of the increased stock. The analytical parts of chapter 4 will emphasis the flow effects mainly because monetary planners have to deal with these every year. These flows also explain why the money stock changes in planned economies.

The third reason for monetary growth arises from the balance-of-payments position of a country. For simplicity, assume that the country has a fixed exchange rate (which is a good approximation to the case of an inconvertible currency in a planned economy) and that there is a balance-of-payments surplus at this rate. Domestic residents are earning more in foreign currencies than they are spending for imports. The monetary authorities have to buy these earnings at the fixed exchange rate in exchange for domestic currency, and so the domestic money supply rises. If there were a deficit, the opposite would occur. This is supposed to be a self-adjusting mechanism in market economies. As the money supply rises, for example, prices are supposed to rise, making exports less competitive and imports more attractive and thus reducing the trade surplus. This effect is supposed to offset the expansionary effect on the money supply of a government budget deficit. If there is a budget deficit, this increases aggregate demand and domestic prices, encouraging imports and causing a balance-of-trade deficit. This latter effect causes a contraction in the money supply to offset the expansionary effect of the budget deficit. Anyway, that is the theory. Whether the two effects work in this way in planned economies is an interesting question, which will be examined in the case of China below.

All these three factors contribute to monetary growth in planned economies also, although the mechanism is slightly modified. The first major difference is that we are interested in explaining the growth of narrow money (cash plus household savings deposits), not a broader measure that would include enterprise deposits or government deposits. This is because these deposits have different degrees of moneyness, which we cannot assess, and do not effect household behaviour. The second difference is found in the reasons for borrowing in planned economies. Some of these reasons are the same as in a market economy. In a reformed planned economy enterprises may have to borrow from the banking system if they wish to invest in new equipment. In the traditional system they would get a budget grant tied to their investment plan. However, many state enterprises have to borrow because they make losses. This is very often due to the prices they must pay and receive, which are set by planners. They become permanent deficit units and must be subsidised by the budget.

The basic reason for changes in narrow money in planned economies is well summarised by a Chinese economist as: loans minus cash equals deposits (Li, 1986–87: 6), which implies that loans minus deposits equals cash. Here Li is referring to new loans and deposits and the increase in cash. New loans that do not result in new deposits (including household savings deposits) must show up as increased cash holdings. Banks in planned economies also have a credit plan, which is supposed to plan their granting of loans and the expected increase in deposits (Garvy, 1977: 43–4; Chai, 1981: 39–42). As a Chinese source puts it, 'from the point of view of the country as a whole, the credit plan's balance is identical with the amount of currency put into or withdrawn from circulation' (Ma, 1982: 479).

We can use the banking system's accounts to provide another accounting explanation of changes in narrow money. This will be done using Chinese data on the total amounts of loans outstanding (the assets of the system or the 'use of funds', *zijin yunyong*, as the Chinese call them) and the liabilities of the banking system (the 'sources of funds', *zijin laiyuan*). Currency and savings deposits are items on the liabilities/deposits/sources-of-funds side of the balance. The accounts show total assets and liabilities at the end of each year. Therefore, the annual increases in use of funds (essentially loans) minus the annual increase in sources of funds (essentially deposits), net of the change in currency itself, must equal the change in currency. At this aggregate level this tells us very little except that loans granted minus deposits received equal the change in currency. However, we can group together the loans and deposits of various sectors of the economy to show their relative contributions to narrow monetary growth. If we wanted to explain the increase in cash plus savings deposits we would have to deduct the increase in savings deposits from the increase in deposits in any year.

I have grouped the items in the following way to explain the annual changes in currency in circulation:

$$\text{CURRENCY} = (L - D) + G + R + IMO - F - O - B \quad (2)$$

where all items are annual changes. The first item $(L - D)$ is the excess of new loans over deposits received, including savings deposits. It is mainly loans to the state industrial sector and state enterprises. The item G is government borrowing net of any change in government deposits. The accounts I have used show government balances with the bank. When the government draws on such balances in the form of cash it is contributing to an increase in the narrow money supply, and vice versa when it increases its deposits. By netting out this item I differ from the approach of Huang Xu (1988a; 1988b), but I think that it is necessary. Item R is the change in the banking system's holdings of gold and foreign currency reserves. When this item increases the banks must have issued domestic currency in return, thus contributing to an expansion of narrow money. *IMO* is the change in China's net holdings at international monetary organisations, any increase in which contributes to the expansion of currency. Item F is the banking system's own funds, which increase when it makes an operating profit that withdraws currency from circulation. O is the item 'other' in the accounts. It is entered on the sources-of-funds side of the balance sheet, so increases in it serve to restrain currency growth. This item is very large for some years, meaning that we cannot accurately identify the real reasons for currency growth. Item B is the sale of bonds by the specialised banks established in 1984. Such bond sales obviously act to withdraw currency from circulation.

Table 3.4 shows the contributions of these factors to the growth of currency in China for the period 1979–88. The general picture of the importance of the various contributions is similar to that in Tsang (1990: 230) although not identical as an alternative data source was used. Some interesting conclusions emerge.

The government's activities had a strong expansionary effect on currency in circulation in 1979 and 1980 when it ran a sizeable budget deficit;[4] it ran down its deposits in 1979 but increased them in 1980. The foreign position had an expansionary effect on currency growth over the period 1981–83. The latter two years of this period were years of balance of trade surpluses (*Statistical Yearbook of China 1987* p. 519). In 1984 it was the excess of loans over deposits that principally contributed to currency growth. In 1985 the government had a restraining effect on currency growth, an effect noted by Tsang (1990: 230) although we differ slightly on the size of this effect.[5] In both 1984 and 1985 the foreign sector exerted a contractionary effect, which was most marked in 1985 when there was a huge balance-of-trade deficit. This episode is most interesting. In 1984 there was a large increase in the state wage bill, and it grew in 1985 also; this is reflected in the large excess of loans over deposits in 1985. There was a record grain harvest in 1984. To deal with the resulting expansion of money incomes of 29.5 per cent in 1984 and 26.7 per cent in 1985 (*Statistical Yearbook of China 1987* p. 480) the government ordered the importation of many consumer goods such as televisions and other electronic products. These were sold on the consumer goods market to absorb part of the excess purchasing power caused by the growth in wages. Equation 1 shows directly how this policy would restrict the growth of currency by increasing VRS on the right hand side. Equation 2 and Table 3.4 reveal how this policy shows up in the banking system's accounts. The government had to run down part of its reserves of gold and foreign currency (item R in equation 2), converting them into foreign goods and then converting these goods into its own fiat currency, thus restricting the rate of growth of narrow money.

An important lesson of Table 3.4 is that the government's budget deficit is not always the dominant factor in causing narrow monetary growth. In China after 1984 the main cause of such growth was excessive lending to state enterprises, which allowed rapid wage

Table 3.4 Explaining annual increases in currency in circulation, China, 1979–1988

(annual increases, billion yuan)

Year	1 CURR[a]	L — D	2 G	3 R	4 IMO	5 F	6 O	7 B
1979	5.57	-5.37	12.89	0.63	0	4.92	-2.34	0
1980	7.85	6.84	6.42	-2.90	0.42	2.58	0.35	0
1981	5.01	0.88	-3.29	9.78	-1.26	2.58	-1.48	0
1982	4.28	-4.05	1.84	12.81	-0.11	5.30	0.91	0
1983	9.07	1.48	0.52	4.84	1.80	4.62	-5.05	0
1984	26.23	36.72	7.49	-0.25	0.36	5.54	12.55	0
1985	19.57	59.72	-12.44	-17.05	0.67	8.03	2.48	0.82
1986	23.06	53.85	15.19	-5.50	-3.19	9.54	25.89	1.86
1987	23.61	27.49	14.94	9.40	1.87	12.22	14.69	3.18
1988	67.95[b]	57.41	9.76	2.63	3.29	12.29	-3.25	1.70

[a] CURR equals $1 + 2 + 3 + 4 - 5 - 6 - 7$

Note: [b] The explanatory items add to only 62.35 billion yuan. This is because the source used gives the total of funds used as 1154.14 whereas the items add to only 1148.53. This is explained in a footnote as due to the omission of 5.59 billion yuan from the item 'other'.

Source: Calculated from data in Fenjinde Sishi Nian 1949–1989 (pp. 429–31).

growth. After 1984 the absolute budget deficit was lower than earlier, but the proportional increases in currency in circulation, and hence the absolute increases, were much higher than previously in the 1980s (Peebles, 1990b: 77–9).

Although the government's budget position was not responsible for rapid monetary growth in China, we can say that rapid growth was all the government's responsibility, or fault. State enterprises were allowed to borrow in order to pay bonuses to workers; grain procurement agencies made losses and were subsidised, as were unprofitable enterprises. The source used for Table 3.4 can be used by interested readers to account for currency changes for earlier years back to 1952.

To the best of my knowledge it was not until the publication of ZGTJNJ90 with its new separate section on 'Finance and insurance' (Jinrong he baoxian) that statistical yearbooks carried actual data of the banking system's ex post cash plan, as described in, for example, Ma (1982: 478–9). The data appear as two tables labelled 'State bank cash receipts' and 'State bank cash expenditures' respectively (ZGTJNJ90 p. 667). They show us the form in which the banking system received cash in the years 1980 and 1985–89 and how this cash was disbursed. The difference between the total amount of cash disbursements and receipts in any year is of course equal to the increase in currency in circulation in that year. This is true of these data, and this can be shown by checking these data against the data of the absolute amounts of currency in circulation at the end of each year in the banking system's balance sheet (p. 666). The tables thus provide an alternate way of looking at causes of growth in currency in circulation.

The largest item of bank cash receipts was retail sales, except in 1989 when saving deposit receipts exceeded this item for the first time. Of course there was also a large withdrawal of savings deposits, and the net contribution of savings deposits in moderating currency growth was much less than the amount withdrawn through retail sales. For example, in 1989 bank receipts from retail sales were 548.25 billion yuan (36 per cent of total cash receipts) and the amount received as savings deposits was 572.67 billion yuan (38 per cent of total receipts), but 502.55 billion yuan of savings deposits were withdrawn, making a net increase of 70.12 billion yuan.[6] The extent to which money had become more important for Chinese households is reflected by the fact that in 1980 they deposited 29.61 billion yuan in savings deposits, withdrawing 22.5 billion yuan, whereas the amount deposited in 1989 was nearly twenty times as much as households were able to deposit in 1980. The main item of cash disbursements by the banking system was in the form of savings deposit withdrawals (33 per cent of the total in 1989, for example) and wages and other payments to individuals (24 per cent). Payments for agricultural procurements constituted 10.1 per cent of total cash disbursements in 1989 as against 14.7 per cent in 1985. Money provided to rural credit co-operatives made up 11.8 per cent of total disbursements in 1989.

A recent and important Chinese statistical source, *Zhongguo Shangye Waijing Tongji Ziliao 1952-1988* (1990, pp. 11-2) provides complete time-series data of the total amounts of cash distributed and recalled by the banking system together with two main items on either side of the balance.These data provide another accounting method for explaining annual changes in currency in circulation. They show the importance of retail sales in withdrawing currency and allow us to see the turnover of savings deposits, not just the annual changes in this stock shown in other statistical sources.

The availability of long runs of monetary data from China has made possible econometric studies of money. In China there are studies of the demand for money, as during the 1980s monetary relations changed and it was important to try to determine the demand for money in order to formulate monetary policy. Outside China, Western economists have studied such issues as the supply and demand for money, the direction of causation between money and income, and which monetary variable should be the target of the government's monetary policy. Peebles (1991: ch. 5) reviews some important such studies. Here we can review two different approaches: the theoretical and the non-theoretical.

Feltenstein and Farhadian (1987) studied the determinants of changes in broad money (currency and savings deposits) over the period 1954–83. Their study can be termed theoretical as it is based on Chinese institutions and elements of both equations 1 and 2 above. They regressed annual changes in broad money on the state wage bill, the total paid out for agricultural procurements, the current account of the balance of payments, and the government budget deficit not including the wage bill and agricultural procurement payments. Their main finding was that all variables had the correct sign, that the coefficient on the current account was not significant and that agricultural procurement payments had a greater expansionary effect on broad money than did the wage bill.

Santorum (1989) takes a non-theoretical approach to explaining changes in currency in circulation. Her basic hypothesis is that planners react to anticipated changes in the currency stock by increasing the supply of consumer goods and to unanticipated increases by increasing output or prices. She thus needs a money supply equation on which planners are assumed to base their expectations of currency growth. She regressed annual increases in currency on its previous increase, the currency stock two years earlier, the previous increase in savings deposits, the increase in savings deposits two and three years earlier as well as the increase in nominal consumption in the previous year. This equation was used because it 'seemed to be the best obtainable description of the process governing monetary growth over the period 1956–83' (p. 33). It was obviously obtained as a result of experimentation with other forms (as it is the 'best') and is just a statistical description, not an explanation of why currency grew. The resulting residuals from this money supply equation were then used in two other equations to explain changes in consumer goods supply and in the price level. The latter equation suggests that planners did increase retail prices in response to unexpected increase in currency stocks in the previous year (p. 34). When the money supply equation was used to forecast (which is usually the main purpose of such non-theoretical autoregressive econometric exercises) it performed very badly. It forecasted currency growth rates of 11 and 2 per cent for 1984 and 1985 respectively (p. 35) when the actual growth rates were 50 and 25 per cent respectively (*Fenjinde*

Sishi Nian 1949–89 p. 429).[7] Chen (1989) used Bayesian vector autoregressive analysis to analyse the relationships between money, income, prices and other variables in China over the period 1951–85.[8] His conclusion is that there is bidirectional causality (feedback) between currency and overall economic development, the budget deficit and the trade deficit and one-way causality from currency to total inflation. He concludes that monetary policy in China should be aimed at controlling currency.

It would be very useful to reproduce the explanation of Table 3.4 for each of the countries under study. As far as I know this is not possible, and I have never seen anyone else attempt it for these countries for a long period. On the basis of various assumptions and guesswork, Grossman (1986) examines the banking system's accounts in the Soviet Union to identify the unexplained changes in net liabilities. As he points out (p. 188), this is not necessarily equal to the extent of currency issue, but he takes year-to-year fluctuations in it as evidence of fluctuations in currency issue for the period 1978–83. He is unable to arrive at an estimate of currency in circulation. For the Soviet Union, the most common way of estimating changes in currency has been by reconstructing the balance of money incomes and expenditures of the population (Birman, 1981: Peebles, 1981).

An interesting attempt to assess the impact of the Soviet state budget on narrow monetary growth has been made by Harrison (1986), but only for the period 1945–55. He draws on the ideas of Birman (1981) and searches for hidden and unidentified revenues. His main conclusion is that, although the official figures consistently showed a surplus, the actual situation was one of some surplus years and some deficit years. Deficits were mainly financed by bond sales. An important conclusion is that currency growth was not caused by budget deficits, except possibly in 1954. This is another example of monetary growth not caused by budget deficits.

Harrison estimates the Soviet stock of currency in 1958 (average for the year) as 64.1 billion roubles (presumably pre-1961 roubles, so 6.41 in post-1961 roubles). The average of Peebles's (1981) estimates for the beginning of 1958 and 1959 is 5.92 billion roubles, a difference of 8 per cent, which given the different methods used is quite close. Powell (1972) gives a reconstruction of the Soviet State Bank's balance sheet for selected years from 1928 to 1967. He also gives estimates for currency in circulation for a few postwar years. He gives 1956s currency as 5.6 billion roubles. Peebles (1981) takes this as the base for the currency estimates for subsequent years. Earlier,

Ames (1965: 167) also reconstructed the banking system's balance sheet but was unable to derive any estimates of absolute amounts of currency in circulation.

The Soviet Union is the country most deficient in its publication of monetary data. It does not publish currency data but does publish data of savings deposits regularly in the section 'Growth in the standard of living of the population' in the statistical yearbook. Data of currency in circulation and savings deposits are available for the other countries under study in their national statistical yearbooks and are collected in *Comecon Data*. Monetary data for Hungary and Poland are published by the International Monetary Fund (IMF) in its monthly *International Financial Statistics* and this journal's *Yearbook*. They are classified according to IMF definitions ('money', 'quasi-money' and so on).[9] Chinese data are available from China's own statistical publication (the national economic yearbooks are available in both Chinese and English) and, for recent years, from the IMF sources mentioned above.

3.7 ECONOMIC REFORM AND BANKING REFORM

Planned economies have been continually trying reforms of various kinds since the Second World War. Pick up any book on reform in socialist economies and it will be almost exclusively about reform in industry, industrial management incentives, distribution of retained profits, determination of prices and so on. Very little attention, if any, will be paid to monetary and financial issues. This is because these economies did not consider there to be any need for drastic reforms to their monetary systems until the 1980s, when they contemplated major changes to the co-ordinating mechanism of the economy. The introduction of market elements into the economy—attempts to make enterprises deal with each other rather than take orders from planners, generate their own funds for investment or borrow such funds from banks—entailed necessary major reforms to the banking and financial systems.

China was the first country in the 1980s to implement changes to the structure and operation of its banking system. The traditional banking system had a limited number of functions, the main ones being to issue currency, to oversee the cashless transactions between state enterprises, to provide savings deposits for individuals, to distribute investment funds to enterprises from the budget, to handle the government's budget transactions and to monitor cash payments from enterprises to the population. The main thrust of reforms has been to make enterprises responsible for their losses and to allow them to keep larger parts of their profits, so that they will be provided with an incentive to produce and encouraged to rely on repayable loans to finance investment.

In the Soviet Union, as early as the mid 1960s the object was to make units economically accountable by stressing the application of the economic accounting (*khozraschet*) principle. This was supposed to be applied even to entire ministries, but the reforms did not go very far. In the 1980s the stress was on the need to make enterprises behave according to complete economic accounting (*polnii khozrachet*) and self-financing (*samofinansirovaniye*).

This principle of commercialising the activities of state enterprises has been applied to the banking system itself. The main reforms have been to turn the single state bank (the monobank) into something more like a Western central bank, separate from the Ministry of Finance, and to create or revive separate, commercially oriented banks to carry out day-to-day banking business with enterprises and the public. The central bank is now supposed to control the lending activities of the new commercial banks using economic levers such as reserve requirements and interest rates. It remains responsible for issuing currency, controlling credit extended by the other banks, managing foreign reserves and so on.

China pioneered this change in structure. In September 1983 it was announced that the People's Bank of China would become the central bank with effect from January 1984 and that four specialised banks would carry out basic banking functions (Tam, 1986; Wilson, 1986; Barnham, 1988; Chang, 1989). The most important of these banks for domestic business was the new Industrial and Commercial Bank of China, which became the bank for all enterprise loans and deposit transactions, providing short term loans to enterprises and dealing with individuals. All these banks remained state owned of course, but they were to be judged and rewarded by their performance, earning interest from the loans they made to state enterprises and to the newly emerging township enterprises and small private businesses.

This desired commercial orientation of the banks was captured in the Chinese expression that they be turned into enterprises (*qiyehua*). A commentator on similar attempts in Hungary later in the 1980s states that the new commercial banks were 'expected to operate in a competitive, profit-orientated manner' (Zalai, 1988: 64). A Western perspective shows why this approach is supposed to improve the efficiency with which savings are channelled to investors by creating true financial intermediaries that are not just state accounting houses taking profits from some state enterprises and redistributing them according to the plan to other state enterprises. The commercial principles of profit and loss were to be applied to these new banks so that they would have an interest in ensuring that the enterprises to which they lent money could actually make a profit and repay the loan. It is felt that a competitive commercial banking system reduces the costs of bringing together the surplus money units (savers) and deficit units (investors). By reducing these transaction costs the banks can offer a higher interest rate to savers and charge a lower interest rate to borrowers, thus increasing both saving and investment. The banks' commercial orientation was supposed to ensure that they lent only to profitable borrowers, thus increasing the average return on the funds invested and through this boosting economic growth.

Other planned economies followed China's lead in banking reform. Hungary announced that from 1 January 1987 it would operate a two-level banking system with the Hungarian National Bank becoming the central bank and its business functions being taken over by new banks. Five banks were established, but three of them still do about two-thirds of all banking business in Hungary (*The Economist* 20 October 1990, p. 96). In 1988 a new independent bank, Post Bank Ltd, was created to compete with the Hungarian National Savings Bank. In Poland in 1989 the first private joint-stock bank, the *Savim-Bank Depozytowo-Kredytowy SA*, was established. It was owned 40 per cent by individuals and 60 per cent by a housing investment company. In the first five months of 1990 thirty-two new bank licences were issued and there were at least that many applications outstanding (*MNBPB* no. 1035, 20 June 1990, p. 24). In co-operation with the French *Centre de Formation de la Profession Bancaire* a new banking school is being planned for Katowice to train the required banking personnel.

Changes in the structure of the Soviet banking system have been very marked, and the whole system is in a state of flux with its eventual structure yet to be determined. Before 1988 the banking system was the traditional monobank with specialised banks to administer separate areas of the economy. The monobank was the state bank of the USSR (*Gosbank*), under which were the USSR Bank for Capital Investments (*Stroibank*), the USSR Bank for Foreign Trade (*Vneshtorgbank*) and the USSR Savings Bank (*Gostrudsberkassy*). Their respective titles indicate which aspects of Soviet economic life they were supposed to administer. This structure was said to reflect 'administrative methods of management, which emphatically under-estimated the money–commodity relations under Socialism' (Ponomarev, 1989: 16).

From January 1988 a new structure came into effect with *Gosbank* as the central bank and under it five specialised state-owned banks:

Bank for Foreign Economic Affairs of the USSR (*Vnesheconombank*)
USSR Personal Savings and Credit Bank (*Sberbank*)
Agri-Industrial Bank of the USSR (*Agroprombank*)
USSR Bank for Industrial Construction (*Promstroibank*)
USSR Bank for Municipal Services and Social Development
(*Zhilsotsbank*). On 10 July 1990 it was announced that this bank
would be transformed into a joint-stock commercial bank called
the Bank for Social Development (*Sotsbank*).

These banks specialise in the areas of activity indicated in their titles. A major change to this two-level system came into effect after August 1988 when co-operative banks, with state-owned agencies, co-ops, local authorities and federal departments as shareholders, were allowed to do business. It was planned to allow 180 such banks, and by 1 August 1989 there were 140 such banks (Ponomarev, 1990: 17) or, according to another source, about 85 commercial banks and 51 co-operative banks (*MNBPB* no. 1025, 16 August 1989, pp. 20–4). By 3 August 1990 there were 247 commercial banks and 111 co-operative banks registered in the Soviet Union (*MNBPB* no. 1038, 17 October 1990, p. 24). April 1990 saw the publication of the first annual report of a commercial bank in the Soviet Union when the commercial innovation bank *Inncombank-Interznaniye* reported a profit from its business of granting short term credits to industry. It is now felt in the Soviet Union that this three-level banking system (central bank, specialised state banks, and commercial and co-operative banks) should be simplified to a two-level system comprising the state central bank and the commercial banks. This is the proposal of the draft banking laws being developed during 1990.

According to Viktor Geraschenko, chairman of the board of *Gosbank*:[10]

> It is important during this phase to encourage the creation of
> organisations that will promote economic development. This can take
> place the more quickly if the new banks are allowed without
> restrictions to mark out an area of operations and become efficient.
> The State Bank will, of course, supervise closely, especially where a
> lack of experience and professionalism is evident. But it will clearly be
> the market which decides which of these new banks will develop, how
> many will survive and how many fail.

This quite clearly shows the intention to use market discipline to determine which forms of banking organisation there should be and how many banks can survive in the transformed market-based Soviet economy. What structure emerges and what effect this will have on the state banking sector is yet to be seen. Viktor Gerashchenko believes in the necessity of making the central bank truly independent so that it 'should not be answerable to government, but rather to the Supreme Soviet, following to some extent the example of the central banks in Germany and the United States (p. 25).' An optimistic Soviet view is that already 'Money in the USSR is slowly becoming real money, and banks real banks' (Fedorov 1989: 461).[11]

Generally, it seems that Hungary has been most prepared to allow foreign banks to buy into its newly emerging banks, and Poland has had greatest access to foreign advice and support in creating a new banking system. Both Poland and Hungary received IMF loans in early 1990. The Polish government is being advised by a group of leading Western central banks brought together for this purpose by the IMF. In addition, the US Treasury created a fund of US$1 billion at the beginning of 1990 to support the zloty when it is made convertible. Twelve Western counties contributed to the fund, including Japan, Portugal and Turkey (*MNBPB* 1030, 17 January 1990, p. 20). Czechoslovakian banking reform seems to be the slowest to get going. The first non-state bank in this country, the *Agrobank*, was established in Prague in early 1990. It is intended to support entrepreneurial activity in the food industry and agriculture and is expecting to involve foreign capital from France and Austria. In early 1990 Czechoslovakia signed an agreement to join the IMF in late 1990.

3.8 CONTROL OF THE MONEY SUPPLY DURING REFORM

This section will examine the problems involved in controlling the narrow money supply during reform in a planned economy. China and the Soviet Union will be taken as examples as they are the most prominent of our countries.

Economic reform started in China in 1979 with the introduction of monetary incentives for farmers under the compulsory purchase system. Further reforms were the granting of more independence to enterprises by substituting tax payments for the delivery of profits to the budget, the introduction of bonuses for workers, the allowing of non-state enterprises, the decontrol of many prices and the introduction of a two-tier pricing system, and reform of the banking system. The positive impact of these reforms on real output and the standard of living, as well as the negative impact on nominal variables such as the budget position, balance of trade and inflation, have been obvious (Perkins, 1988; Peebles, 1990a).

In 1988 holdings of cash and saving deposits were 9.4 times their 1979 level, rising from about 33 per cent of that year's retail sales to 73 per cent of 1988s. Real national income rose 126 per cent and was accompanied by an 85 per cent rise in the cost of living index.[12] Currency growth rates were high and erratic, with the currency stock rising by nearly 50 per cent in both 1984 and 1988, for example. The cost of living rose 12 and 21 per cent in 1985 and 1988 respectively. Of course, part of the large increase in the stock of currency would have been justified by the monetisation of the economy due to reforms that led to the opening of many markets and trade outside the state non-cash sphere of circulation. It was against this background that a severe credit squeeze was introduced in September 1988. This credit squeeze is credited with ensuring that in 1989 the growth rate of currency in circulation, said to be 14.5 per cent, was the lowest since 1984 and 32 percentage points lower than the rate in 1988.[13] My own calculations show that the amount of currency in circulation at the end of 1989 was only 9.8 per cent higher than at the end of 1988. *International Financial Statistics* (September 1990, p. 166) gives the series 'Currency outside deposit money banks', which is the same as currency in circulation in Chinese sources (for example, *Huobi Liutongliang* in *Fenjinde Sishi Nian 1949–1989* p. 429). The rate of increase of the retail price index in 1989, at 17.8 per cent, was much the same as the 18.5 per cent rate in 1988. The rate of inflation is said to have fallen significantly in 1990, however (Delfs and Bowring, 1990: 40). The reasons for slower currency growth are said to be the lower rate of growth of money incomes achieved in 1989 and the greater extent to which households accumulated savings deposits. This is seen as a change in the relative roles of retail sales and savings deposit accumulation in withdrawing currency from circulation. The latter became more important, and this could be attributed to the indexing of some savings deposits to the rate of inflation during the credit squeeze.

It is interesting to note that this explanation can be easily understood in terms of equation 1. Despite reforms this slightly old-fashioned way of looking at the money supply process still makes sense and is the framework often used to explain narrow monetary growth. When accounting for the large increase in the money supply in 1990 Chen Yuan, vice-governor of the People's Bank of China, pointed to 'the need for additional funds to purchase agricultural products' because of the record harvest (Delfs and Bowring, 1990:

40). This shows how monetary growth follows credit issue, which results from the government's need to meet its purchase commitments. We saw above that there was a large increase in currency issue in 1984, which had a then record harvest. The banking system cannot predict such events and really has to make government commitments possible by extending credit. These commitments result in cash payments to the rural population and are identified in equation 1.

I have remarked on these macroeconomic and monetary developments elsewhere and tried to show their interrelationships (Peebles, 1990a; 1990b; 1991). To identify the problems the reformed banking system had in controlling monetary growth I will refer to an independent assessment by Tsang (1990). He identifies four main reasons for the lack of control over monetary growth during China's economic reforms:

1. The People's Bank of China lacks autonomy in its decision making. It is subject to pressure from the Treasury and other ministries to 'cater for their expansionary ambitions' (p. 230). Under reform, greater power has been given to local authorities in decision making, and these authorities constantly pressure local bank branches to extend credit for their favourite tax-generating projects. Local authorities 'even have a say in the appointment of and remuneration to bank officials.' (p. 230).

2. It has been difficult for the banks to predict the behaviour of the demand for money, and they have tended to oversupply money for fear of causing short term recessions that are visible and can be blamed on the banking system.

3. The determinants of the narrow money supply are 'very complex, many of which are beyond the control of the central bank' (p. 230). This important point was made earlier and is highlighted by equation 1 above.

4. Tools of monetary control are largely ineffective because 'the specialised banks have yet to establish themselves as entities with independent operational status and sufficient resources of their own'(p. 232).

When the credit squeeze was implemented it did not use indirect economic levers like bank reserve requirements, open market operations and interest rate adjustments. It placed quantitative quotas on bank lending.

Two other commentators (Bowles and White, 1989) assess banking reform in China very negatively and conclude that the reforms may have even weakened, not strengthened, the credit constraints facing enterprises (pp. 487–8). They stress the weakness of the central bank's control over the new specialised banks (as does Tsang) and give examples of the tendency to approve virtually all loan applications irrespective of profitability.

Such views are reflected in those of a Chinese economist (Li Yunqi, 1989: 666–7), who argues that the following reforms are still necessary:

1 The People's Bank of China should become a truly independent bank, with its governors appointed by the premier of the State Council. It should itself determine the required rate of growth of the money supply based on economic and financial conditions.

2 The American banking structure of 'regional branches' should be considered for China.

3 The central bank must be separated from the Ministry of Finance and the latter should borrow only by selling Treasury bonds, not by automatically drawing on its overdraft.

4 The system of reserve deposits required of the specialised banks must be improved, and interbank lending must be controlled by making the banks go through their reserve accounts with the central banks when doing this.

5 More financial institutions should be set up, and existing and new banks should be 'truly independent enterprises'.

In the case of the Soviet Union it is much more difficult to identify what has been going on with respect to the money supply process and the relationship between economic reform, the government budget, monetary expansion, price changes and so on. However, we can say something on the basis of fragmentary data and some Western reconstructions and estimates. Grossman (1989: 31) argues that most of the currency stock was created in the late 1970s and early 1980s. It seems clear that narrow monetary growth was rapid during the 1980s, particularly so in 1989 and 1990. There are no precise figures, but the following give some indication. Gorbachev's statement at the June 1987 plenum that the quantity of currency in circulation had increased 3.1 times over the period 1971–85 has been noted (Grossman, 1989: 31). On the basis of Peebles's (1981: 63) estimate of 29.17 billion roubles for the beginning of 1971, this implies an amount of about 90 billion for 1985. This figure is hard to reconcile with Lokshin (1990: 74), who puts the population's holdings of cash (*nalichniye den'gi*) at about 70 billion roubles for the beginning of 1989. Perhaps Peebles's estimates were underestimates, which would imply that Birman's (1981) were as well.

For more recent developments, Parker (1990: 12) states that the money supply (no definition given) increased 56 per cent in 1989. It has recently been stated that at the beginning of October 1990 the Soviet population held about 124 billion roubles in cash and 358.8 billion roubles in savings deposits. Using the figures of 70 and 296.7 billion roubles for these concepts respectively for the beginning of 1989 (Lokshin, 1990: 74), we can see that, if the figures are accurate, cash holding grew 77 per cent and savings deposits 21 per cent in just over eighteen months. Elsewhere, it is said that the quantity of money issued during the first nine months of 1990 was 1.7 times the amount issued during the same period of 1989. The growth of unsatisfied demand of the population for the same period was 19 billion roubles when the population's money incomes were 461 billion roubles—an increase of 14.4 per cent over 1989 against a planned growth of 7.1 per cent.[14] The consumer price index in the first nine months of 1990 increased 3.7 per cent over the previous year (same period), with state prices rising 3.6 per cent.[15] These figures show an over-plan increase in total money incomes, an increase in unsatisfied demand and a large increase in unspent purchasing power. All this can be understood in terms of equation 1. How these phenomena can be interpreted in a consistent comparative framework will be discussed in the next chapter.

Izvestiya (21 October 1990:) reported that:

> The monetary and financial imbalance in the country's economy is getting worse, money issued has increased and there has been a noticeable rise in prices for consumer goods. The faster growth of the population's money incomes against the manufacture of output is increasingly exacerbating the situation in the consumer market.

Proponents of the excess demand hypothesis would say that this has always been the situation. What role did economic reform play in exacerbating these problems? An interesting hypothesis has recently been advanced by the well-known monetary economist Ronald I. McKinnon to highlight the main factor behind rapid monetary growth and the implications for policy necessary to stabilise the rouble and eventually make it fully convertible.

McKinnon (1990) lays the main blame on the nature of reform under Gorbachev and the effect this had in increasing the budget deficit. On the basis of estimates by Jan Vanous, McKinnon (1990: 133) puts the budget deficit in 1984 as 2.0 per cent of gross national

product (*GNP*) and 13.1 per cent in 1989. He attributes the widen-
ing deficit after Gorbachev's coming to power in 1985 to the fall in
total revenue from 47 per cent of *GNP* in 1985 to 38 per cent in
1989. As we saw above, most of Soviet budget revenue is remitted by
state enterprises. Reforms meant that enterprises were allowed to
retain more of their profits and non-state units and local governments took over state industrial assets and remitted less of their
profits to the central budget. Soviet sources point out that the plan
for turnover tax remissions has not been fulfilled since 1982, receipts
from foreign economic activities have fallen (oil markets were
depressed) and revenue from alcohol sales slumped because of
Gorbachev's anti-alcohol campaign after 1985 (Kagalovsky, 1989:
447). McKinnnon sees this as the eroding of the 'implicit tax collecting mechanism' (p. 133) of the central government. It was implicit as
under the old system of ownership and management the government
just ordered its enterprises to remit profits. There was no need to
have a formalised tax system clearly specifying tax rates and the
obligations of legally independent producers and income earners. For
MacKinnon the monetary implications of this are clear as 'the
government fiscal deficit is responsible for the major and rapidly
growing part of money and near-money owned by households' (p.
134). McKinnon recognises that in order to estimate the true extent
of the 'monetary overhang' it is necessary to add 'the huge stocks of
partially blocked enterprise credit money (about which information
is scare) ... but on less than a one-for-one basis' (p. 134). This is
passive money held in the accounts of enterprises, and as it is less
liquid than cash it should be discounted in arriving at some total of
broad money.

Now, all this is correct. However, when we examine reasons for
changes in narrow money in the form of cash and savings deposits,
we must remember that the money must at some time be withdrawn
from enterprise or government accounts and become household
money income and then not be withdrawn from circulation, as
shown in equation 1. The reasons for money growth are shown in
this equation just as much as in budget deficit figures. Over the past
few years money incomes of the population have been growing rapidly, at annual rates of 9.2 and 12.9 per cent in 1988 and 1989
respectively, and in the first nine months of 1990 incomes were 14.1
per cent higher than in the same period of the previous year. As
narrow monetary growth results from money income creation, the
approach taken in the analytical section of the next chapter will
focus on this aspect of the money supply process as shown in
equation 1.

3.9 *PRIVATE FOREIGN-EXCHANGE MARKETS*

This is a fascinating topic for the economist, which has not been much researched because of data and other problems. Visitors to the six countries under study often bring back interesting observations of foreign exchange activities. Often they are surprised by the extent to which trade in foreign currencies between tourists and local buyers occurs even on street corners and near hotels under the eyes of the police when they have been told that such activities are illegal, as they have been (Cowitt, 1986: 20–2; Mojzisková, 1987/88). This is an interesting observation for the economist to explain. This section summarises the arguments and findings of Vanous (1980) concerning various aspects of foreign currency transactions in Eastern Europe and the Soviet Union as an example of the phenomena that can be observed, and also points out their implications for the analytical sections of the next chapter.

Vanous (1980: 18) argues that in fact many buyers of foreign currency are buying on behalf of the State Bank. This explains why they are not harassed by the police. It also implies that the government recognises that the tourist rate of exchange overvalues the domestic currency and that it is willing to pay a higher price for foreign exchange informally. In all the countries covered by Vanous for the period before 1980, private trade in foreign currency was illegal, but the degree of enforcement of the law varied with Poland being the least keen to enforce the law.[16] This was mainly because the Polish government was willing to supply domestic residents with goods in exchange for foreign currencies, as noted in chapter 2. Allowing private trade in these currencies redistributed access to these goods to people who could not directly obtain foreign currencies from abroad. The Soviet Union and Hungary were the most keen to enforce their laws. In the case of Hungary this was to prevent the Austrian schilling from becoming a second currency. However, by the end of the 1980s Hungarian forints were being accepted from Hungarian tourists in Austria, but at half the official exchange rate (Résésv, 1990: 2) This trade was illegal (Kornai, 1990: 42). In East Germany, the fear of the West German marks taking on a second-currency role led to further restrictions on trade in foreign currencies in 1979 at the same time as Hungary was tightening its laws.

The different degrees of enforcement of the law played a role in determining the black market rates in different countries. Poland has always had the highest black-market rate for the US dollar among all the countries under study.[17] This was mainly due to the fact that no questions were asked about the source of currency when Polish residents deposited foreign currencies in their accounts, the ease with which the dollar could be traded in Poland, and the high demand for the dollar because it could be freely spent in government stores. Together with shortages in official shops this easy official attitude ensures a high demand for foreign currencies in Poland. Vanous derives a measure of the deviation of the black market rate from the official rate for each country, which shows the relative profit a tourist can make and the extent to which each country tries to attract tourists by allowing the free market rate to exceed the official rate. The excess is greatest in the Soviet Union, East Germany and Poland, less in Czechoslovakia and much less in Hungary.[18] In Vanous's view this reflects the relative degree of openness of each economy to tourism and Hungary's concern to eradicate a black market.

The Soviet Union's financial problems were really brought to world attention when there was a major adjustment of the tourist rate of exchange in late October 1989, from 0.64 roubles per US dollar to 6.26 roubles — a massive devaluation (McKinnon, 1990: 135). I have been told that in 1989 the black market rate was anything between 20 and 25 roubles.

In China, the increase in international trade during the 1980s and the decentralisation of trading activities to enterprises meant that informal markets in foreign currencies emerged. These were recognised by the government from about early 1986 onwards when official foreign-exchange swap centres were opened in major cities, at which registered enterprises, not individuals, could bid for foreign exchange at auction under local government supervision. In the Soviet Union the first similar auction was held in November 1989, organised by the Bank for Foreign Economic Affairs. During the 1980s the Chinese currency was devalued a number of times, with the major devaluations occurring in July 1986 and December 1989.[19] In November 1990 there was a further devaluation, which brought the official rate nearer to the free market rate and signalled the possibility of making the currency convertible, although this has not been accepted by all Chinese leaders. China seems more willing than the other countries under study to keep adjusting its official rate to the free market rate that it can conveniently see being paid at the official swap centres. In September 1988 the Chinese government instituted a severely restrictive credit squeeze, an interesting result of which was that a few months later the *Renminbi* appreciated against the US dollar on local foreign-exchange markets, showing its increased relative scarcity. It still traded at a discount, however, at about 5–6 yuan to the US dollar (it had been over 7 earlier) compared with an official rate of 3.7221 yuan. Demand and supply were having their effect in this market. Hsu (1989: 179) discusses the effect on the Hong Kong dollar/*Renminbi* exchange rate of rumours of a devaluation of the latter in August 1988, but Hsu gets the exchange rates the wrong way round, with Hong Kong people supposedly paying more for the yuan than the official rate[20]—and this at a time of the latter's expected devaluation. I do not think that this has ever happened.

The case of Poland provides difficulty for any comparative monetary analysis because of the free use of foreign currencies in domestic trade and as a store of value remarked on in chapter 2. This issue has been ignored in comparative studies such as those of Peebles (1981) and, more recently, Winiecki (1988) and Farrell (1989), when the problem was likely to be much more important. It must be impossible to quantify accurately the extent of foreign currency holdings in Poland. IMF sources on Poland list an item 'Time, savings and foreign currency deposits' valued in zlotys, thus lumping foreign currency deposits together with zloty deposits, presumably having converted them by some acceptable exchange rate. One view is that 'By 1987 in Poland the majority of savings deposits and cash held by the population were in hard currency (valued at the black market rate of exchange)' and that these holdings amounted to about $7 billion (presumably US dollars) (Rostowski, 1989: 281–2). Rostowski's estimates imply that these holdings increased from $2 billion in 1982 to $7 billion in 1987. Sokil and King (1989: 23) put the amount in foreign exchange accounts at US$3 billion (no year specified). The main sources of these currencies, which are mainly US dollars and West German marks, are remittances by Polish workers working abroad, gifts from relatives and friends abroad, and foreign currencies earned by Polish traders in neighbouring countries who only accept the 'hard' currencies of Western countries.

As we saw in chapter 2, Polish zloty holdings in real terms are the lowest of the countries under study. The question we must ask is whether the availability of foreign currencies makes any difference to our subsequent analysis of government policy and whether Polish individuals can somehow reduce their zloty holdings by obtaining foreign currencies, independently of government actions. Let us take this last question first. I think that in the most likely circumstances we can assume that it is not possible for Polish households to reduce their zloty holdings because of the existence of stocks of foreign currencies and regular additions to these stocks. If a Polish individual buys foreign currency on the private market, the zloty stays in circulation and there is no reduction in the zloty money supply. Only if Polish individuals physically exported zloty notes in return for foreign currencies (unlikely), or if the government sold foreign currencies in exchange for zloty banknotes, would this trade be able to reduce the zloty money supply. From the point of view of government actions to control the growth of the zloty money supply, the use of foreign currencies has no effect on policy. As long as the government tries to limit the growth of zloty holdings, the existence of foreign currency holdings makes no difference to the subsequent analysis except to the extent that the government can sell foreign currency to the population. However, this sale is possible in all the countries under study and does not depend on existing levels of foreign currency holdings. The holdings of foreign currencies may explain why Polish zloty holdings are so low, but the question we will face in the next chapter is how the government ensures that these holdings are so low.

As households hold foreign currencies as a store of value the liquidity of the Polish household sector may be higher than is indicated by considering the zloty money supply alone. For example, the ratio of private savings deposits to annual retail sales given by Winiecki (1988: 63) for 1983 is 0.29. This figure can be derived from official sources whose data are reproduced in *Comecon Data*. The figure for private savings deposits was 1058.2 billion zlotys in 1983. It is not clear whether this figure includes foreign currency deposits or not. From IMF data we can obtain a figure of 1034.2 zlotys for demand deposits and 1292.3 zlotys for 'Time, savings and foreign currency deposits' (*International Financial Statistics Yearbook 1987* p. 565). There is no way of knowing what proportion of this total was held by individuals. If all of it was held by individuals, this implies a *Liquidity SD* ratio of about 0.66, if we take *SD* as including all types of savings deposits (demand, time, savings, foreign currency). This can be regarded as a possible maximum liquidity ratio for households, ignoring cash holdings.

3.10 CONCLUSIONS AND IMPLICATIONS FOR ANALYSIS

The simplest and most direct way to understand the money supply process is expressed in equation 1. It concentrates on the actual flow of money into circulation and the return flows through which money returns to the state sector. It shows us that narrow monetary growth is determined by a number of factors, most of which are not under the control of the central bank. It also shows us what reactive policies monetary planners can take when these variables are likely to produce higher rates of narrow monetary growth than the planners desire. The banks' accounts allow us to identify the extent to which the enterprise sector, the government or foreign exchange transactions contributed to narrow monetary growth, if we had complete data for all the countries under study.

In the next chapter we will attempt to explain the possible consequences of excess demand, for consumer goods in these countries, how planners reacted to excess demand, and the different rates of monetary growth and open inflation that resulted from different reactions.

4 Analysing money and prices

Any adequate historical analysis of money and prices would have to show why there were different rates of monetary growth in the different countries being studied and the nature of the relationship between money and prices. Why did prices rise at different rates in the different countries, and with what consequences? Before proposing a simple way of answering these questions it will be helpful to look at the implications and application of one of the oldest of monetary theories to these problems. This is of course the Quantity Theory of Money.

4.1 MONEY AND PRICES: THE QUANTITY THEORY APPROACH

The basic idea underlying this theory is that there is a stable relationship between the amount of real money people wish to hold and a few major macroeconomic variables, the most important of which is taken to be real income. People wish to hold money both for transactions purposes and as an asset. The higher their real incomes, the more transactions they will make and therefore the more real money they will need to hold. At higher real incomes people will hold more wealth in the form of monetary assets. The real money supply equals the nominal money supply (M) deflated by the aggregate price level (P). Let real output be Q and the proportion of money people wish to hold be k, say, 25 per cent. Then

$$M/P = kQ$$
or
$$MV = PQ$$
where
$$V = 1/k$$

Here velocity (V) is equal to 4. The expression $MV = PQ$ is called the equation of exchange.

The assumption is that people are always holding the desired amount of money and that the observed value of V is the equilibrium value showing people's demand for money; that is, it is equal to $1/k$. If M were to increase without there being any corresponding increase in PQ, then V would fall. The Quantity Theory would interpret this ex post as there being a shift in the demand for money (k increases). In such circumstances predictions of MV and hence PQ on the basis of changes in M would be incorrect. This instability of V occurred in the United States and the United Kingdom in the early 1980s when there was rapid monetary growth and no corresponding increase in PQ, meaning that observed V had to fall. This has been referred to as the period when velocity (of $M1$ in the United States) 'fell off the rails' (Gordon, 1987: 372). Despite such episodes quantity theorists believe that there is a stable relationship between M and MV, hence between M and PQ over the long run.

The second important issue related to the interpretation of the equation of exchange is how the economy adapts to a change in spending (MV). Does the response consist mainly of an increase in P, an increase in Q or both; and if the latter, what determines the proportions in which P and Q change? This is the attempt to turn the identity into a theory that says: if M increases by so much, P and Q will increase by so much (the effect on V is assumed to be minor or at least predictable).

The equation of exchange is used in the following way. The extra assumption is added that changes in M are determined largely independently of changes in PQ, meaning that they occur first and that the rest of the economy must adapt to these changes. Assuming that V is relatively constant, or does not fall dramatically when M rises, an increase in M must increase PQ. The increase in PQ will increase the demand for the extra nominal money so that people will be holding it all voluntarily. When M first increases people are holding more real money than they wish, and so they try to reduce their excess money holdings. A crucial aspect of the theory is based on the institutions of the market economy. An individual can reduce his or her money holdings by buying goods, but society as a whole cannot do this because the money stays in circulation as it passes from buyer to seller. The only way people's money holdings will be voluntarily held is if the demand for money increases. There are only four ways in which equilibrium can be restored when there is an increase in M: either V must fall, P must rise, Q must rise or a combination of all three must occur. How the economy adapts to the initial rise in M is controversial and cannot be answered by the equation of exchange. It requires a full macroeconomic model of the supply side of the economy to show how demand increases Q or P and what time profile these events will take. This is the area of controversy. To simplify dramatically, we can say that quantity theorists use models that predict that eventually the entire effect of the increase in M will be reflected in an increase in P, and not in an increase in Q or a fall in velocity.

From the equation of exchange $MV = PQ$ then

$$P = V(M/Q)$$

meaning that, if V is constant, the price level (P) is proportionate to the ratio of money to real output (M/Q). The crucial aspect of the theory is that changes in the money stock are taken as the first, initiating, factor to which the price level must respond. As we can see, a change in M/Q is capable of bringing about a change in P, and so it is not just changes in nominal money that can cause changes in the price level.

4.2 APPLYING THE QUANTITY THEORY TO CHINESE DATA

Because of the availability of long runs of macroeconomic and monetary data for China the Quantity Theory of Money has been applied to Chinese data by Chow (1987) for the period 1952–83. This makes a very interesting case study, showing the limitations and lack of explanatory power of the theory when it is applied to a planned economy.

First Chow examined the demand-for-money formulation of the theory by regressing the natural logarithm of M/P on the natural logarithm of real output (national income available). His monetary variable is currency in circulation (end-of-year figures). He obtained a slope coefficient of 1.162, which he interprets as the income elasticity of demand for money. This means that velocity fell in China. He explicitly assumes that actual real money holdings were always equal to the amounts people wished to hold. There are problems with the model in the form of positive serial correlation, and after another regression he concludes that the quantity theory 'provides a reasonable first approximation in explaining the demand for money in China' (p. 325). He then turns to the question of the dependence of the price level on M/Q.[1] He uses the retail price index as his price level. This is sensible as it is the price index that we would like to explain. Chow recognises that many consumer goods prices have been controlled in China and so 'may not adjust to monetary forces as they would in a market economy. However, the theory could still provide a good explanation of the general price level if the remaining, uncontrolled prices were able to adjust sufficiently' (p. 322). This is a crucial assumption necessary for the theory to work. He is assuming that the weighting of free market prices in the general retail price index is sufficient to provide a relationship between P and M/Q. He will have only one explanation of why prices actually changed in China: they were market prices and so rose in the face of excess demand just as prices do in a market economy.

A regression of ln P on ln (M/Q) produced a slope coefficient of 0.2687, and Chow concludes that the explanatory variable, the ratio M/Q, 'does provide a good explanation of the price level P, as the quantity theory predicts' (p. 325). This is because the t-statistic is over 11 and the coefficient of determination fairly high (0.8217). As he further remarks, 'However, the co-efficient . . . is only 0.2687 and very much below unity, contradicting the quantity theory' (p. 325). A regression of the first differences of the logs of the variables yielded a slope coefficient of only 0.1266. These results show a very weak quantitative relationship between the money ratio and the retail price level in China for this period. Whatever one may say about statistical significance, the relevant question is the size of the quantitative link, and these are very low co-efficients.[2] Chow went on to add various other lagged variables and concludes that ln (M/Q) is a significant variable in explaining ln P.

This interesting case study shows the weaknesses of the Quantity Theory. First, it starts from changes in the money ratio and argues that the main response is a change in the price level. For the purpose of historical narrative it is of no help in explaining why the money supply or money ratio changed in the first place. This is just assumed to occur. Second, the theory assumes that the retail price level is virtually the same as a free-market price level and so does not ask *why* it changed. It cannot therefore answer Chen and Hou's (1986: 817) question as to why the government increased prices, thus contributing to inflation in the early 1980s. Third, the theory ignores the nature of the institutions of the planned economies. In particular, it does not ask why the money supply changed and, more importantly, it ignores a crucial difference between the institutional assumption on which the Quantity Theory is based and the reality of the institutions in planned economies. This difference is that in market economies an individual act of spending cannot reduce the aggregate money supply, whereas in a planned economy it can if the money is spent on state-supplied goods. Fourth, the theory does not allow for any other cause of changes in the price level. In particular, the macroeconomic theory underlying the supply side of the economy used by quantity theorists does not allow for an independent effect of the level of money wages on the price level. This is because quantity theorists assume a competitive economy with a competitive labour market where the money wage has to adapt so that it produces the required full-employment real wage. In other words, the money wage is just another price, which is determined by the real wage and the general price level, which is determined by the money supply. In such a model there is no role for independent changes in the money wage. Now, in planned economies it is blindingly obvious that there are no competitive labour markets as they are understood in market economies and that the money wage (interpreted broadly as average money income paid out by the state sector) is determined by the government. The government can easily decree a 10 per cent increase in average money incomes. We want to know the consequence of this for the price level and the money supply. The Quantity Theory cannot tell us, even in its model let alone in the real world. Chow recognises that the wage bill may influence the price level in the institutional context of China but does not offer a theory for this. He tested for this possible effect by adding an estimate of the total wage bill to his original Quantity Theory equation. The result was a statistically significant but quantitatively small coefficient (elasticity of only 0.043) (pp. 331–2). This was not really a fair test of the possible impact of the wage bill on the price level (it should really have been total money incomes). By ignoring this effect the Quantity Theory is unable to explain why the price level changes in a planned economy and, more importantly, why the money supply changes. We must offer an alternative explanation — one that explains why the money stock changed, and the relationship between money and prices.

There seem to be two reasons why the Quantity Theory has not been applied to the experiences of other planned economies in such detail. The first is the lack of reliable data, especially for the Soviet Union. The second is the fact that for certain of these countries there has been very little change in the aggregate price level and so, it would appear, very little for the theory to explain. Furthermore, there would be major problems of interpretation if the approach were used to analyse the data from, say, the experiences of the Soviet Union. For illustrative purposes the following analysis can be made. I do not think that it tells us very much about these economies, but it does show the limitations of the theory and the problem in interpreting the statistical results obtained by mechanically applying the theory.

We start with the dynamic form of the theory. Take the equation of exchange $MV = PQ$, take logs of both sides, differentiate with respect to time, and we obtain the following expression, which, like the above equation, is always true:

$$m + v = p + q$$

where lower case letters represent growth rates of the same variables. This equation says that the rate of growth of the nominal money supply plus the rate of change of velocity (which together equal the rate of change of nominal expenditure and incomes) must always equal the rate of inflation plus the rate of growth of real output. We can rearrange to obtain

$$p = (m - q) + v$$

or
$$(m - q) = p - v$$

The expression in brackets, the difference between the rate of nominal monetary growth and the rate of real output $(m - q)$, can be called the rate of excess monetary growth. The equation tells us that this will be reflected in two variables: the rate of inflation and the change in velocity. If over a long period and on average $m = 10$ per cent per annum and $q = 2$, then $(p - v)$ must equal 8. There are any number of outcomes. For example, if $v = 0$ then $p = 8$; or maybe $p = 4$ and $v = -4$; or maybe $p = 0$ and $v = -8$.

Whatever the outcome, for a market economy the quantity theorist would interpret this as an equilibrium relationship. The change in the demand for money explains the behaviour of v and, given m and q, the rate of inflation will show up as the residual. The growth of demand for real money is q plus the fall in v. The nominal money supply is growing at rate m, therefore inflation must equal the difference in order to reduce the nominal money supply to equal the real quantity demanded. For example,

$$p = (m - q) + v$$
$$4 = (10 - 2) + (-4)$$

The excess rate of money growth is eroded by a 4 per cent inflation rate and a 4 per cent fall in velocity, that is, by an increase in the demand for money and hence an increase in the ratio of money to output.

Now, the crucial issue is the determinants of the proportions in which $(m - q)$ is reflected in either p or v. For a market economy the answer from a quantity theorist would be clear. Given m (determined by the monetary authorities, or determined independently of their wishes by the banking system) and given q (determined by the supply side of the economy and the growth of labour force, capital stock, technical progress and so on, which are all independent of m), and given also the income elasticity of demand for money, which determines v, then p follows as a residual. A textbook approximation is that V is constant, meaning that v is zero. This corresponds to the case where the income elasticity of demand for money is unity. In this case all excess monetary growth shows up as inflation,

$$p = (m - q)$$

Many economists use this approximation for countries for which they think that the income elasticity of demand for money is approximately unity. In the above numerical example p will be 8 per cent per annum. The crucial assumption is that any value of v reflects households' choice, meaning that they are always holding desired real money stocks.

With these relationships in mind let us look at the variables from three of our six countries, chosen because they represent two extremes and a median position. The issue is how a quantity theorist would interpret the results and how we interpret them. Rough estimates of the required statistics are contained in Table 4.1.

The fourth column of Table 4.1 shows the rate of inflation divided by the rate of excess monetary growth, thus showing the extent to which the latter is transformed into open inflation. The lower this ratio, the greater the fall in velocity. For Hungary we can see that excess monetary growth was reflected entirely in open inflation, meaning that velocity was roughly constant. At the other extreme there was no open inflation in the Soviet Union, and so excess monetary growth showed up as a large fall in velocity. Similar results would be obtained from East German data. In China there was an open inflation response of about 30 per cent, so the majority of excess monetary growth showed up as a fall in velocity.

Now, no-one would accept these countries as market economies where the change in v was a pure reflection of demand conditions, although one might be tempted to do so for Hungary and one analyst has done so for China. If we were to interpret the relationships in this way, the implications for the income elasticity of demand for money would be interesting. Roughly speaking, for Hungary the income elasticity of demand for money is obviously about unity; real money grew at about (9.4 — 3.8) 5.6 per cent per annum on average and real income at 5.7, giving an estimate of 5.6/5.7 =0.98. For China the rough estimate would be (19.4 — 3.5)/7.7 = 2.1, and, interestingly, a similar figure would be obtained for the Soviet Union,

Table 4.1 Monetary and price indicators for selected countries

(average annual growth, per cent per annum)

Country	m^a	q^a	p^a	$p/(m-q)$	Period
Hungary	9.4	3.8	5.7	1.02	1971–85
USSR	13.1[b]	6.7	0.06	0.009	1956–78
PRC	19.4[b]	7.7	3.5	0.30	1970–88

Notes: [a] m for Hungary is based on 'money' (IMF definition) and for the USSR it is cash plus savings deposits; p is based on the consumer price index for Hungary and the official retail price index for the USSR and China; and q is based on real GDP for Hungary and real national income produced for USSR and China.

[b] The real growth rates seem particularly large for the USSR and China, but these are the figures implied by the data. The growth rates were obtained from semi-log regressions against time.

Sources: Calculated from the following data sources.
Hungary: International Financial Statistics Yearbook 1987 (383–7).
Soviet Union: Peebles (1981), Narodnoye Khozyaystvo SSSR (various years), and Clarke and Matko (1983: 7, 19–29).
China: ZGTJNJ89 (pp. 30, 598–9, 688.)

$(13.1 - 0.06)/6.7 = 1.95$. Presented with these statistics and no information on where they came from a quantity theorist might accept them as reasonable. Many developing countries have income elasticities of demand for money near to and even in excess of 2 and hence rapidly falling velocity. In fact, one of the early demand-for-money studies for the United States, for the period 1870–1954 (Friedman, 1959: 328–9; Friedman and Schwartz, 1963), concludes that the income elasticity of demand for money was on average 1.8, making money a luxury. Velocity would therefore fall over the long run.[3] The above results for the Soviet Union, presented 'blind' and with no information that they came from a price-controlled economy, might be interpreted as coming from an economy with a very high income elasticity of demand for money. On hearing that they were from a price-controlled economy, a quantity theorist would probably estimate the true price level (after taking into account the extent of queuing time, necessary bribes to shop staff, cost in searching for sources of supply and so on).[4] Whatever use the Quantity Theory made of the above relationship it still could not explain why the money supply grew at the rate it did; this would always taken as external to the relationship. The quantity theorist takes m and q as given and takes the resulting p as an equilibrium response, given v, therefore predicts p on the basis of the past behaviour of v. The prediction becomes very wrong if v turns out to be very different from its past trend.

The approach taken below can be explained in terms of the dynamic equation of exchange. We want to explain m so cannot take it as given. What is more important is explaining the inverse of v, that is, how much real money measured in terms of output (or something else) there is and why this ratio has changed. I argue below that in the planned economies q is given, planners choose p in the face of a given extent of excess demand, this determines the resulting v, and this tells us how rapidly narrow measures of m will grow in comparison with Q or something highly correlated with Q. As the equation above implies, the larger the fall in V, the smaller p can be; that is, there is an inverse relationship between inflation and monetary growth. In the planned economy context I will show that the lower the value of p the planners chose, the more likely it is that v will be negative and the ratio of money to real variables will rise. Anyway, the thing that cannot be taken as given is m; this is to explained. In a market economy people's behaviour determines v and, given $(m - q)$ p follows. This result follows because there is nowhere else for the excess money to go. In a planned economy q is given, planners chose p, and these two factors together determine the rate at which currency is withdrawn from circulation and hence plays a role in determining m, which when compared with q will tell us how v will behave.

The 'trick' of the Quantity Theory is to define velocity (V) as PQ/M and to assume that whatever value velocity is observed to be it is that value because that is what people want it to be. This argument is based on the demand-for-money version of the theory. There is no reason to assume that this is true of velocity in planned economies. In the decades following the publication of J.M. Keynes's *The General Theory of Employment, Interest and Money* in 1936, velocity fell from favour as a tool of analysis. In the United Kingdom it was referred to as 'just a number', and in the United States a leading Keynesian such as Alvin H. Hansen could disparage the concept. The counter-revolution in monetary economics, led by Milton Friedman and co-researchers and dating from the late 1950s, used extensive empirical analysis to try to show that there is a close and stable relationship between M and PQ over long periods of time. This evidence in itself tells us nothing about the direction of the relationship (M could be determined by PQ, for example). This counter-revolution preceded a period of high and unstable inflation in market economies, and so its policy aspect, 'monetarism', became a common policy and a household word. This relied on control of the money supply to control PQ and hence the rate of inflation. Now, in this application it was important to show which monetary concept was correlated with PQ, so that by controlling it the government could control aggregate spending. It was a policy to restrain PQ. It was reasonable to assume that V could not become larger and larger in the face of monetary restraint and so frustrate the intention of controlling PQ through control over some concept of M.[5] Given the transactions technology of the economy, it was felt that there is some monetary measure that has a stable relationship with PQ and that there is an effective maximum to its velocity. Although we can concede that there is probably a maximum limit to the velocity of some existing monetary concept in market economies, the argument cannot be applied when we examine planned economies because the situation is completely the opposite. It is not a possible *maximum* limit to V that concerns us but its *minimum*. This has nothing to do with transactions technology or the demand for money; it concerns the tolerance of money holders. The chronic–excess–demand hypothesis has argued that velocity can fall steadily regardless of people's desired monetary holdings. People are assumed to make other adjustments, until velocity is so low (the liquidity ratios are so high) that, in the crisis version of the hypothesis, the government just gives up and abandons the traditional monetary system.

4.3 AN ALTERNATE APPROACH: ITS REQUIRED ASSUMPTIONS

To provide an alternate explanation of the relationship between monetary growth and changes in the price level, and the consequences of such changes, we need to make some simplifying assumptions about the institutional context of these changes. These assumptions are based on the nature of the economic system of the planned economies under study and the nature of their money supply process. The assumptions are as follows:

1 The narrow money supply changes because there is a gap between the amount of currency paid out in any period and the return flow to the combined state sector. The principal item of money income is state wages, except in China where payments to the rural population are more important. In all countries retail sales constitute the main channel of currency recall.

2 Monetary planners have a rough idea of an acceptable ratio of household monetary assets to annual retail sales. This liquidity ratio is an indicator of the extent of the real debt of the state sector, measured in consumer goods, owed to the population. If circumstances indicate that there is potential for a large rise in this ratio, we assume that they will take action to prevent it.

What reactions they make is an empirical matter.

3 Planners cannot always control the payments side of the balance of money incomes and expenditures of the population. They therefore have to adopt reactive policies aimed at withdrawing currency from circulation. Some of these policies can be used for only a short period. Such policies include increasing direct tax rates, selling from government stocks and selling imported consumer goods. If imbalances persist over a long period, other policies will have to be adopted every year. Retail sales are the main way of withdrawing currency from circulation with savings deposits being the next most significant method.

4 The official price indexes of these countries are dominated by the prices of state-supplied goods. Therefore, major changes in these indexes are due not to changes in market prices (which have only very small weighting) but to changes in government pricing policy.

This fourth assumption warrants further discussion. It is often thought that Hungary and China have gone furthest in freeing retail prices. Yet Tardos (1988: 66–8) states that the main part of any observed change in the price index in Hungary is due to changes in government pricing policy. Central control is 'strict' and extends to the 'so-called free prices' (Tardos, 1985: 32). For Hungary, Balassa (1959: 118) argues that inflation is deliberate. In Hungary during the period 1976–80, two-thirds of the annual rate of inflation of 6.3 per cent was due to measures taken at the centre (*Vengerskaya Narodnaya Respublika* p. 361). In China the weighting given to market prices in the retail price index is about 12–15 per cent (World Bank, 1990: 35, fn. 6). Peebles (1990b: 78) shows that changes in the general retail price index in China mirrored changes in government-determined list prices during the 1980s. Chen and Hou (1986) ask why the government increased retail prices during the early 1980s in China and thus contributed to inflation; they provide no answer. In the Soviet Union about 95 per cent of prices included in the official index are state-determined prices. Many of the significant episodes of retail price increases in Poland occurred when the government initiated changes in retail prices. Although 46 per cent of consumer goods sold in 1986 were at state-fixed prices, there remained a great degree of state control over the 52 per cent sold at contracted prices (Józefiak, 1989: 60–1). In 1988 the government in Poland was still talking about the need for substantial increases in retail prices, which would have to be made by the government (Myant, 1989: 23).

On the basis of these reasonable assumptions derived from the common institutional features of the countries under study, we can begin to provide an explanation of the relationship between monetary growth and price increases. We must focus on the consumer goods market. Figure 4.1 shows the situation facing monetary planners in a particular year. Assume that planners have an accepted rate at which households can be allowed to accumulate monetary assets in terms of the proportion of money incomes remaining unspent. In a market economy this proportion will be determined by the voluntary decisions of the millions of income earners in the economy. In the planned economies this proportion is both the saving rate of households and therefore the determinant of the rate at which narrow money accumulates. In a situation of excess demand its size is influenced by planners' reactions to monetary developments.

Figure 4.1 shows how the situation on the consumer goods market determines the rate of monetary and liquidity growth. The example is illustrated with numerical examples for clarity. Assume that the proportion of money incomes that planners aim for households to accumulate is s^* [5 per cent] and that household money incomes in any year are MIP_1 [100 monetary units, *mus*]. Then $(1 - s^*)MIP_1$ [95 *mus*] is the amount of money incomes planners expect households to spend on consumer goods. This is shown as a rectangular hyperbola. Aggregate demand grows at the same rate as MIP. Assume that the available supply of consumer goods is S_1 [95 physical units] and that the current official price level is P_1 [1.0 *mu*], where the aggregate demand curve intersects the supply curve at point X. We can call this a situation of balance; all goods are sold at the state-determined price, consumers realise their consumption and monetary accumulation plans, and monetary planners realise their plans. Now assume that MIP increases by 10 per cent to MIP_2. Aggregate demand is now $(1 - s^*)MIP_2$ [104.5 *mus*], and if there is no increase in retail supplies there is excess demand to the extent of XD (in physical units). This is how excess demand is usually conceived (in real terms), but we are interested in its monetary consequences.

If planners make no reaction, households will not be able to realise all their desired expenditures and 9.5 *mus* will remain unspent, as shown by either shaded rectangle under the aggregate demand curve. This excess monetary accumulation will be in addition to the 5.5 *mus* households will willingly accumulate. Households will be left with a proportion of money incomes unspent that

Figure 4.1 Excess demand for consumer goods and the planners' dilemma

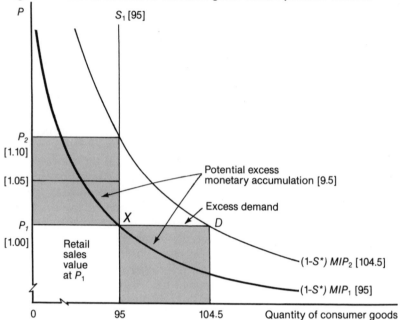

Potential excess
monetary accumulation [9.5]

Excess demand

$(1-S^*)\ MIP_2\ [104.5]$

$(1-S^*)\ MIP_1\ [95]$

Retail
sales
value
at P_1

Quantity of consumer goods

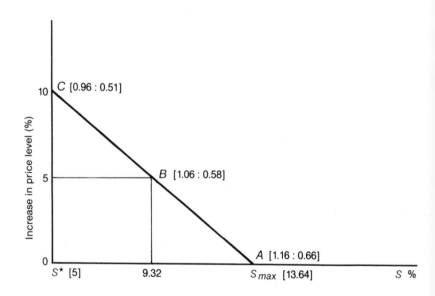

exceeds s^*, equal to s_{max} [13.64 per cent = 15/110], and there will be rapid narrow monetary growth. Narrow monetary growth will be more rapid than planners want if they do nothing. Planners could react to such a situation by increasing the price level to P_2 [1.1] to clear the market. If they do so, households will accumulate narrow money at the approved rate of s^*.

Planners face a dilemma. If they repress the inflation and make no price increases, s will rise; if they sacrifice price stability and increase prices by 10 per cent, s will equal s^*. This trade-off between open inflation and narrow monetary accumulation is shown in the lower part of Figure 4.1. Points on the line show the resulting value of s for any given percentage increase in prices chosen by planners. For example, a 5 per cent price increase increases the value of the fixed real supply of consumer goods and withdraws part of the potential excess monetary accumulation from circulation, thus reducing the value of s to 9.3 per cent.

How planners have actually reacted in the different countries is an empirical question. We can see, however, the clear implications of different reactions. If they choose points like or near A, excess demand will show up as rapid monetary growth. If they choose points like or near C, excess demand will show up as open inflation in the sense that the official price index will rise and there will be moderate narrow monetary growth. If they compromise and choose a point like or near B, there will be both open price increases and rapid narrow money growth. As Portes and Winter (1980: 146) put it, 'There is no obvious single indicator of excess demand in a CPE, partly because the way in which excess demand affects observable variables depends on the planner's behaviour.' Here I have indicated two possible symptoms of excess demand: open price increases and rapid monetary growth. The relative proportions in which we observe the indicators will depend on the nature of the planners' reactions. These reactions in turn will depend on the priorities of the political leaders who instruct the monetary planners in the light of their assessment of the consequences for the economy of the different reactions. We can refer to points near A as showing a low open-inflation response to excess demand and to points near C as showing a full or high open-inflation response.[6]

Figure 4.1 shows the implications for liquidity growth of possible choices by planners. These are shown in square brackets at such responses as zero, 5 and 10 per cent increases in prices. The first figure shows what will happen to liquidity if it was initially equal to 1.0, and the second if it was 0.5. As can be seen, increasing prices restrain liquidity growth in the face of excess demand. If prices are left unchanged (point *A*), the liquidity of the household sector will increase to 1.16 or 0.66 from 1.0 or 0.5 respectively. If there is a price increase equal to the full extent of the increase in income (10 per cent), liquidity will become 0.96 or 0.51 respectively, virtually remaining constant in this example. Price increases restrain liquidity growth through two means: they reduce the extent of monetary accumulation (the nominator of the ratio), and they increase the nominal value of retail sales (the denominator of the ratio). This analysis thus shows the motive for increasing state prices: they can be used to restrain household liquidity growth.

If we observe both price increases and rapid growth of money in any year, these are the consequence of excess monetary demand and the nature of the planners' reactions. We cannot just take monetary growth as a separate independent cause of the open inflation; both are caused by a third factor, which is excess nominal demand for consumer goods. Any strong positive correlation between annual rates of growth of narrow money and the rate of inflation tells us nothing about the direction of causation between the variables.

The above analysis has shown that imbalances on the consumer goods market can cause either open inflation or rapid monetary accumulation or a mixture of both. Before examining the nature of planners' responses to excess demand on the consumer goods market, we need a simple operational measure of excess demand. It must be easy to compute from available sources and it must include variables that determine both the demand and supply sides of the market. It must also be such that we can reasonably assume that planners in these economies can monitor its development throughout each year. I propose a simple measure called purchasing power imbalance (*PPI*).[7] This is simply the difference between the percentage increase in each year's *MIP* and that year's rate of growth of real national income. This latter supply-side factor is being taken as proxy for the rate of growth of real supplies of consumer goods. Hence, I am ignoring the possibility of meeting excess demand by such short-run policies as selling from stocks, importing consumer goods or ordering factories to switch production from investment goods to consumer goods.[8] These could all be further reactions to *PPI*. A positive *PPI* value gives an indication of the extent of excess demand as shown in Figure 4.1. *PPI* will be positive if *MIP* grows more rapidly than real national income, if national income falls but *MIP* remains constant, or if both *MIP* and national income fall but the fall in output is greater than the fall in *MIP*. In the example of Figure 4.1, *PPI* will be 10.[9]

It is reasonable to assume that planners can monitor the development of *PPI* each year. On the nominal side they have the ex post cash plan of the banking system, or even daily reports, showing how much cash has been paid out in each planning period in the form of wages and so on. The extent of plan fulfilment in production and records of deliveries of retail supplies will give them indications of retail supply availability.

Positive values of *PPI* can be caused by both supply side factors and nominal income growth. For most of the period under study positive *PPI* values were due to nominal income growth's being greater than positive real output growth. The question is: How did planners react to imbalances? Did they increase prices or not? What were the different consequences of their reactions in different countries?

4.5 THE EXTENT OF IMBALANCES (PPI)

Before examining planners' reactions, let us get a feel for the extent to which imbalances differed across our sample of countries. Table 4.2 shows the extent of *PPI* for the period 1970–89 (1971–88 only for Poland). Several interesting features are clear.

First, imbalances increased in all the European countries after 1985. Depending on which years we take for comparison we can obtain a slightly different picture, but it is fair to say that the extent of increases was most marked in the Soviet Union (compare 1989 with 1984), Poland (1988 with 1984) and Hungary (1989 with 1984). In China imbalances became marked in 1979 and 1980 (the first years of economic reform), were controlled somewhat over the period 1981–83, but increased in 1984 and after when urban wage and tax reforms and financial system reforms were implemented. Imbalances peaked again in 1988, the most inflationary year in China since the early 1960s, but were reduced significantly in 1989. The austerity programme of late 1988 reduced the rate of growth of *MIP* to 12.6 per cent in 1989 compared to 26.8 per cent in 1988, thus playing a role in reducing *PPI*.

Second, in the Soviet Union, East Germany, Czechoslovakia and China there were several years of negative *PPI*, implying that sometimes planners were able to restrain the growth of purchasing power to be less than the growth of potential retail supplies. This never occurred in Hungary or Poland.

Third, in the Soviet Union, East Germany and Czechoslovakia the average value of *PPI* was small, being 1 less. These are the countries in which liquidity rose rapidly, so we can see that *PPI* itself does not

Table 4.2 Purchasing power imbalance, 1970–89

Year	USSR	GDR	Czecho-slovakia	Poland	Hungary	PRC
1970	-2.1	-2.5	-1.1	n.a.	5.3	-16.7
1971	0.4	-1.0	0	2.3	1.9	4.4
1972	2.3	0.5	0.3	3.0	1.0	5.8
1973	-2.8	0.7	1.2	3.4	2.6	0.9
1974	1.1	-1.4	-1.3	4.3	4.2	3.4
1975	1.9	-1.1	-2.5	4.5	3.6	-0.5
1976	0	0.2	0.8	5.3	3.1	8.1
1977	-0.1	0.4	0.3	7.3	2.7	-1.4
1978	0	-0.1	-0.6	5.9	3.9	-0.7
1979	1.7	-1.0	0.5	12.2	7.4	11.6
1980	1.6	-1.9	1.1	18.1	10.1	14.7
1981	0.6	-1.7	2.7	43.1	5.6	3.4
1982	0.3	0.2	4.1	70.4	4.7	2.0
1983	-0.2	-2.3	0.8	17.0	8.2	3.7
1984	0.2	-1.6	-0.9	12.7	6.7	15.9
1985	2.2	-1.2	0.2	19.9	10.6	13.2
1986	2.0	1.3	0.6	14.3	7.2	12.8
1987	2.2	1.4	1.2	24.1	4.3	9.2
1988	4.8	1.1	1.7	78.3	13.7	15.7
1989	10.5	1.0	2.0	n.a.	22.0	9.3.
Summary statistics for 1971–88						
Maximum	4.8	1.4	4.1	78.3	13.7	15.9
Minimum	-2.8	-2.3	-2.5	2.3	1.0	-1.4
Mean	1.0	-0.4	0.6	19.2	5.6	6.8
Coefficient of variation	1.6	2.8	2.6	1.2	0.6	0.9

Note: Purchasing power imbalance (PPI) is the percentage increase in money incomes of the population minus the percentage increase in real net material product (NMP).

Sources: European countries: increase in money incomes from ESE p. 390 net material product, ibid. (p. 387).
China: increase in money incomes calculated from ZGTJNJ89, (pp. 596, 599); increase in real national income, ibid. (p. 31); see also Peebles (1991).

explain liquidity developments. Even though the average value of PPI was low in the Soviet Union, East Germany and Czechoslovakia its coefficient of variation was largest. This shows that there were larger annual variations in its value, implying that monetary income planning was less consistently co-ordinated with real supply availability. Although the average value of PPI was larger in Poland, Hungary and China it was not so volatile on an annual basis, as is shown by the lower coefficient of variation there. In these countries PPI was consistently large, yet there was not rapid liquidity growth. We will have to explain this.

Table 4.3 Price reactions to _PPI_

(regressions of percentage increase in consumer prices on _PPI_)

Country	Slope	t-statistic	R^2	DW	d.f.	Period
USSR	0.202	2.36	0.234	1.36	18	1970–89
GDR	0.035	0.36	0.007	1.15	18	1970–89
Czechoslovakia	0.350	1.87	0.163	1.53	18	1970–89
Poland	1.011	8.56	0.822	2.05	16	1971–88
Hungary	0.752	7.57	0.761	1.61	18	1970–89
PRC	0.360	3.41	0.406	0.95	17	1970–88

Sources: European countries: data on consumer price increases from _ESE_ (p. 392).
China: increase in government list prices calculated from data for 1970–83 from _Zhongguo Maoyi Wujia Tongji Ziliao 1952–1983_ (p. 373); other years from various issues of _Statistical Yearbook of China_ and _ZGTJNJ89_.
PPI from Table 4.2.

4.6 EVIDENCE ON PLANNERS' REACTIONS TO PPI

So, there were imbalances facing the monetary planners. How did they react? We can answer this question in relation to price changes in a simple way. If the extent of the open inflation response is roughly constant each year, open inflation will be a positive function of _PPI_. If we run a regression of the annual changes in consumer prices against _PPI_, we will get an average measure of the price response indicating which countries chose points near A, B or C of Figure 4.1. Table 4.3 reports the results of such regressions. Apart from the case of East Germany the results are reasonable. The slope coefficient indicates the average price response to _PPI_.

First, the results show that there was a positive correlation between the annual rates of increase in consumer prices and the extent of _PPI_ for all countries except East Germany. This is shown is by the uniformly positive slope coefficient with t-statistics that indicate significant positive slopes at at least the 5 per cent level of confidence. Years of large _PPI_ produced large open-inflation responses and vice versa. For Poland and Hungary there was a very clear positive relationship. In East Germany there was no relationship because there were hardly any changes in the official price index to correlate with _PPI_. Second, the results show a clear difference in the nature of planners' price response to _PPI_. In East Germany, the Soviet Union and Czechoslovakia the average response was equal to or less than 0.35 of _PPI_. This puts these countries in the range between A and B in the lower part of Figure 4.1. Third, Poland and Hungary showed much greater price responsiveness to _PPI_ with coefficients of 1.0 and 0.75 respectively, putting them near C in Figure 4.1. Fourth, this difference in price responsiveness was directly linked to the extent of growth of household liquidity. In those countries with low price responsiveness the liquidity ratio rose most rapidly and at the end of our period was the highest in East Germany, Czechoslovakia and the Soviet Union. In contrast, as we have seen, liquidity growth was restrained in Poland and Hungary by large price rises in the face of large values of *PPI*. This shows that it was not the size of *PPI* that determined the extent of liquidity growth but the extent to which planners responded by ordering increases in official prices.[10] A significant price response produced high open inflation but moderate liquidity growth. China shows a picture of large *PPI*, moderate price response and rapid liquidity growth in the 1980s.

We cannot offer an explanation of why some countries chose points like *A* and others points like *C* except to say that the choice must have been determined by political leaders. Their choices reveal their preferences. They seem to have preferred price stability in the Soviet Union, East Germany and Czechoslovakia even in the presence of increasing excess demand. Aslund (1989: 130–3) reviews Soviet discussion of the necessity to increase retail prices in the mid 1980s. From the discussion the extent of opposition to such moves to abandon the traditional policy of retail price stability is clear. Reasons for opposition seemed to be fear of political and social instability and even some Stalinist romanticism for the postwar period of retail price reductions. The consequences of price stability in the face of rising *PPI* were rapid liquidity growth and the need for large price rises in the late 1980s and early 1990s. In the case of East Germany and the Soviet Union the reforms included the abandonment of the traditional monetary system.

An aspect of this approach is that, if *PPI* is positive, the ratio of *MIP* to output will rise. The theory offered here is that in some countries prices will be increased, hence we should observe a relationship between price level and the ratio *MIP/Q*. For China over the period 1952–85 the slope coefficient of a double-log regression of *P* on *MIP/Q* was 0.49. This shows that a 1 per cent increase in the ratio of purchasing power to real output was associated with a 0.5 per cent increase in the general retail-price level. This coefficient was 82 per cent greater than the coefficient from a Quantity Theory regression that showed that there would be only a 0.27 per cent increase in the price level when the money ratio (M/Q) rose 1 per cent (Peebles, 1991: ch 6 and 7). Of course, the Quantity Theory approach does not explain why the money ratio changed.

Among the countries under study, Poland has had the most rapid nominal monetary growth and open inflation in recent years. It may be thought that the Quantity Theory would provide a good description of this relationship. There seems to have been a reasonable relationship as shown in the following regression result (t-statistics are in brackets):[11]

Poland 1970–85

$$\ln P = 1.2144 + 0.7792 \ln(CASH/Q)$$
$$\quad\quad (5.0351) \quad\quad (16.5740)$$

$R^2 = 0.9515$
s.e. = 0.1530
DW = 0.5570
d.f. = 14

Now, this approach does not explain why the explanatory variable itself $(CASH/Q)$, changed. On an annual basis there was a close association between the percentage rate of change of cash and the price level, with a simple linear correlation coefficient of 0.845. This may seem to be further support for the Quantity Theory approach. However, we cannot draw any conclusions about the direction of causation between these variables on the basis of this evidence.

The PPI approach explains both why prices were increased and why cash grew in Poland. From Figure 4.1 we would expect there to have been a close relationship between PPI and the rate of growth of cash in any year. Although price increases were used to moderate the rate of growth of cash, they could not prevent rapid cash growth when PPI was large. Moderating s when PPI was large means that there was still a large amount of cash remaining unspent, because s is a proportion of a large MIP. In fact, there was a clear positive relationship between the annual percentage increase in cash $(dCASH/CASH)$ and PPI, as shown by the following result:

Poland 1971–1985

$$dCASH/CASH = 13.6662 + 0.5077\ PPI$$
$$\quad\quad\quad (9.3432) \quad (8.1734)$$

$R^2 = 0.8371$
s.e.= 4.3076
DW = 1.0135
d.f.= 13

This means that both the rate of growth of cash and the rate of open inflation were closely positively correlated with PPI on an annual basis. This explains why there was a positive association between the rate of growth of cash and the rate of open inflation and why the Quantity Theory appears to produce an explanation of the link between money and prices. However, it is not an explanation, because both cash growth and open inflation were caused by PPI and because the Quantity Theory offers no explanation of cash growth in the first place.

Data are not sufficient to show for long periods for all countries under study whether annual changes in narrow money were correlated with annual values of *PPI*. In the case of China, annual absolute and proportionate changes in narrow money were significantly correlated with *PPI* and the rate of inflation (Peebles, 1991: chs 6 and 7). This is because China's reactions to *PPI* are represented by points like *B* in Figure 4.1. During the 1980s both the rate of growth of currency in circulation and the rate of open inflation clearly followed developments in *PPI* (Peebles, 1990b: 77–9).

Interestingly, a Soviet writer (Grinberg, 1990) has recently classified socialist countries according to whether their inflations show up as price increases or shortages. He classifies inflation as open inflation or suppressed inflation. The former he calls the quantitative devaluation of money and the latter the qualitative devaluation of money, which is suppressed inflation and is reflected in an increasing degree of shortage. The data he has used to make these distinctions are not very clear, but he makes the following classifications. Open inflation is the dominant form in Hungary and Yugoslavia, where there is no suppressed inflation. In the Soviet Union, Bulgaria and Romania the qualitative devaluation of money predominates and there are stable prices. There is a relatively equal combination of both types of inflation in Poland, China and, to a certain degree, Vietnam. He thinks that East Germany and Czechoslovakia seem to have neither type of inflation, but in his view their 'inflation potential is also building up in these countries' (p. 46). These classifications do not differ from those resulting from the above analysis.

4.7 PRICE REACTIONS AND LIQUIDITY GROWTH

Price increases restrain liquidity growth. They do this in two ways. One is that they withdraw currency from circulation. However, this does not mean that we have to observe a fall in the volume of currency in circulation to justify this argument. Price increases also restrain liquidity by restraining the rate of growth of unspent purchasing power (the nominator of the liquidity ratio) and also increasing the value of a given volume of retail supplies (the denominator of the liquidity ratio). To show the extent to which price increases have restrained liquidity growth in the European planned economies we can refer to the statistics of Tables 4.4 and 4.5.

Table 4.4 shows the average rates of open inflation and growth in the *Liquidity SD* ratio for the five countries, by subperiods of the period 1961–85. Except for the case of East Germany, there is an inverse relationship between these statistics. This shows that periods

Table 4.4 Relationship between open inflation and growth in *Liquidity SD*, by subperiods, 1961–85

(average annual growth rates, per cent per annum)

	1961–65	1966–70	1971–75	1976–80	1981–85	
USSR						
Inflation	–0.1	–0.1	–0.1	0.7	1.0	*r*
Liquidity growth	4.6	10.7	7.5	5.6	4.1	–0.76
GDR						
Inflation	–0.1	–0.2	–0.4	0.1	0	*r*
Liquidity growth	10.1	5.9	2.3	2.0	2.7	–0.06
Czechoslovakia						
Inflation	0.7	1.9	0.1	2.1	2.0	*r*
Liquidity growth	8.4	2.5	5.3	0.8	3.7	–0.70
Poland						
Inflation	2.2	1.6	2.4	6.8	32.5	*r*
Liquidity growth	15.0	5.4	8.5	0.3	–5.8	–0.80
Hungary						
Inflation	0.5	1.0	2.8	6.3	6.8	*r*
Liquidity growth	24.3	6.6	3.6	1.5	3.0	–0.59

Sources: Inflation rates from *Comecon Data 1981,* (p. 301), *1985,* (p. 308) and *1987,* (p. 302).

Growth of *Liquidity SD* calculated from data in Winiecki (1988: 63), supplemented with estimates of the ratio for after 1983 from data in *Comecon Data 1987:* (pp. 294, 410).

of high open inflation were periods of slow liquidity growth, and vice versa. The time trend is for the inflation rates to increase and the growth of liquidity to slow down. As we have seen, this is most apparent in the cases of Poland and Hungary after the early 1970s; inflation rates became substantially higher and liquidity growth slowed. Even though there were not such marked increases in inflation rates in Czechoslovakia and the Soviet Union, these rates did rise after the mid 1970s; liquidity growth rates fell steadily in the Soviet Union and were lower in the 1980s in Czechoslovakia than at the beginning of the 1970s. In East Germany the official price index showed no reductions after the mid 1970s; liquidity growth rates remained roughly constant until 1985, although lower than they had been in the 1960s.

Figure 4.2 shows the inverse relationship between *Liquidity SD* in 1985 and open inflation over the period 1970–85 in the upper section, and the inverse relationship between the growth rate in liquidity and open inflation over the same period in the lower section. Table 4.5 presents the necessary data. The figure shows clear evidence of this inverse ratio; countries that followed a policy of stable prices experienced rapidly growing liquidity and, more importantly, higher liquidity in 1985 than countries that increased retail prices.

The argument presented above is that liquidity growth is an

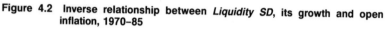

Figure 4.2 Inverse relationship between *Liquidity SD*, its growth and open inflation, 1970–85

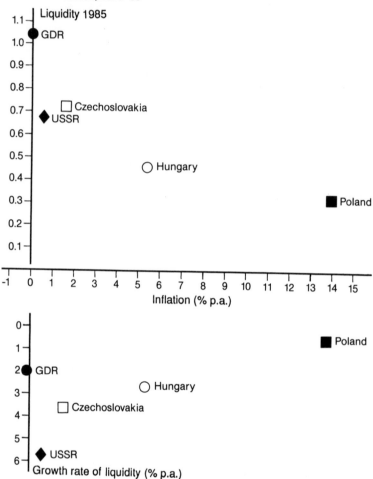

inverse function of price increases because of the existence of excess demand for consumer goods. An equilibrium theorist could interpret this evidence in another way. The argument would be that liquidity developments represent household desired rates of monetary accumulation. In inflationary countries people will not want to hold large monetary balances, whereas in countries with stable prices (which also happen to have the higher levels of income per capita) they will be prepared to hold larger real money balances. This view is

Table 4.5   Relationship between open inflation, *Liquidity SD* and its growth, 1970–85

Country	Liquidity SD in 1985	Growth in Liquidity SD (% p.a.)	Inflation (% p.a.)
USSR	0.68	5.6	0.6
GDR	1.10	2.0	−0.01
Czechoslovakia	0.73	3.5	1.6
Poland	0.33	0.7	14.3
Hungary	0.47	2.8	5.5

Sources: Liquidity SD in 1985 calculated from data in *Comecon Data 1987* (pp. 294, 410). Growth in *Liquidity SD* calculated from data in Winiecki (1988: 63), supplemented with calculations using *Comecon Data 1987*: (pp. 294, 410).
Inflation rates calculated from consumer price indexes in *Comecon Data 1981*, (p. 301), *1985*, (p. 307) and *1987* (p. 299).

consistent with the inverse relationship. We could ask whether it is consistent with monetary collapse in East Germany and crisis in the Soviet Union — the two countries with particularly high liquidity ratios.

4.8 EXPLAINING PPI

The above attempt to show the true direction of causation between variables in the planned economies has evoked the simple concept of *PPI* as the first, or prime mover, to explain money and price developments. A full economic history of each of these countries would have to explain what determined *PPI* in each historical period under study. This is beyond the scope of this short book,[12] but some indicators can be given here.

Some periods of imbalance were caused by supply shocks. This is clear in the case of China when political disruptions led to falls in real output in 1967, 1968 and 1976. Economic collapse in 1960–62 caused large imbalances and open inflation, and planners also reacted by increasing prices. As this policy was judged to be successful they readopted it when imbalances re-emerged in 1979 and 1980. Of the other counties, Poland is the only one where periods of falling real output contributed to imbalances. This occurred during the period 1979–82. In all the other countries the general reason for positive *PPI* was nominal money income growth's outstripping real output growth. A number of factors could have caused this and would have to be identified and explained in any fuller study. Excess wage growth is the most likely explanation. In addition the role of compensatory wage increases must be investigated. These occur when state prices are increased and the government feels compelled to compensate the population. These were an important cause of money income growth in Poland in the 1980s, to such an extent that the proportion of remuneration in total incomes fell from 60 per cent to 48 per cent over the period 1979–86 (Socha, 1989: 46–8). In the case of Poland the high rates of open inflation and these compensatory income increases complicated the relationship between *PPI* and open inflation. It could be argued that *PPI* was becoming a function of the rate of inflation, hence the close contemporaneous relationship between them. If this was indeed the case, *PPI* becomes more an explanation of narrow monetary growth.

The direction of causation is: imbalances, price rises, compensatory (or partially compensatory) money income or wage increases, large *PPI*, further price rises in reaction and rapid nominal monetary growth. In explaining why the narrow money supply grows it is necessary to identify how the money actually gets into circulation in the form of money incomes and why it is not withdrawn by government policy reactions.

Studies of the macroeconomics of planned economies (especially recent China studies) often contain statements like: 'In such-a-such year there was a restrictive credit policy (or deflationary monetary policy), and so in the next year currency growth rates fell and inflation was lower.' This is stated but never demonstrated. Given the institutions of these economies, this can happen only if the rate of growth of *MIP* is restrained compared to the rate of growth of real output. This will reduce the extent of *PPI*. If there is a roughly constant price reaction to *PPI* by planners (that is, if $(dP/P)/PPI$ is roughly constant from year to year), a lower *PPI* will mean a lower rate of inflation and probably a lower rate of growth of currency in circulation. The *PPI* concept allows us to see whether restrictive policies do reduce the extent of imbalances. Movements in *PPI* in China during the 1980s accord with what are said to be changes in monetary policy (Peebles, 1990b: 77–9).

Emphasising the role of the wage bill, or more generally the size of *MIP*, in determining developments in the price level and the money supply comes naturally to observers of planned economies. They recognise the primacy of such developments for monetary and price changes. Such a recognition is also found in the works of Keynesian and Post Keynesian economists, who stress cost factors in determining the price level and advocate an incomes policy to control inflation. In contrast, quantity theorists would advocate control of the money supply to control total spending and hence inflation and money wage growth. They see no independent role for money wages in determining prices. It is interesting to note Kornai's (1990: 142–45) views on the necessity of bureaucratic control over state sector wages in his liberalisation programme for Hungary. Maintaining wage discipline is the 'Achilles' heel of the stabilisation operation' (p. 145). Despite a whole list of liberalising policies it is recognised that wages must be administratively controlled, as in planned economies, even in Hungary, restrictive monetary policies do not, and cannot be expected to, restrain wage growth (p. 144). Kornai cites the time when he and James Tobin (a US Keynesian economist) urged direct control of the wage bill on Chinese economic reformers in the mid 1980s. He believes that ignoring this advice led to inflation in China (p. 145, fn. 49). The above analysis has clarified the way unbalanced money-income growth leads to open inflation or liquidity growth and sometimes both.

4.9 CONCLUSIONS

This chapter has argued a number of important points about the nature of the relationship between monetary growth, prices and liquidity in the planned economies under study. The Quantity Theory of Money is no real help in understanding why different economies had different rates of narrow monetary growth as it starts with this rate of growth as given. The analysis has identified the nature and determinants of excess demand for consumer goods, considered its consequences given different reactions by planners, proposed a simple operational measure of it and estimated it for all six countries. In circumstances of excess demand for consumer goods planners face a dilemma. Repressing inflation leads to rapid nominal monetary growth and rapid liquidity growth. Increasing state prices restrains nominal monetary growth (which can still be rapid if PPI is large) and can restrain the rate of growth of liquidity. If we assume that planners aim to restrain liquidity growth, we can obtain a theory of why prices are increased. The evidence cited shows that, in those countries where there was a full or medium open-inflation response to PPI, open inflation and monetary growth were correlated with annual values of PPI. In economies where excess demand was ignored and there was a low open-inflation response to PPI, liquidity grew rapidly. PPI explains open inflation on an annual basis for certain countries and, given the nature of the open inflation response, the pattern of liquidity growth for all countries in the long run. Investigating developments in PPI allows us to see to what extent restrictive policies succeed in reducing imbalances and hence open inflation and liquidity growth. Control over the growth of MIP has implications for control over imbalances, inflation (or price adjustments) and monetary growth in these economies.

5 A methodological review

This chapter surveys the still growing literature on the monetary and macroeconomic aspect of the planned economies. Its purpose is simple: to discover which methodologies predicted the financial crises of East Germany and the Soviet Union, which did not and, more importantly, how they did or did not do this. What tools of analysis, data sources and preconceptions were used by different economists in analysing the monetary systems of the planned economies? This is a question about methodologies, not ideologies or personalities, although these latter two factors may explain why certain analysts adopted certain methodologies.

5.1 THE PURPOSE

In asking to what extent economists predicted the crises now evident there are major problems of interpretation to be faced. As will be shown below, it is easy to show who predicted crisis and to discover the methodology they used. It is far less easy to discuss the works of others who just indicated problems within the monetary systems of these economies. Many of these writers did not specifically discuss future events in terms of the likelihood of crisis. On the other hand, some writers did specifically challenge the applicability of the term 'financial crisis'. However, they might now argue that their works were compatible with the later emergence of a crisis or that the crisis emerged for reasons different from those their works were concerned with. In short, it can be shown that some people clearly said that there would be a financial crisis, whereas very few said that there would definitely not be a crisis. The latter argued that events said to foreshadow crisis either could be interpreted in other ways or were being interpreted on the basis of a refuted hypothesis. By their claiming to have refuted the hypothesis on which the prediction of crisis was based, these studies can, however, be interpreted as arguing there would not be a crisis. I have interpreted in a generous light the writings of those whose works suggest to me that a crisis was unlikely (as they could always argue that such things are never impossible). However, it is clear, I think that there were many writers whose publications suggested a very low probability of financial crises and drastic reforms. One indication is the lack of discussion of the works that specifically predicted crisis. If such economists now claimed that the radical reforms being observed in Eastern Europe are not the result of monetary developments, we could conclude that they believe that monetary developments are not particularly important causes of change, despite the major efforts they have put into studying such phenomena. Furthermore, we could ask them what factors did cause the current radical reforms; 'agricultural crisis', 'productivity crisis', 'political crisis' or whatever could be cited. To many analysts these problems have been exacerbated by the monetary problems of these countries and are not separate causes.

5.2 CATEGORISATION OF DIFFERENT METHODOLOGIES

I will divide studies relating to monetary issues in planned economies into three categories. Emphasis is placed on the European countries as they have reacted to their problems in the most extreme way. The sample of studies covered will not be exhaustive but is sufficient to identify the different approaches to the basic question raised in this chapter: Which methodologies predicted a crisis, and which did not? Three groupings are used:

1 Clear predictions of crisis (section 5.3). In this section I will also discuss the critics who specifically challenged these predictions of crisis.

2 Studies that presented evidence consistent with the chronic–excess–demand hypothesis but did not specifically discuss or predict a crisis (section 5.4).

3 Studies that suggested that there was no real problem of chronic excess aggregate demand in the centrally planned economies (CPEs). By their claiming to have refuted the theory on which the prediction of crisis was based, these studies can be interpreted as arguing that crisis was very unlikely. As suggested earlier, it could now be argued that the present crises are the results of factors not analysed in these studies (section 5.5).

5.3 PREDICTORS OF CRISIS

As was shown in chapter 1, Igor Birman's work on financial aspects of recent Soviet development is omitted from nearly all discussions of the excess demand problem in CPEs. It is easy to identify clear predictions of financial crisis in the Soviet Union in Birman (1980a; 1980b; 1983) and Birman and Clarke (1985). Birman (1980a), written in 1977, is entitled 'The financial crisis in the USSR' and argues on the first page (p. 84):

> But it would be a serious mistake to underestimate the role of finances in the Soviet economy and in Soviet life in general—their role is distinctive but by no means insignificant. Research which I have completed . . . shows not only that deep financial crisis is developing in the Soviet Union but that its consequences are extremely serious.

Birman concludes (p. 99) by predicting, among other things, that:

> There is no basis for the hope that the total volume of consumer goods and services will grow to an extent that the population spends more than it receives and thus reduces existing savings; at best it might be possible only to check their rapidly increasing growth. Therefore, a continuing and sharp increase in consumer-goods prices is practically inevitable. In addition the surplus of non-cash money will unavoidably call for a further increase in wholesale prices, and this will also lead to increasing retail prices.
>
> Thus, a rapid growth in consumer-goods prices must take place, but this alone will not be enough. It looks as if any serious attempt to improve the situation must include the liquidation, or at least 'freezing', of a substantial part of the savings of the population. Some measures to accomplish this can certainly be expected in the near future, and they will lead unavoidably to discontent among the population which cannot even be compared with the dissatisfaction of a small group of Moscow intellectuals.

Perhaps the prediction of drastic policy shifts 'in the near future' caused readers not to cite this work during the mid 1980s as such policies had not been adopted by then.

How did Birman come to these conclusions? His approach was simple beyond belief and had no real theoretical foundation. His main argument and piece of evidence was the rising ratio of house-hold financial assets to household annual money incomes. In his reply to Pickersgill (1980a) Birman (1980b: 591) christened this ratio *ALB* and called it 'the ratio of savings accumulated by the population at any given moment to the annual income of the population'. This is a slightly misleading definition as the figures he actually presented were derived from figures of what he calls 'internal debt', that is, savings deposits plus 'cash saving' plus 'others' (principally government bonds and deposits in *Gosbank*). In 1960 this ratio was 19 per cent, in 1970 it was 43 per cent, and by 1976 it had reached 66 per cent (Birman, 1980a: 89).

Birman (1980b: 591) states that 'I don't know what rate of *ALB* is normal; further discussion is needed here. It looks as if at most it can normally be something like 0.3. But I do know that *ALB* = 0.7 is extremely abnormal.' Two reasons seem to have supported his certainty. The first was the assertion that Soviet households had very little need to accumulate savings deposits or cash. There were no opportunities for household investment, and there was no need to save as an insurance against illness or unemployment. Hence 'it can safely be said that an overwhelming part of all savings is forced; they grow—and grow rapidly—primarily because people are unable to spend their money rationally' (Birman, 1980a: 88). The second reason for his certainty was that 'this belief of mine [that savings deposit holdings are excessive] is shared by responsible Soviet authors'. Furthermore, Birman (1980a: 89–90) presented evidence, which he called 'well-known facts', of the declining ability of monetary incentives to secure agricultural sales to the state, to induce mobility of labour to Siberia or to allocate labour by profession and workplace.

Wimberley (1981) added some support to Birman's viewpoint by providing simple comparative evidence of the ratios of money to gross national product (*GNP*) and of money plus quasi-money to *GNP* (both being the inverse of the respective velocities of these definitions of money) for four market economies in the years 1963 and 1978. As these ratios were relatively constant, implying an income elasticity of demand for money not much different from unity, this suggested to him that the experience of the Soviet Union, where its ratio nearly tripled over a similar period of sixteen years, was exceptional. He thought that the presumption of forced saving, rather than equilibrium money holdings, was 'more plausible' (p. 445). He did not discuss other possible reasons for such a rapid rise in liquidity in the Soviet Union.

Birman and Clarke (1985) used the same methodology as Birman (1980) and cited an *ALB* ratio of 0.7 as abnormally high. Although retaining Birman's earlier definition of *ALB*, which used the population's annual income as denominator (p. 499), they cited ratios, also called *ALB*, that had annual monetary expenditures as the denominator because official expenditure data were more reliable (p. 499 and note 16). They state that a ratio of 0.4, reached in the early

1970s, 'was already abnormally high' (p. 502). All Soviet policy should be aimed at reducing *ALB* and they predicted the following policies (p. 503). They did in fact call these policies 'options . . . for dealing with the situation', but in the context of their work I think it fair to call them predictions:

1. a drastic cut in military expenditure;[1]
2. a radical economic reform in industry and/or agriculture;[2]
3. a sharp increase in retail prices;
4. some kind of monetary reform designed to destroy most of the accumulated savings: by freezing deposits in savings banks, or by a currency reform under which each citizen is permitted to exchange only a strictly limited amount of old currency for new. This could be accompanied by changes in prices and wages. There might also be a simultaneous economic reform of some kind (p. 503).

Except for the fourth one, these policy options are all part of current Soviet reforms. Of course, one can try to dispute the extent to which they were caused by the financial crisis alone rather than by an agricultural crisis or by something else caused independently of the financial situation. However, they are in sharp contrast with the views of Portes (1982) with respect to the Soviet situation, which will be quoted below.

Birman (1988: 146) predicted not just crisis but 'collapse of the Soviet economy (and of the regime)'. By collapse he meant 'a situation of *negative* growth rates, with the economic situation worsening rapidly'. In his view there 'is no real possibility for rapid improvement in the situation, even if Gorbachev decides on real radical reforms, i.e. on the introduction of private property'. The first quarter of 1990 almost certainly saw falling output in the Soviet Union although there are claims that in the second quarter output recovered.[3]

Birman claimed novelty for his methodology in that he was able to use official Soviet statistics to estimate household cash holdings. Birman (1980a) presented estimates of household currency holdings by estimating the ex post balance of money incomes and expenditures of the population over the period 1960–76. Detailed estimates and methodological discussion are contained in Birman (1981). Birman pointed out that all attempts at estimating incomes and expenditures using official Soviet statistical sources showed that annual expenditures consistently exceeded incomes—a situation that could not last for more than a few years. However, he used a common source that on this one occasion only, I believe, gave total money incomes of the population (*MIP*) in actual prices (*denezhniye dokhodi naseleniya v fakticheskikh tsenax*) for each of the three five-year plan periods during the period 1961–75 in *Narodnoye Khozyaystvo SSSR v 1975 godu* (p. 55). He allocated the total figure for each five-year plan period to individual years by decomposing the totals so that each resulting annual figure stood in the same proportion to its total as each of his estimated figures did to its total. This was not necessary to identify the extent of currency accumulation over the long run. His conservative estimate was that at the end of 1975 households held 50 billion roubles in cash. His cumulative difference between money incomes and expenditures over the period 1961–75 implied an accumulation of 74.4 billion roubles, but he assumed that he might have overestimated by one-third so reduced the figure to 50 billion roubles.

As Peebles (1981: 59) pointed out, any estimate of currency accumulation using this method is very sensitive to error. As the annual increase in currency equals the difference between two estimated series, both of which are susceptible to wide margins of error, the annual increases, and hence the total accumulated over any period, may be wildly overestimated or underestimated. If incomes are consistently overestimated and expenditures underestimated, for example, the resulting currency stock can be widely overestimated, and vice versa. Peebles (1981) also presented a reconstruction of the balance of money incomes and expenditures of the population, but for the period 1955–78, most of which work was done before the end of 1975, that is, before the publication of *Narodnoye Khozyaystvo SSSR v 1975 godu*. These estimates implied a currency stock of about 34 billion roubles at the beginning of 1976 compared to Birman's conservative 50 billion roubles for end-1975.

Critics of Birman's viewpoint were not slow in challenging either his facts or his logic. Pickersgill (1980) did both. She rejected any use of ratios of monetary assets to incomes as an indicator and relied on her methodology of estimating household savings functions econometrically (Pickersgill 1976; 1980b). As these estimates produced a marginal propensity to save (*MPS*) of about 0.1 for the period 1965–78, well within the range found for a large number of countries, she concludes that Soviet household saving behaviour was normal. Pickersgill's time series saving function regressions used only the accumulation of savings deposits as the saving variable. As she noted, if the ratio of currency to savings deposits is falling, her *MPS* estimates will be biased upwards if we define saving, as it should be defined, as refraining from consumption, which in the Soviet system means the accumulation of financial assets by households. She took advantage of Birman's currency estimates to calculate the ratio of currency to savings deposits for the period 1961–76. Although this ratio increased over the period 1961–66 it fell steadily from 1966 to 1976. Although I do not agree with Pickersgill's methodology in establishing this important point, Peebles (1981: 70–2) showed that the ratio of currency to savings deposits did fall in the Soviet Union after 1965, just as in the other planned economies. Pickersgill concludes that her estimated marginal propensity to save was an overestimate and that 'the currency series estimated and used by Birman weakens rather than strengthens the case that liquidity in the hands of the population is reaching crisis proportions' (1980a: 584). She states that it is reasonable to expect household savings holdings to grow as incomes increase but that deciding what constitutes a 'reasonable' level of currency and savings deposit holdings is 'more difficult to discern' (p. 584). Her whole criticism of Birman ignored the issue of his *ALB* ratio (which is liquidity), and she confined herself to the margin, discussing only households' likely marginal propensity to save. Of course, moderate marginal propensities can produce rapidly rising household stocks of currency and savings deposits. The problem lies in interpreting what these stocks mean for the behaviour of a non-market economy.

Birman (1980b), in reply to Pickersgill (1980a), rejected Pickersgill's methodology entirely, stating:

> MPS has nothing to do with Soviet realities . . . she operates within the limits of the theory and does not pay enough attention to the facts of reality. It cannot be a coincidence that in her papers and articles on the subject she hardly quotes Soviet sources. Unfortunately for her the theory does not fit the realities. I would say so much the worse for the theory; her opinion, unfortunately, is quite different.

Birman argued that Soviet households did not have the same need to accumulate savings deposits as households in market economies. He repeated that the reason for such Soviet accumulation was shortages of goods and that 'for the most part Soviet savings are forced' (Birman, 1980b, p. 588). He referred to the opinions of some unnamed Soviet economists that three-quarters of all deposits in savings banks were due to unsatisfied demand for goods and services. He stated (p. 590)

> I am forced to confess that we have no way of measuring even approximately what share of Soviet savings is, so to speak, normal and what share is abnormal or forced. I am absolutely sure that those Soviet economists who venture to say that three-quarters of savings are

forced have no 'hard data' to support the view. Such estimates can be based only on intuition which is not bad by itself but is not, of course, reliable. My own intuition tells me that the estimate can be only an underestimation, but, alas, I cannot prove it.

Rosefielde (1988) is one of the very few economists who thought Birman's later forecasts of Soviet collapse worthy of serious analysis. Birman's statements after about 1983 were more apocalyptic in nature, being based on the marked decline in productivity growth and the low or possibly negative per capita consumption growth. He tended to put the monetary reasons for such phenomena in the background of his latter arguments, but these reasons were clearly the main cause in Birman (1980a) and Birman and Clarke (1985). They are given prominence in Birman (1983: 70–93), where they are analysed as a 'threat' (*ygroza*) to the government. These earlier monetary works are important for understanding Birman's later arguments.

Rosefielde's basic approach was to subject Birman's predictions to the test of logic by trying to establish a theoretical argument that would demonstrate that collapse must be the consequence of the phenomena identified by Birman. Rosefielde treated Birman's prediction as an hypothesis (the cumulative disequilibrium hypothesis) that was consistent with the facts of Soviet economic life and was logically consistent. Rosefielde did not analyse Birman's earlier monetary works, but he clearly appreciated that this analysis was the foundation for all Birman's pessimistic forecasts (Rosefielde, 1988: 227–8). He did not automatically accept that the prediction of collapse followed from Birman's assumptions. He tested Birman using neoclassical economic analysis of shortage phenomena and excess demand. He concludes that 'No theoretic evidence however has been adduced to suggest that the system is dynamically unstable.' (p 231). Furthermore, 'With the possible exception of the labour market, the Soviet system appears to be in a state of controlled disequilibrium.' (p. 231). (The last statement is accorded a footnote in which Rosefielde says that he sees no evidence that there will be an 'imminent run on the ruble'.) Rosefielde (p. 234) put probabilities on various possible outcomes given possible rates of growth of per capita consumption.[4]

He concludes (pp. 234–5):

> These illustrative computations suggest that Birman's hypothesis is unlikely to be confirmed at prevailing rates of per capita consumption growth, but that any further decline in the CIA's estimates and/or official Soviet series could radically alter the likelihood calculus. . . . Careful analysis has revealed that although he might be right on all

scores, neither neoclassical theory nor the preponderance of the evidence at present validate his surmise.

In other words: Given what we know, I think that Birman's predictions will not be borne out; but if things change, the outcome may be different.

Nove (1988) criticised both Rosefielde's methods and his ignoring of Soviet statements about the extent of hidden inflation. Birman (1988) commented on Rosefielde's interpretation.

The interpretation of the rising monetary stock in the Soviet Union was the main issue raised by Birman. An alternative explanation of why these stocks were large and rising in the planned economies and represented no monetary problem was offered by Farrell (1989) in his critique of Birman and Clarke (1985). Farrell's title, 'Financial "crisis" in the CPEs or "vsyo normalno"?', immediately suggests his argument (*vsyo normalno* means 'everything is normal'). Parts of his conclusion are quite ironic when viewed with hindsight. His basic argument was that monetary holdings in the Soviet Union—which he termed the liquidity ratio, M/Y, where Y is household income—were normal when put into the context of the holdings of the four other planned economies studied in this book and their relative levels of development. Among other comparative evidence he showed a scatter diagram of all five countries' liquidity ratios plotted against GNP per capita (in US dollars) in 1980. There was a clear positive relationship: the higher the GNP per capita, the higher the liquidity, with East Germany being the richest and most liquid and Poland the poorest and least liquid. The Soviet Union fell roughly in the middle with the range of estimates for its M/Y straddling a regression line for the sample. Although citing Peebles's (1981) lower estimates for currency than Birman's, for 1975 Farrell adapted Birman and Clarke's (1985) figures to derive a Soviet M/Y ratio in the range 0.6 ± 0.05. Farrell (1989: 7) concludes that 'Birman's and Clarke's notion of what M/Y would be tolerable (0.2–0.3) is inordinately low, again, by international CPE standards'.

This conclusion was based on the methodological position of '(a)ccepting the four CPEs as a standard'. This was a crucial assumption. It might be argued that as Farrell's data in his regression were for 1980, recent events could invalidate his conclusions. He was willing to publish these conclusions at the end of 1989, however. Furthermore, I think that his methodology would lead him to the same conclusion even if data for the late 1980s were used. Even if these countries experienced limited growth in GNP per capita in US dollars and even if liquidity growth became more rapid, the relative positions of the countries would not change much. Farrell's regression line would just move upwards. The Soviet Union's liquidity would not appear abnormal compared with that of the other countries. The parameters of any implied demand for money function might possibly increase as more real money was being held per unit real GNP, but Farrell's methodology would not permit the argument that this was a sign of excessive holdings.

On the basis of the time trend of M/Y in East Germany Farrell states 'The GDR is in a class of its own. As the most developed of the four, it may be the vanguard country whose pattern of financial development will be followed by the others.' (p.4). Within a few months of the publication of this statement East Germany did indeed seem to be in the vanguard of a trend in financial development in the CPEs, but one very different from that implied by Farrell: East Germany gave up its currency.

Brooks (1990: 34–6) used the term 'financial crisis' but confined it to the problems of the Soviet agricultural sector. These problems were the large debt burden of farms and continuing demands on the state budget resulting from price subsidies for many agricultural products.

Another predictor of crisis in the Soviet Union is Goldman (1983). Although not specifically concerned with financial aspects of crisis he referred to the more rapid growth of savings deposits than retail sales over the period 1975–80 and attributed this to frustrated purchasing power (pp. 55–6). Like Birman, Goldman had no model suggesting that such disparate rates of growth were definite evidence of sustained excess demand. Durgin (1984a), in a critical review of all aspects of Goldman's book, took the methodological position of showing that, for everything Goldman counted as bad about Soviet economic performance, things were as bad or even worse in the United States. For instance, Goldman saw the Soviet Union's importation of grain and meat as evidence of inefficient agriculture and impending crisis. Durgin argued that, although the United States was a net importer of agricultural produce and Canada imported two-thirds of its fruit and vegetables, no-one took this as evidence of crisis; it resulted from comparative advantage having its play (p. 104). Goldman (1984a: 114) replied that although the Soviet Union might import meat it was hardly seen in the shops, even in Moscow and Leningrad. Durgin (1984a: 104) showed that in the United States also savings deposits grew more rapidly than retail sales. In reply, Goldman (1984a; 113) argued that such comparisons just could not be made because the two economic systems were not comparable. He argued (p. 113) that it was:

> ... widely appreciated by both Western and Soviet economists [unnamed] that the rapid recent growth of private savings in the USSR is associated with suppressed inflation, scarcities of desired consumer goods, and a weakening of the incentive effectiveness of the money wage system. Variation in household savings behaviour in the US has no equivalent, adverse significance for the American economy.

Shelton (1989) wrote of 'The Coming Soviet Crash' (her title). I think it fair to say that this book is a popularisation of Igor Birman's work and views intended for the US business community and politicians. She relied on him for the methodology for investigating Soviet budget accounts and for several sources.

There are other writers who pointed out the consequences of sustained excess demand in Soviet-type economies (STEs). Cassel (1990) insisted that in the countries of administered socialism inflation was an everyday phenomenon that appeared not as open inflation but as 'cash-balance inflation'. He argued that such cash-balance inflation did have 'system-specific effects on allocation, growth, and distribution, which reduce the officially utilizable capacity, impair the long-term development prospects, and harm the political and social climate in the socialist countries' (pp. 32–3). Because of the seriousness of these problems difficult policy decisions had to be made. In particular, the supply of newly issued money had to be stopped and either a currency reform or a once-and-for-all rise in the price level was necessary. Cassel seems to have been referring to all the planned socialist countries. Although Cassel did not discuss the necessary reforms in terms of a financial crisis, he made the point that reforms might even overturn the system. This is compatible with the way I have defined crisis above. There were no doubt other appreciations of the seriousness of the financial situation of the STEs that concluded that radical reforms were necessary. Birman and Clarke (1985) and Birman (1980a; 1980b), however, gave the clearest predictions of this state of affairs.

When it comes to predictions of East German financial crisis it is harder to identify clear predictions. On the basis of the long run rise in the ratio of cash and non-cash financial assets to household incomes over the period 1955–79 (represented by a fall in income velocity) in four Eastern European countries and, for non-cash financial assets, for the same four including the Soviet Union, Pindak (1983: 125) argued that 'the GDR emerges as the country with the most virulent repressed inflation'. Nuti (1989: 120) believed that this claim was 'contrary to casual observation and other evidence'. In the event, the evidence of financial collapse in East Germany has proved consistent with Pindak's view. Pindak also concludes, without citing any data of Soviet household cash holdings, that in the Soviet Union 'the available figures suggest quite a dramatic intensification of repressed inflation in the seventies' (p. 125).

A symposium on East Germany (*Comparative Economic Studies* Summer 1987, pp. 1–70) chose to concentrate on international trade and energy use aspects of the economy and ignored financial aspects of the economy almost entirely, only briefly mentioning the consumer goods situation (p. 33).

There was no indication of the possibility of the events of 1989 and 1990 in such works as Jeffries and Melzer (1987).

5.4 PRESENTERS OF EVIDENCE CONSISTENT WITH THE CHRONIC-EXCESS-DEMAND HYPOTHESIS

This methodology looked for evidence compatible with the hypothesis of sustained excess demand by examining both monetary and price developments in a number of STEs and their relationship. This evidence would be in the form of the inverse relationship between liquidity growth and open inflation discussed in chapter 4 above.

Portes (1989: 39–40) criticised Winiecki (1985) for using such 'theoretically unjustifiable measures like the ratio of savings (flow) to change in income, or wealth to retail sales (consumption flow)'. The former measure is certainly meaningless, as was argued in section 1.3. As far as I can see Winiecki (1985) made no reference to such an indicator, and anyway his argument does not depend on it at all. There is nothing wrong in using the latter measure if we wish to understand planners' behaviour. Planners are not concerned with whether a measure is theoretical justifiable or not. If they are concerned with the possible excessive growth of this ratio, we can expect them to take action to restrain its growth. One such policy reaction is to increase retail prices.

The claim that a model could be built showing that in a country with a higher rate of inflation the wealth/income ratio will be lower than in a country with similar income growth but lower inflation (Portes, 1989: 40) does not invalidate this approach. The approach at least tries to show precisely why there is a lower wealth/income ratio. If we want to explain the trend in this ratio and the way it affected planners' aggregate retail pricing behaviour, we must use this ratio.

In a review of papers from a symposium on labour markets in STEs Peebles (1984a) pointed out that the authors did not take into account the debate about the differing incidence of excess demand

and the extent to which this might influence labour market participation and work efficiency in the different economies studied.
Peebles pointed out that 'there are some differences between the
"traditional" economies [meaning the USSR and GDR] where retail
prices are relatively stable and liquidity is rising and the "modified"
economies of Poland and Hungary where there is more open inflation
and slowly rising liquidity' (p. 76).

Winiecki (1985: 45–7) made the same point, illustrating it with
estimates of the ratio of savings deposits to annual retail-trade turnover at current prices. Countries with stable prices have high ratios,
and those with open inflation have lower ratios. As we have seen,
there are problems with using savings deposit figures to illustrate this
point. Currency generally grows less rapidly than savings deposits.
This latter figure will overestimate the true rate of growth of total
household liquidity, and it is this growth rate that is influenced by the
existence of chronic excess demand.

Peebles (1986a) presented data for total household liquidity for
the four Eastern European countries studied in this book and for the
Soviet Union and corroborated this point. Countries with high rates
of open inflation tended to have lower liquidity ratios and slower
rates of liquidity growth over the period 1965–79. Peebles (p. 90)
argued that:

> This latter inverse relationship is exactly what you would expect if you
> believe in the existence of sustained excess demand in all five countries
> and accept that official retail price rises can be used to withdraw
> currency from circulation. Where this latter policy is not used excess
> demand will be reflected in relatively rapid liquidity growth.

He concludes (p. 90) that:

> The inverse relationship between the extent of liquidity growth and
> open inflation referred to in my review of Jan Adam's book and
> partially quantified by Winiecki can be taken as a feature of these
> economies. Whether it is accepted as an indication of repressed
> inflation and possible explanation of other systematically different
> phenomena[5] has to be decided by detailed comparative work that
> avoids the problems of single-country studies.

Brada and King (1986) related labour supply behaviour to their estimate of repressed inflation econometrically in four Eastern European
economies and found a significant disincentive effect on labour of
supply shortages. This was consistent with one of the implications of
the chronic-excess-demand hypothesis and was more sophisticated
support for the point Peebles (1984a; 1986a) was trying to make.

Winiecki (1988: 62–4) returned to this theme and, still using only savings deposit data, showed that this empirical regularity held for the period 1960–83. This relationship was shown in section 4.7 above.

None of the economists discussed in this section drew the conclusion that there would be financial crises in the countries with high liquidity. East Germany had the highest liquidity at the end of the 1980s and was the first to abandon its currency.

5.5 ARGUMENTS THAT CHRONIC EXCESS DEMAND DID NOT EXIST

Here there are difficulties of interpretation as the studies to be considered did not discuss the likelihood of financial crisis. However, these studies have been taken as a basis for arguing that the claims of chronic excess demand, on which the prediction of crisis was based, were mistaken. In particular, the study by Portes and Winter (1980) has been cited, even in Soviet studies, to challenge or qualify the view of chronic excess demand. The research programme that argued that excess demand was not a characteristic feature of the STEs will, for the sake of brevity, be referred to as the Portes–Winter approach. Portes (1989) summarised the approach and detailed the publications of himself and his collaborators that argued this case. He clarified what they were actually claiming, pointing out misinterpretations and exaggerations of their claims. This chapter will not discuss their methodology in detail. Interested readers are referred to Portes and Winter (1980), Portes (1989), Davis and Charemza (1989) and van Brabant (1990) for a general discussion.

Portes and Winter (1980), taking a different approach from that in their earlier equilibrium-based studies (Portes and Winter, 1977; 1978), made the first significant claim that excess demand was not endemic to the STEs. This claim was based on disequilibrium macroeconometric estimates of the consumer goods markets in the four Eastern European countries studied above for the period 1955–75. Their data are in Rudcenko (1979). The results were put in the form of estimates of the probability that there was excess demand for consumer goods in any particular year. On the basis of these probabilities Portes and Winter (1980: 156) conclude that:

> ... the evidence here and in our earlier papers clearly justifies rejecting the hypothesis of sustained repressed inflation in the market for consumption goods and services since the mid-1950s in our four CPEs. Even in the GDR, the one country where excess demand appears to have been the dominant regime, the excess demands are

fairly small (and exceed twice their standard error in only five of 17 years), and four years show excess supply.

It was this conclusion that caused controversy and led Kornai (1982: 35) to opine that 'In my opinion, the conclusion is absurd. All four countries should be considered chronic-shortage economies all through the period under examination.' Kornai's view was that Portes–Winter methods can show only fluctuations in the extent of shortage around the normal rate of shortage, not switches from excess demand to excess supply regimes.

In summarising Portes and Winter's conclusion Winiecki (1985: 42) incorrectly stated that they found excess *demand* to be the dominant regime in three out of the four countries studied. He probably found it difficult to write that they were claiming that excess *supply* was the normal situation.

Portes (1989) replied to such criticisms and defended the methods used and their interpretation of the results. He was careful to point out exactly what he and his colleagues were claiming. Briefly, there are two kinds of criticism of Portes–Winter.

One form of criticism just rejects the results as implausible and therefore the method as wrong. This is what Kornai was doing in the quotation above. In reply, Portes (1989: 28) took as 'no longer acceptable':

> . . . unsupported assertions, purely a priori reasoning, 'stylized facts' not based on the data, and confident, elaborate verbal arguments founded on the most casual empiricism. For a theorist to use 'obviously' in argument or to dismiss empirical results as 'absurd' is one level below offering various general qualitative considerations to support essentially quantitative propositions.

Furthermore, 'Disagreement over empirical issues can be resolved only by testing well-defined hypotheses.'

The other form of criticism is criticism of the method of disequilibrium macroeconometrics itself, in which criticism Kornai (1980), Winiecki (1985; 1988) and Podkaminer (1989) were prominent. Briefly, their view was that many markets suffer excess demand, many excess supply, and that no aggregate macromeasure of demand can measure this: 'there is no aggregate excess demand to be measured' (Winiecki, 1985: 55). Kornai (1980: vol. B) originally dismissed the applicability of the concept of excess demand and the empirical possibility of excess supply in STEs. Podkaminer (1989) continued these criticisms, arguing that the minimum condition[6] on which the disequilibrium approach was based was inapplicable at the aggregate level. Winiecki (1988: 55) took an extreme position. He argued that the supply of finance to state enterprises was limitless in STEs because they enjoyed a 'soft budget constraint' — a concept of Kornai's that has received much attention in the study of STEs, including China. Winiecki (1988: 55) argued that enterprises find that their notional demands 'know no limits'; thus 'it may be irrelevant to measure something that knows no limits'. As I argued in section 1.2, I think that this argument is incorrect. Chinese economists have no difficulty in quantifying excess demand for consumer goods in any year, even though they admit the applicability and existence of the soft budget constraint to the enterprise sector and that there was excess demand for consumer goods throughout the 1980s. Peebles (1990a: 24; 1990b: 72) discussed various estimates of excess demand for China in the 1980s.

The Portes–Winter approach had a number of strong points and weaknesses, which will now be outlined.

First, the Portes–Winter approach argued that the existence of excess demand for consumer goods in STEs is an hypothesis, not an accepted fact, and should be tested. This is very reasonable. Portes and Winter's techniques cannot of course test related hypotheses. Birman's proposition that there would be a financial crisis in the Soviet Union can be regarded as an hypothesis, even though it did not emanate from a formal model. Such an hypothesis is impossible to test econometrically; events alone can determine its accuracy. The cause cited by Birman for the crisis, rapidly growing household liquidity because of sustained excess demand, can be examined to some extent and possibly explained in other terms. This was Farrell's tactic.

Second, the Portes–Winter approach applied the same technique to a number of similar economies although the planners' supply functions contain different explanatory variables in different countries. In Czechoslovakia and Hungary deviations of agricultural output from its trend play a role in planners' supply adjustments, but not in East Germany and Poland.

Third, a weakness of the Portes–Winter approach was that it did not include the Soviet Union, probably because of the lack of official currency data. Birman's estimates could have been adapted and used in a trial of the model for the Soviet Union but as far as I know no-one has tried this. However, Portes did have his views on the situation there and wrote:

Western estimates of the hidden (that is, actual) inflation in the USSR show an annual rate of 0.8–1.2 per cent for 1955–72, and although the rate seems to have accelerated during the 1970s it would be very difficult to argue that it has exceeded an annual 1.5–2 per cent. This is partly because since 1955 disposable money incomes have grown annually at only about 5 per cent per head, while even conservative Western estimates of real consumption per head give growth rates of about 4 per cent a year, leaving little room for price inflation. This last point also partially rebuts allegations of widespread and severe repressed inflation. Of course there are shortages of some goods, as is to be expected when prices are not allowed to respond to excess demand; there are also surpluses of many over-priced goods . . . But waiting lists and lines for goods such as meat, automobiles, and high-quality varieties of many commodities are not equivalent to a generalized shortage relative to money incomes and desired expenditure.

Nor is there evidence of chronic generally frustrated demand in household savings or labour supply behaviour. Savings rates do not appear to be abnormally high, and continually rising labour participation rates suggest that people must believe there will be worthwhile ways of spending the extra family income generated by additional earners. Many of the observed lines of people waiting for goods are undoubtedly due to the inefficient and undercapitalized distributive network and to distorted relative prices, and although some shortages do appear to have worsened in the late 1970s there is little evidence that the over-all retail price level has been too low. For most of the period since the mid-1950s, repressed inflation cannot be verified. (Portes, 1982: 363–4)

For just one very different interpretation of the evidence see Wiles (1988a: 236–9), who reviewed the Soviet situation in the early 1980s and concludes that there was a large monetary overhang, suppressed inflation, and a need for general retail prices increases and possibly a confiscatory monetary reform. This suggests that Wiles saw low prices as a cause of the monetary problems: 'It seems that one day neglected inflation will impose a terrible reckoning' (p. 239). It could have been dealt with to some extent by gradual price rises. This contrasts with Wiles's often-quoted earlier view that 'the stability of communist prices shines like a good deed in a naughty world' (Wiles, 1973: 377). Maybe the intention of the deed was good, but the long run consequences have been unintended, unwanted and severe, as Wiles (1988a) argued. Haddad (1977: 44) used Wiles's aphorism as the leading quotation for his article, which concludes that 'Soviet-type inflation cannot be regarded as an evil; it is merely an inconvenience to consumers' (p. 51). Pindak (1983: 94) misquoted 'deed' as 'idea', missing the point entirely.

Portes and Winter (1980: 137) dismissed scholars' use of anecdotal evidence to support the view that there was sustained repressed inflation in the Soviet Union. They also rejected Howard (1976b), who applied the Barro–Grossman disequilibrium model to Soviet data. Howard claimed to have shown that household saving and labour supply behaviour were consistent with the existence of repressed inflation. Portes and Winter (1980: 142–3) rejected this conclusion because Howard *assumed* excess demand and did not, in their view, test for its existence.

Fourth, a further weakness of the Portes–Winter approach was that the main comparative study (Portes and Winter, 1980), the results of which continue to be cited (for example, by Buck and Cole, 1987: 92), covered only the period 1955–75. Portes (1989: 38) specifically states that 'we have not stated any such view [that there is not excess demand] for the period since the mid-1970s, especially with respect of the USSR (to which we cannot extend our econometric analysis because of data problems)'. Portes's comments on the Soviet Union, cited above, related to the early 1980s, were not based on econometric results and were his alone (that is, not Portes–Winter). They were his interpretations of other Western economists' estimates. It could now be argued that these conclusions are completely invalidated by their being specific to this distant time period and overtaken by developments in the 1980s. Grossman (1986: 189), for example, argued that currency growth in the Soviet Union became rapid in the early 1980s, contributing to a 'considerable currency overhang'. Section 3.8 above presented some estimates of the extent of rapid monetary growth in the Soviet Union in the late 1980s.

There has, however, been a very recent direct application of Portes–Winter methodology to East Germany for the period 1957–85 by van der Lijn (1990). Portes and Winter found that East Germany did tend to have an excess demand regime but did not judge it to be a significant exception to the general picture of excess supply in their sample. Van der Lijn (1990: 127) concludes:

> In conclusion we may state that there was not a situation of permanent repressed inflation on the consumption goods market in the GDR in 1957–1985. The dominant regime was one of macroeconomic excess supply. Nevertheless, for a significant minority of years, in the mid 1960s, mid 1970s, and the early 1980s, there is some evidence of excess demand. The problems concerning the existence of shortages, corruption, and black market activity, must therefore be considered to be a result of a combination of other factors, which operate in all years and of repressed inflation which exists in only a minority of

years. (Disequilibrium relative prices is perhaps the most important 'other factor'.)

The words in brackets are from footnote 8 on that page. This is a clear claim of refuting Pindak (1983) (not cited by van der Lijn), who claimed that East Germany suffered from the most virulent repressed inflation among the STEs. We can legitimately ask whether disequilibrium relative prices and all their consequences are sufficient to explain why a country gives up using its own currency and does not just adjust those prices, retaining the existing economic system.

5.6 COMPARATIVE METHODOLOGIES: PREDICTORS OF CRISIS VERSUS THE REST

There are several clear differences in the approaches of those who predicted crisis and those who did not.

Predictors

Predictors have the following characteristics:

First, Birman's work had no theoretical foundation. It was based on the simple ratio of liquid assets to income and its growth. Calling this ratio *ALB* is probably just a means of saving printer's ink as it really is 'a very simple indicator' (Birman, 1980b: 590–1). The question is: What does it indicate? His argument was always that its rapid growth is due to sustained excess demand and that it indicates impending crisis. No other explanation for its rise was contemplated. The rising liquidity ratio was considered sufficient to explain shortages, corruption, dulled work incentives and so on. Birman stated that his estimates were based on 'intuition' and that he had no model.

Second, the predictors consistently claimed that the STEs were so different from market economies that concepts, tools and theories used in the latter were not applicable to them. This is clear in Birman's rejection of Pickersgill's (1980a) appeal to the low estimates of *MPS*: it 'has nothing to do with Soviet realities' (Birman, 1980b: 590). Birman and Clarke (1985: 498) put it more strongly by stating their view that 'it is hard to see whether the *MPS* can bear *any* interpretation in an *STE*' (their emphasis). This obviously put a major methodological division between the work of Birman and Clarke and that of Pickersgill and Portes–Winter. Winiecki (1985: 34–40) also provided a strong critique of this practice in Portes–Winter. This rejection is also clear in Goldman's (1984a) rejection of Durgin's (1984a) use of the United States's experiences to argue that the Soviet Union could not be facing a crisis.

Third, the predictors of crisis often referred to views similar to their own held by economists in the countries under study. This was common in Birman, who often referred to similar views held by Soviet economists. 'Views' are not hard evidence, as Birman admitted. However, if the views of enough senior advisers and planners are that there is crisis, we might expect them to recommend policies similar to those of Birman and Clarke (1985) to deal with it. After all, it is these people who suggest policy. This methodology of predicting crisis is like looking at the statements of the chairman of the Federal Reserve Board, or the governor of the Bank of England or the spokesmen of OPEC, in order to predict the course of the business cycle. In the CPEs, however, the influence of economists on policy is hard to assess. Under a Stalin or a Mao it is likely to be minimal. Now that Mikhail Gorbachev has the power to rule by decree since September 1990 and there are many pro-reform economic advisers, such influence may be great and it may be more likely that new economic policies will be quickly tried out.

Goldman (1984: 113) also appeals to the widely held views of Western and Soviet economists, without naming them, that financial holdings were excessive. If the view of crisis was correct and *Glasnost'* did mean something, we would expect the critical views of Soviet economists to be more common and cited more frequently as things became worse and political life became more open as speaking out was encouraged. I do not know whether this conjecture is correct, but there is no shortage of comments by Soviet writers that read exactly the same as Birman's 1977 view.[7]

Fourth, predictors warned of the danger of accepting official data from the STEs and even official re-estimates such as those by the Central Intelligence Agency (CIA). Birman (1988) was quite clear on the unacceptability of both Soviet growth-rate figures and the re-estimates by the CIA and most Western scholars. All he could offer in their place was his intuition that they were wrong. He did, however, have to rely on Soviet official statistics to estimate currency in circulation and his concept *ALB*. As shown in section 1.2, Winiecki believed that East Germany was the country with 'doctored' statistics, presumably meaning that they were falsified for publication.

Fifth, a further common feature of writers who upheld the chronic–excess–demand hypothesis is that they are citizens or former citizens of the countries they are discussing. Birman from the Soviet Union, Kornai from Hungary, and Winiecki and Podkaminer from Poland all believe that the STEs are sufficiently different economies, that they cannot be analysed using orthodox Western techniques and that they did suffer from sustained excess demand or shortages. Kornai, Winiecki and Podkaminer are all prominent critics of the econometric testing approach for various reasons, some of which I do not agree with.

Critics of crisis predictions

The general features common to the critics of crisis predictions seem to be the four following:

First, critics used comparative methodology to suggest that there could not be a crisis in one country because things were the same or worse in other countries. Sometimes, as with Durgin (1984a; 1984b) when criticising Goldman (1983), a country with an entirely different system was used (the United States versus the Soviet Union). Buck and Cole (1987: viii) used this methodology, also citing the case of the United States. In the case of Farrell (1989), a sample of STEs was used to assess the monetary situation in the Soviet Union. The crucial assumption underlying Farrell's methodology was that somehow all the STEs were normal and that money holdings could be explained in terms of the demand for money and, hence, relative income levels. The first assumption was a feature of Peebles's (1981) comparisons of liquidity in five STEs, which found that the Soviet Union's liquidity was not exceptional. The view of the predictors of crisis would be, presumably, that all STEs were abnormal in terms of their liquidity and that such comparisons could tell us nothing about the normality or otherwise of one country. The stylised facts of Winiecki (1985) and Peebles (1984a; 1986a) showed that liquidity developments in a sample of STEs were compatible with the chronic–excess–demand hypothesis and the institutions of these countries. Farrell argued that the facts were compatible with income developments and were perfectly normal.

This shows the major problem that bedevilled these comparative studies: one study could show that the evidence was compatible with one explanation, and another could show that the same evidence was compatible with another. There seemed to be no phenomena, or even a phenomenon (for one would have been enough), that was compatible with only one hypothesis and could thus refute the other—or, at least, I could never think of one. The only evidence that seems to be able to judge between the two views is financial crisis itself.

Second, users of econometric models that refuted the claim of chronic excess demand tended to study a number of CPEs together using Western models. Portes–Winter and Van der Lijn (1990) used the same model, the former for a number of countries, the latter, however, for just one. Although prefacing their conclusions with many caveats, Portes and Winter (1980) were confident that their views did reject the hypothesis of sustained repressed inflation for a number of countries. Van der Lijn (1990) was very confident in his statement of rejection for East Germany.

Portes–Winter is a good example of how one of the social sciences (economics) that simultaneously incorporates theoretical, general empirical, sometimes econometric and historical methodology has tended to become more like the natural sciences in several obvious features. There is the incidence of multiple authors of the principal research findings. The maximum is four in the case of Portes, Quandt, Winter and Yeo (1987).[8] These authors can be seen as the directors of the research programme, which could be called 'the identification and measurement of the extent of excess demand in various markets in certain CPEs'. Given the nature of modern communications, a collaborative research programme does not require all the principal researchers to be located in the same place. Such a research programme requires laboratory equipment in the form of computer hardware and software. This equipment needs support staff to provide the data and to program it (Portes and Winter, 1980: 156). To run the research programme there is a need for funding from various research councils or private organisations. Preliminary reports are circulated among other researchers for comment, revision and so on. The final results are acknowledged as benefiting from this process. For example, Kornai, among others, commented on Portes and Winter (1980) before publication. Final publications are thus very much the product of extensive teamwork and reflect the features of normal science. None of these features seems to apply to Birman and Clarke to anything like this extent.

Third, critics of crisis predictors often relied on quite dated results and data. The data base of Portes and Winter (1980), frequently cited, extended only to 1975. As far as I know they have not published any similar multicountry results for any period later than the mid 1970s. Portes, Quandt, Winter and Yeo (1987) studied only Poland for the period up to 1980. Their views may have been invalidated by subsequent events that they could not have taken into account. It could be argued that the financial crisis in the Soviet Union was caused by serious monetary developments after about 1985, but Birman and Clarke were in print before that time and Birman long before it. Pickersgill's *MPS* estimates did not go beyond the early 1980s but are often cited. Farrell's (1989) comparative regression used data from 1980. For reasons offered in section 5.3 above, I do not think that Farrell's methodology would have given different results had more recent data been used. However, Van der Lijn (1990), who used Portes–Winter methodology and rejected the hypothesis of repressed inflation for East Germany, the first STE to abandon its own currency, used data from well into the mid 1980s. As far as I know, no one actually predicted the East German crisis as clearly as Birman and Clarke did for the Soviet Union, but Pindak (1983) claimed that East Germany had the most serious repressed inflation problem — a view rejected by Nuti (1986).

Fourth, in terms of the objectives of different approaches it seems that there are the following. Portes–Winter had two main objectives: to show the true macroeconomic mechanisms operating in the CPEs and to suggest necessary policy measures for these economies. For example, Portes (1989: 43–4) argued that the Portes–Winter methodology provided clearer understanding of certain major problems of the CPEs relevant to the formulation of Western policy responses, compared with the insights offered by the conventional wisdom. Portes (1989: 43) saw practical policy implication for the CPEs in their results. Birman, it seems, was primarily concerned to disabuse Western Sovietologists of their blindness to the inaccuracy of Soviet official statistics — and, in particular, of CIA re-estimates: 'The CIA has a monopoly on large-scale research and calculations' (Birman, 1988: 147) — and to the inapplicability of Western models to the planned system. He offered no real hope for government policy measures within the existing system of the STEs to improve the situation. He offered policy advice to Soviet citizens, however: 'If this article were intended for Soviet citizens I would advise them to get out of all forms of accumulation (*nakopleniye*) immediately and to live in debt' (Birman, 1983: 84). This advice was offered of course because he was then predicting a monetary reform that would confiscate private financial assets.

5.7 CONCLUSIONS

I do not belong to the school of economists who take the instrumentalist view that economic theories are solely instruments for making predictions about the world. In this view theories should be judged not by whether their assumptions are 'realistic' but solely by their ability to produce non-refuted predictions. This view encourages the application of models developed for one system to the conditions of another. Ironically, the application of Portes–Winter to the CPEs did not produce predictions. Economics can predict patterns in the behaviour of large numbers of people if we accept that the testing of the theory is based on probabilities and that an acceptably small incidence of exceptions to the pattern does not refute the relationship hypothesised. When it comes to the more usual concept of prediction that economists are often expected to accept — the prediction of such things as an economy's growth rate next year or its exchange rate — failure is almost certain. The quantitative aspects of economic variables in historical processes are impossible to predict. However, it must be admitted that, if one does understand the working of a system, even a complicated national macroeconomic system, one should be able to make more general qualitative predictions. Here, successful prediction *would* be a test of knowledge. Examples of such predictions would be that growth rates will be higher for the next two years, or that the exchange rate will depreciate.

Birman (1980a) and Birman and Clarke (1985) pass this test. They provided qualitative predictions that have been borne out for the case of the Soviet Union: there *is* a financial crisis, and policies very similar to the ones they forecasted are being implemented. Their predictions were quite clear compared with the implications for likely future development emanating from 'harder' methodologies that did not address the question of future events and qualified their conclusions with so many reservations that it is not easy to interpret their views in the context of qualitative predictions. The econometric testers probably had no such intentions. However, they did have the intention of settling the practical question 'with policy implications' of distinguishing 'between the effects of excess aggregate demand and distorted relative prices (or other problems like the inadequacies of the distributive network [references omitted])' (Portes, 1989: 43). Certain of our countries have distinguished between the different effects by adopting policies predicted by the hypothesis of chronic excess demand, not by the problem of distorted relative prices or a shortage of shops. In other words, they decided to change the system.

The methodology of Birman and Clarke unfortunately is not the sort that can be built upon and further developed, based on 'intuition' and 'feel' as it is. It does, however, leave us with three lessons. First, be very wary of applying Western analytical concepts, tools and methods to planned economies; they are different, at least at the macroeconomic level, and on this Stalin was right. Second, listen to what the economists of the countries under study are saying; if *they* talk about crisis, look for crisis policies. Third, determine what are the crucial institutions of the economy for its macroeconomic development. The role of money in the planned economies was ignored for too long at the expense of studies of other institutional arrangements and sectors. Birman's argument was that many of the problems identified in planned economies were due to mismanagement of the monetary sector and cannot be understood alone. This was a complaint of Peebles (1984a) also. The collapse and radical reform of the monetary system has emphasised the importance of correct management of this institution even in a planned economy.

Finally, it is an uncongenial conclusion for economists that 'soft' methodology using intuition based on simple data produced qualitatively correct predictions, whereas 'hard' methodology based on complicated technique, widespread teamwork and extensive data claimed that the arguments producing the correct predictions were unfounded and that the methods used were no longer acceptable. 'Soft' methodology produced clear predictions; 'hard' methodology did not. Unfortunately, the 'soft' methodology cannot be built on. It is too individualistic (and in many ways non-scientific), whereas the 'hard' methodology can be adopted by anyone competent in the field and able to obtain the data. This competence does not require knowledge of the languages of the countries under study. This lack of knowledge often leads to misunderstandings of the nature and sources of the data, the institutions and policies of the country and incorrect interpretations of the results.[9] The results of the alternative methodology, while eschewing predictions, suggest that we should not draw strong conclusions from outdated studies. It is a nice matter of judgment as to what constitutes being out-of-date in a rapidly changing world.

6 Conclusions

Modern money is everywhere debt. Fiat money is the non-repayable debt of the government. In some countries where banknotes were once convertible into some form of commodity money such as gold, the fiction that banknotes can still be so converted is perpetuated by statements on the banknotes that the issuer will convert them (such as those found on Bank of England notes). Despite this, nowadays all the holder will get is another piece of fiat money. In market economies bank deposits are the obligations of, generally privately owned, commercial banks. They are convertible into fiat money. The total of bank deposits existing at any time is many times the amount of fiat money in existence. This means that all bank deposits could not be converted into fiat money if their owners so desired. It is on such a shaky foundation that the monetary system of market economies is based. Generally, this system has contributed to growth and rising living standards in the market economies, albeit with variable rates of inflation.

In the planned economies money is also debt, exclusively the debt of the government in the form of fiat money and savings deposits held by the population. Enterprise money is largely a book-keeping entry. The government tries to meet its debt to the population by supplying consumer goods in return for the fiat money it pays out for labour and labour-produced commodities that are sold to it. In theory, there is a firmer guarantee of the value of money in planned economies than in market economies; in practice, it is the opposite. Stalin was right again. It is perhaps trite to say that socialist governments have found it much easier to print and issue the money than to supply consumer goods, but that is the essence of the problem.

In China, after the austere period of the Cultural Revolution

(1966–76) during which per capita consumption hardly increased, it was recognised that the government owed the population a debt relating to its economic life (*shenghuo fangmian qianzhang*). At the end of the 1970s the Chinese government's policy to meet this debt was to give the people both more money and more goods. Monetary incentives were used to stimulate production and trade, and output and living standards rose. In the Soviet Union it is now recognised that the government owes the people a debt, but there.seems little sign that the government is able to stimulate consumer goods production and raise living standards operating the existing economic system. There are no domestic consumer goods to validate its debt represented by the large amount of fiat money it has issued. We can see the calls for privatisation (*privatizatsiya*) as an alternative way of validating the currency and paying the debt. Instead of supplying consumer goods, the government could supply assets in return and let people get on with the business of using the assets to produce the goods themselves. The government could sell all sorts of assets, ranging from state gold stocks, foreign currencies and the contents of museums, to productive assets such as land, factories and houses. Such assets could be auctioned to individuals or consortia or given to their current users or workers.

One recent call in the Soviet Union has been for the privatisation of productive equipment without payment. One reason is the author's view that it is a myth that the population is holding huge amounts of surplus money that it could use to purchase state property. The second is because the proposer (a candidate in economics, and not the only such proposer) sees the rightful owner of the existing stock of assets as the population, not the government. The physical assets have been built up through deductions from wages since the 1920s and should be returned to their rightful owners. This deduction resulted from the application of Marx's principle that the worker gets back from society that which he or she has contributed after deductions have been made for accumulation and social consumption. Privatisation is necessary because 'If political repentance by the Party before the people is necessary for the continued existence of the Party itself then for the renaissance of the state there must be an "economic repentance" in the form of the return of property to its rightful owners' (Zaichenko, 1990). How privatisation takes place, on what terms and to what extent will be a major part of Soviet economic policy for the future. Kornai (1990) outlines his methods for Hungary, but they could be applied anywhere. Lenin used to say that the main political question was *Kto kovo?* (literally, 'Who whom?'), meaning who had the power and who was ruled. The main question now is *komu?* or perhaps, *Y kovo?* ('Who will get and have the property?'). The answer in turn might then determine *Kto kovo.*

There is one further interesting feature of socialist money that differentiates it from money in market economies that is worth commenting on in detail. We have seen that foreign currencies have been used in these economies alongside, or instead of, domestic currency. Certain governments have encouraged this. Individual Soviet republics want to issue their own money. Good (foreign) currencies were driving out bad (domestic) currencies. In the extreme case of East Germany the bad currency was entirely driven out of existence. The foreign currencies were good because they were able to buy what the domestic currencies were unable to buy and were more generally accepted even among the population.[1] This phenomenon of good currencies driving out bad is the opposite of the proposition known as 'Gresham's law' that states that 'Bad money drives out good.'[2] Gresham's law, like the Quantity Theory of Money, is a very old proposition in monetary economics and sometimes still gets discussed in textbooks. It relates to a world of commodity currencies where currencies have some intrinsic value. It is sometimes held up as a universal principal. Lipsey, Steiner and Purvis (1987: 614) state that it 'has stood the test of time' and is 'as applicable to the twentieth century as it was to the sixteenth century'. It cannot be taken as a general principle, however, as the events in Eastern Europe show. It is applicable to commodity monies that have intrinsic value; they are the good currencies.

It is worth a diversion to show the assumptions on which the proposition is based. Imagine an economy that uses silver coins where a coin stamped $1D$ contains an amount of silver equal to $1S$. Silver is valuable as a commodity, and this value is sufficient to buy a basket of goods of value $1B$. This ratio is determined by the real forces of demand and supply for commodities. Now, assume that the government debases the coinage by producing coins stamped $1D$ that only contain $(\frac{1}{2})S$. No one will supply $1B$ for such a coin; suppliers will insist on $2S$ in order to obtain the true silver value of $1B$. In other words, there has been an inflation and the price level has doubled. A given stock of silver could produce twice as many coins and the price level would double. This is how Marx saw the question of money as he accepted the Quantity Theory. Now, anyone who has an old (good) coin that contains $1S$ will not offer it in exchange for goods as it is still stamped $1D$ and will only buy $(\frac{1}{2})B$ whereas its true value is $1B$. People will melt down such coins, obtain the silver and thus be able to obtain 1B. As Gresham put it, the bad (debased) coins will drive the good (non-debased) coins out of circulation. They will simply disappear. If there were pieces of paper labelled 1D circulating, they would stay in circulation but would depreciate and could also be classified as 'bad'.

Lipsey, Steiner and Purvis (1987: 615) use Gresham's law to explain why inflationary countries, such as Chile, do not use coins but small-denomination paper notes. No one would offer valuable metal coins with low denominations in exchange for hardly any goods when the metal itself is worth much more in terms of goods.

Gresham's law is not a general principle that can be applied to all modern economies. In the planned economies Gresham's law does not apply. In what he calls 'an extension of Gresham's law' Nordhaus (1990: 305) argues that it does apply to the Soviet Union. He argues that overvalued things (roubles) are driving out undervalued things (goods). I think that this phenomenon can be understood without trying to extend Gresham's law outside the field of monetary circulation for which it was developed. In the planned economies, good money drives out bad. Here again Stalin was correct: 'With us, its the other way around.' This reversal of Gresham's law has long been recognised 'Hence in monetary conditions characterized by a great distrust in the national money the principle of Gresham is reversed, and *good money drives out the bad*, and the value of the latter continually depreciates' (Bresciani-Turroni, 1937: p. 174, italics in original).

Let us summarise the monetary situation in our six countries towards the end of the 1980s by comparing the values of various variables in 1989 with their 1980 values. This is shown for certain important relevant variables in Table 6.1. Poland stands out as the country with the lowest increase in real variables (for example, in net material product, *NMP* and real income per capita) and with the highest increase in nominal variables (a consumer price level 34 times that of 1980, for example). This is good evidence that inflation above a certain rate is inimical to economic growth. China shows the greatest increase in real output by far and increases in nominal variables more similar to those of Hungary than to those of the other European countries. Its high open inflation rates do not seem to have retarded growth and development. They caused much hardship for those on fixed incomes, redistribution of income and popular protest. The policies taken to deal with inflation in 1988 certainly slowed growth. It seems that China just did not have the monetary institutions and experience capable of reducing inflation without

Table 6.1   Selected variables, ratio of 1989 to 1980

Variable	USSR	GDR	Czechoslo-vakia	Poland	Hungary	PRC
Real NMP (Q)	1.30	1.41	1.19	1.08[a]	1.10	2.20
Consumer Prices	1.14	1.02	1.12	33.80	2.15	2.00
Money (SD)	2.15	1.60	1.78	6.63	2.51	10.1
Nominal Wages	1.42	1.29	1.22	33.90	2.60	3.39[b]
MIP	1.61	1.39	1.34	39.20	2.41	4.27
Real Incomes per capita	1.20	1.42	1.21	1.06	1.13	n.a.
MIP/Q	1.24	0.99	1.13	36.30	2.19	1.94
M/Q	1.65	1.13	1.50	6.14	2.28	4.59

Notes:
[a] *1980–88.*
[b] Staff and workers' average wage.

Sources: European countries: ratios for *NMP*, prices, nominal wages and real incomes per capita, calculated by compounding the growth rates given in *ESE*, (pp. 387, 389, 391–2), to obtain 1989 or 1988 figure; savings deposits from *ESE* (Table B-18).
China: calculated from data in *ZGTJNJ89* and *ZGTJNJ90, passim.*

reducing growth—but then, there were some market economies that were not able to do this in the 1980s either.

The last two lines allow us to see a remarkable correlation between nominal variables and the consumer price level across the sample of European countries. The ratio MIP/Q shows the extent to which money incomes of the population increased in relationship to real output in these countries. The simple linear correlation (not including China) between this ratio and the consumer price ratio is 0.999.[3] This means that the extent to which the consumer price level in 1989 exceeded its 1980 value is strongly correlated with the extent to which the level of money incomes was allowed to rise in relationship to real output. In other words, the price level mirrors movements in the ratio of money incomes of the population (MIP) to real output (Q). This is an implication of the *PPI* approach discussed in chapter 4. In East Germany this ratio did not rise and so the price level hardly rose, whereas in Poland the ratio rose to be 36 times its 1980 level and the price level rose to 34 times its 1980 level. Of course, there is also a correlation between the ratio of money to real output and the consumer price level ($r = 0.985$), but the theory underlying such a relationship does not explain why money changes nor why prices are increased.

Although the *PPI* approach rejects the Quantity Theory of Money as a useful tool for writing economic history, it recognises the importance of the quantity of money for developments in nominal variables in these economies. It reverses the direction of causation between nominal variables and money, however. The *PPI* approach starts with developments in nominal incomes (which can occur as a result of both deliberate policies and uncontrolled factors), shows how these developments cause imbalances on the consumer goods market, identifies planners' reactions, and shows how these reactions lead to different combinations of nominal money growth and retail price increases. The quantity of money and its control are important matters, even in the traditional command economies. This is also true in models of market socialism being proposed for the planned economies (Brus and Laski, 1989: 117–8).

Money was not well managed in the planned economies, and now they are reaping the harvest of monetary mismanagement. The harvest has brought open inflation to most (hyperinflation in Poland), economic and political instability (to say the least), and a complete loss of faith in the command economic system among the population and the leadership. A question for historians, and those who like counterfactual questions, is whether the command system could ever have designed monetary institutions or rules to ensure reasonable monetary equilibrium in a system using essentially what was labour token money. Let us not forget that monetary management in market economies is not particularly successful at times either, but it has not in the postwar period directly brought economic collapse. Perhaps future economic historians will try to assess the extents to which monetary matters were responsible for the abandonment of command planning and the different extent of abandonment of single-party communist rule in these countries.

The countries under study here fall into three groups in terms of the nature of their reactions to their monetary problems. China stands alone as the country that has retained its modified planned system and dealt with inflation by a restrictive administrative monetary policy, sacrificing real growth. The administrative nature of the policies used to achieve this have been endorsed by a World Bank team (World Bank, 1990) only as a temporary policy. East Germany has used a unique approach to solve its monetary problems through monetary union that hands this responsibility to the West German central bank. The remaining Eastern European countries and the Soviet Union have decided to abandon planned socialism and adopt a market system of co-ordination. There are major problems in achieving such a transformation and I will not speculate on the likely outcome. The transformation from feudalism (to which the command system is very similar in certain significant ways) to capitalism took a number of centuries of evolution in Western Europe. The planned economies are trying to achieve this within decades. They are doing it in an world where they can see how market economies function, what institutions are necessary, what roles they play and how Western economist analyse their behaviour. Knowing the functions of these institutions is a far cry from creating them. They will, to various degrees, draw on the advice of outside economists and agencies and the experiences of their economies.

Some aspects of transformation may be easy in economic terms but difficult politically. Small scale trade and production can be legalised and liberalised easily. What was previously smuggling now becomes an import–export business; what was previously speculation becomes commerce. Large amounts of money can be made from such activities that were formerly thought of as unproductive and immoral under the influence of Marxism. Private entrepreneurs who make money in such economies are in a precarious position. Their new fortunes, based perhaps on luck, connections, bribes and so on, cause resentment.[4] If every town in these economies could get a supermarket of the standard found in the most modest of Western economies, resentment at private trade could disappear quickly. The Chinese experience has fostered the view that collectivised agriculture should be abandoned in favour of private family farming and all that this entails for marketing and price reform. Such things as maintaining a transport network, co-ordinating the flows of goods in the economy and creating a stable monetary system will be much more difficult.

The main legacy of the planning system is that most resources are being employed in the wrong branches of the economy and in an inefficient way. There is no easy mechanism for reallocating them. The market solution of forcing market discipline on enterprises will bankrupt many and cause unemployment that may be long-lasting. With distorted prices and the fact that it is impossible for any planning mechanism to obtain the needed information, the use of command to reallocate resources has to confront the problem of knowing which enterprises should expand and which close, which industries should be abandoned, which products are exportable and so on.

Let us conclude with a brief survey of the political and economic situation of these countries towards the end of 1990. In Poland, Czechoslovakia, East Germany and Hungary the ruling Communist Parties abandoned one-party rule between October and December

1989 and committed themselves to multiparty elections, which were held in 1989 or 1990. These changes were generally peaceful and certainly so in comparison with the changes in Rumania in December 1989. The Communist Parties changed their names or announced that they would do so and contested the elections, doing badly in all countries. East Germany was absorbed by West Germany in October 1990. Poland's presidential elections in November and December 1990 were bitterly fought. Its serious economic problems remain. All these countries are committed to introducing a market economy. Poland and Hungary are undertaking rapid privatisation programmes. Poland's approach has been called the 'big bang' approach of trying to do it all at once. It is said that the average standard of living in Poland fell 42 per cent between December 1989 and April 1990 (Marrese, 1990: 58). I do not know how this estimate was made. The Soviet Union, whose president, Mikhail Gorbachev, can be credited with, or blamed for, letting all this happen, is wrestling with the problems caused by its fundamental political and economic reforms in the face of the independence movements of its major republics. He is attempting to rule by decree and is continually being blamed for being both indecisive and a dictator. Some analysts see the Soviet Union fragmenting, with independence for each republic, which opens up the possibility of their creating their own monetary systems.

In China, events have been very different. The Communist Party remains in control after the violent suppression of student and popular protest in June 1989. The existing system has been retained, but quiet adjustments are being made to remove important financial distortions. During 1990 some retail prices were raised to reduce budget subsidies, and other increases (possibly the retail price of grain) are being discussed (Delfs and Bowring, 1990: 40). The successive devaluations are aimed at reducing export subsidies (Bowring and Delfs, 1990: 42). Throughout the latter half of 1990 there seemed to be paralysis in political decision making, with the Seventh Plenum of the Thirteenth Central Committee, which was to ratify the eighth five-year plan and a ten-year growth strategy, being postponed a number of times. The fate of China's economic reform programme is unknown under the present leadership. There have been strong statements recently that China will never privatise its economy.

Such were the fates of the countries using socialist money. How they manage their new systems, which *will* be new to them, is yet to be seen.

Endnotes

1 In October 1990 the Ukrainian Republic started to issue its own ration coupons to Ukrainians. These could be regarded as an alternate form of money as they were required to obtain virtually all goods. If they circulated widely on private markets, they could be called money. If they replaced Soviet rouble notes, they would be a new money. Such a method is an easy way for the Ukraine to establish its own currency. This is an illustration of a general principle that anything that is given official exchange value could circulate as money. In China, food ration coupons became a common means of exchange during the 1980s. High income families could easily afford grain and would exchange surplus grain coupons directly for industrial products on private markets. They were demanded by the emerging itinerant population seeking jobs in urban areas who did not have residence permits and were willing to offer sideline products, among others. As the coupons circulated they became money. In the Chinese case it was probably never intended that they should circulate in this way.

2 Birman's work was almost completely ignored. For example, of all the essays in Davis and Charemza (1989b) only Nuti cites Birman (1980a; 1980b), but even Nuti ignores Birman's 1981 book and does not discuss his predictions in any detail. In their introduction, Davis and Charemza (1989a) refer to only Birman (1983) (published in Russian), ignoring his substantial book of 1981 (in English) and his earlier articles. Kaser (1990) ignores Birman. Buck and Cole (1987) do not discuss Birman's prediction of financial crisis although they devote an entire chapter to the problem of excess demand and growth of Soviet savings. Ellman (1989) includes Birman (1981) in his 'Suggestions for further reading' but does not discuss his ideas, even though they concern the complete failure of Soviet monetary planning. Rosefielde (1988) takes Birman's predictions as an hypothesis, discusses it extensively, but does not support it. Birman (1990: 28–9) discusses the problems he had in getting his work published. Peebles (1984) complains that students of labour markets in the planned economies had

not taken into account the debate about the differing extent of repressed inflation and the nature of 'socialist money' and how this affected work incentives citing Birman (1981). Peebles (1981) discusses Birman (1980a).

3 'U nikh, u kapitalistov [. . .] U nas naoborot' ('With the capitalists [this is how it is]. With us, it's the other way around').

4 The concept of repressed inflation was first used to analyse wartime market economies (Charlesworth, 1956) and was applied to the young People's Republic of China (Jao, 1967/1968).

CHAPTER 2

1 This is about three months' average salary in the state sector (ESE p. 389).

2 That is, 1,000,000,000,000,000,000,000,000,000 to 1. Gurley (1953: 81) puts it at 400 octillion flat pengo to 1. This is the correct rate using the US definition of octillion (1,000 raised to the power of 9, which is 1 with 27 zeros after it). Berend and Ranki (1974: 190) give the rate at 400,000 quadrillion to 1.

3 Most writers refer to Marx's views expressed in 'Critique of the Gotha programme' of 1875. See Marx and Engels (1968: 315–35). Similar visions of a moneyless economy with no commodities, therefore no trade, where everything produced is available from state warehouses and workers receive a non-circulating certificate or token can be found in Bolshevik writers. Arnold (1937: 105) discusses such views.

4 The Chinese economist Sun Yefang also took this view.

5 In May 1979 East German citizens were forbidden to use their West German marks directly to buy in these shops, and all had to obtain certificates first and explain how they had obtained the foreign currency.

6 I refer to the law as applied to ordinary citizens. There have always been rumours that leaders maintain foreign bank accounts.

7 The figures given in Table 2.1 are from ESE (p. 113) and relate to the proportion of net material product (NMP) used. Higher ratios for the proportion of gross domestic product (GDP) allocated to gross investment are reported in World Development Report 1988 (p. 231) for certain reporting countries. For Hungary and Poland, for example, the proportions in 1986 were 26 and 29 per cent respectively.

8 ESE gives both 254 per cent (p. 392) and 244 per cent (p. 136).

CHAPTER 3

1 Such a separation of monetary flows can be found in other centralised systems. Crump (1981: pp. 203–4) quotes a case where state accounts were made in units of barley ('documentary barley') purely as an accounting device and the people used silver. This was in Ur more than 4000 years ago.

2 In China the English-language statistical sources refer to 'Bank credit

receipts and payments' but the Chinese-language sources refer to 'State credit receipts and payments' (*Guojia xindai shouzhi*). See *Statistical Yearbook of China 1981* (p. 408) and *Zhongguo Tongji Nianjian 1981* (p. 399) respectively.

3 The planners' choice of the retail price given the wholesale price determines the tax rate. The retail price is not determined as the state wholesale price plus some known predetermined tax rate.

4 Official Chinese budget figures include domestic and foreign borrowing as revenue. Hence the deficit is the unfunded part of the deficit.

5 Tsang (1990: 231) also says that the amount of currency in circulation in 1985 was lower than in 1984, but this is not correct as his own figures show.

6 I cannot reconcile this increase with data for end-of-year savings deposits for 1988 and 1989.

7 Santorum (1989: 54) presents a table showing annual percentage increases in M0 (which must be currency) for the period 1978–86, but these are very different from the correct rates.

8 Chen's currency series comes from a number of sources, including Chow (1987), who presents a wrong figure for 1952

9 These sources do include an item 'currency outside banks' which is useful but it differs by about 1–2 per cent each year from the item 'money in circulation' published in *Comecon Data*.

10 In an interview given to *Corriere della Sera* published on 22 November 1989 (English translation in *MNBPB* no. 1031, 21 February 1990, pp. 24–7).

11 A year later the Ukrainian Republic began to issue ration coupons to its citizens. This could be seen as a first step towards replacing Soviet roubles with a Ukrainian currency.

12 All these statistics were derived from data in *ZGTJNJ89 (pp. 29–30, 598–9, 688)*.

13 I am relying on a translation of an article by Wang Yaping in *Jinji Cankao* (19 March 1990), translated in FBIS-CHI-90-072-S (13 April 1990, pp. 34–6).

14 Gorbachev also stated that the population's money incomes grew 2.1 times over the period 1971–85. Peebles's (1981: 63) *MIP* estimate for 1971 was 202.81 billion roubles implying a figure for 1985 of 426 billion roubles. Aslund (1989: 86) estimates total money incomes for 1985 at 351.6 billion roubles but is not very clear on the method used. In the first nine months of 1990 these incomes were 461 billion roubles, implying roughly 615 billion roubles for the year. On the basis of the *ESE* (p. 390), which gives annual growth rates for *MIP*, Peebles's 1985 figure would grow to 569 billion roubles in 1989 and Aslund's to only 469 billion roubles.

15 The data and statistics in the discussion come from the report on the economic results for the first nine months of 1990 in *Izvestiya* of 21

October 1990 and from the issue of *Selskaya Zhizn'* of 20 October 1990, as translated in *Summary of World Broadcasts*, (SU/W0151, pp. A/6–9).

16 The complexity of the laws relating to the ownership of foreign exchange in the European countries in about 1986 is covered in Mojziskova (1987/88).

17 Vanous (1980) bases his estimates on reports of monthly black market exchange rates published in *Pick's Currency Yearbook*. He is very suspicious about their sources and accuracy (pp. 59–60) and advises 'considerable caution' in accepting them. *World Currency Yearbook* continues to publish such data even for China.

18 I have omitted reference to countries Vanous (1980) includes if they are not covered in this book.

19 The official rate against the US dollar went from 1.4962 yuan in 1979 to 4.7221 yuan in 1989 (end of period figures). The December 1989 devaluation took the official rate from 3.7221 to 4.7221 yuan, suggesting that the principle used for the devaluation was just to change the first digit. The November 1990 devaluation changed the rate to 5.2221 yuan.

20 Hsu (1989) says that the rate 'shot up from the usual 0.78 Hong Kong dollars to about 0.9 Hong Kong dollars per renminbi yuan compared to the official rate of 0.47 Hong Kong dollars per renminbi yuan (p. 179).' At that time the black market rate was about 1 yuan per Hong Kong dollar (1/0.9) and the official rate was 0.476 yuan per Hong Kong dollar (*Far Eastern Economic Review* 1 September 1988, p. 68). The Hong Kong dollar only bought about 0.47 yuan because it was linked to the US dollar at a rate of 7.8 Hong Kong dollars (Peebles, 1988: 180–1). Thus a Hong Kong dollar would be worth approximately 3.7221/7.8, which is 0.477 yuan. The year 1988 was the most inflationary year in China during the 1980s.

CHAPTER 4

1 Chow (1987) uses y to represent Q but I have not followed his notation here.

2 I extended the analysis to the periods 1952–85 and 1952–88 using correct currency-in-circulation data. Chow (1987) is not very clear on his sources, and his figure for 1952 is nearly 40 per cent greater than the figures published in official Chinese sources (Peebles, 1990a pp. 25–6; 1991: ch. 6). The maximum slope coefficient obtainable was 0.322, still very much below unity.

3 This estimate led Friedman and Schwartz (1963, p. 700) to predict the resumption of the secular decline in velocity in the United States after 1963. In fact velocity continued to rise quite steadily until it collapsed in the early 1980s.

4 This approach is found in the work of Feltenstein, Lebow and van Wijnbergen (1980).

5 Keynesian models did make V a positive function of the rate of interest so

that PQ could expand even if M remained constant as long as the rate of interest rose.

6 Figure 4.1 shows the situation for only one year. If imbalances persist then increasing prices can only prevent s from rising above its existing rate, which may now exceed s^*.

7 Peebles (1986b). The *PPI* measure has been adopted by Gardner (1988, p. 39) and adapted by Hsu (1989: pp. 151-5), but they do not use it to explain anything. They take it to be of interest in itself. Chinese sources have recently described the excess demand problem in terms very much like the *PPI* concept (Peebles, 1990a: pp. 23-4; 1990b: pp. 72-3). Naughton (1986: pp. 107-14) estimates excess demand for China before 1979 with an approach that is essentially equivalent to estimating the gap XD in Figure 4-1. This requires subtracting an estimate of desired saving from purchasing power in every year in order to estimate demand and comparing it with real supplies. This cannot really be done for a longer period as there are no data on actual supplies of retail goods, only data on realised sales and changes in inventories.

8 Portes and Winter (1980: pp. 144-5) assume that planners do adjust the supply of consumer goods to monetary developments. They identify this latter effect as the deviation of current monetary stock from its trend growth rate. This does not explain why the monetary stock grew faster than its historical trend in any year. Santorum (1989: p. 34) extends this by making price increases a reaction to unanticipated increases in currency stocks in the previous year but does not explain the motive for increasing prices when nominal money rises unexpectedly.

9 Of course, the objective of monetary planning is to prevent excessive monetary growth by controlling MIP to meet increases in supplies. If the objective is to keep s constant then MIP should only be allowed to grow at the same rate as real supplies. If the objective is to keep liquidity constant with constant prices, the dependence of the growth of MIP on the growth of supplies is more complicated. For example, if the existing liquidity ratio is unity and planners are told to maintain this ratio and that supplies will grow 10 per cent then they can increase MIP by 14 per cent. If supplies grow 20 per cent they can increase MIP by 33 per cent. The formula $m = -5.0 + 1.9g$ (where g is the growth rate of real supplies and m is the growth rate of MIP) shows the permissible rates of growth of MIP for any increase in supplies, in this numerical example.

10 If an economy starts with a liquidity ratio of 0.8, a value of s of 0.05 and a *PPI* that is continuously only 1, and there is no open inflation response, liquidity may increase to 1.02 within four years and to more than 2.00 within eleven years.

11 $CASH/Q$ is the ratio of cash to real Net Material Product (NMP), in 1977 prices. Data sources were *Comecon Data 1981* (pp. 47, 301, 420) and *1987* (pp. 50, for growth rates of real output used for extending the series, 299, 412). There is evidence of positive serial correlation. Assuming it to be of

the first order and running a Cochrane–Orcutt regression, the results con-firm a close relationship with $R^2 = 0.9786$ and a t-statistic on the slope (which was 0.9027) of 4.66.

12 See Peebles (1991) for the application of *PPI* to China for the period 1952–88.

CHAPTER 5

1 Current reductions in Soviet defence expenditure are specifically aimed at increasing the supply of consumer goods by means of the 'economic con-version' of defence industry factories to produce desired consumer goods in order to 'saturate the consumer market', in the words of Abel Aganbegyan, cited from Kincade and Thomson (1990: 85), who give many examples of this aspect of reform. Bova (1988) shows why the military were early supporters of economic reform.

2 The current radical reforms in agriculture are discussed in Brooks (1990).

3 *The Economist* (6 October 1990, p. 86). For a full report of economic results for the first nine months of 1990 I have used the British Broadcast-ing Corporation's *Summary of World Broadcasts: Soviet Union Report* SU/W0151 A/5 of 26 October 1990 (pp. A/5–A/7), which is a translation of the report from *Izvestiya* of 21 October.

4 Birman (1983: 208) had pointed out that it is not necessary for there to be a revolutionary party for there to be a revolution, noting that the February revolution in Russia was not organised by revolutionary parties but occurred 'when there were no bread supplies in Petrograd for three days'.

5 Peebles (1986a) is referring to the difference in labour productivity growth over time, which is inversely related to liquidity and its increase. This is consistent with the chronic–excess–demand hypotheses but with other things also.

6 This is the proposition that when there is disequilibrium the quantity traded will be the minimum of either the quantity demanded (excess supply) or the quantity offered for supply (excess demand).

7 A commentator in *Izvestiya* (10 September 1989) writes:
In plain language, when there is nothing to be bought with the rubles which have been paid out, they gather dust either in savings accounts or in 'mattresses.' Thus deposits with the Savings Bank increased by 17.7 billion rubles during the first six months of [1989] and reached the impressive amount of 314 billion rubles.

A large proportion of this money is certainly not being put aside for 'a rainy day'. We are talking about really forced savings. After all this money today is, for all intents and purposes, not [matched by saleable goods.] It is impossible to underestimate the danger of this phenomenon. The incentive to work is being lost. What is the point in working well if there is nowhere to spend the money earned as a result? (FBIS-SOV translation cited from Kincade and Thomson, 1990: p. 84)

No doubt political considerations colour writing of this type. Economists, however, express similar viewpoints.

Leonid Abalkin says that:

... one should not try to build popularity among the people and give them money that is not worth anything and is not backed by goods. If would be better not to issue this money, though the forced nature of such measures would necessarily have to be explained to the public." (cited from Rumer, 1990: 77)

Abalkin considers the need to examine the possibilities of freezing part of the public's savings—a feature of the necessary policies envisioned by Birman (1980) and Birman and Clarke (1985).

The necessity of general price rises is discussed by L. Piyasheva in *Izvestiya*, (19 April 1990, p. 3), where she states that 'the total disparity between prices and the money supply has become acute in today's economy'. Furthermore:

... there is a very high probability that the government will forgo its principles and set to work solving the 'surplus-savings' problem by sacrificing 'low prices.' The problem of 'surplus savings' can be solved quite simply: Through high prices the state can take in everything that it paid out in the past when prices were relatively low but the corresponding goods and services were lacking.' (Cited from *The Current Digest of the Soviet Press*, Vol. 42, No. 18, p. 17)

L. Piyasheva is described by *Izvestiya* as a 'Candidate in Economics'. She also writes in the Soviet press under the name Larisa Popkova, arguing for the introduction of full private property rights and capitalism in the Soviet Union.

8 I once saw reference to a paper in a medical journal that had thirteen authors. Four is the maximum I have seen in economics.

9 Birman (1988: 147) makes this criticism of Western students of the Soviet Union. More recently, it is probably more relevant to modern macroeconometric studies of China, where many researchers do not use Chinese language sources. Much of this work suffers from the shortcoming of ignoring historical analysis, not understanding the coverage of the data and relying too readily on the 'regression meat grinder' (Cagan, 1989: 118). Chinese data are not generally available from databanks, but they are available in English-language statistical yearbooks.

CHAPTER 6

1 Moscow taxi-drivers at the international airport say they will not drive for what they call 'wooden roubles' (*derevyanniye rublyi*) and accept only foreign currencies. This is a not uncommon phenomenon elsewhere.

2 Named after Sir Thomas Gresham (c. 1519–79), Elizabethan financier and businessman and adviser to Queen Elizabeth I (Powell, 1987; Harris, 1987).

3 This is not a spurious correlation. It is, however, dominated by the extreme case of Poland; without Poland it is 0.995. It is based on cross-sectional data, not data for individual countries. Furthermore, it is not based on an

identity within each country, The names of the variables are deceiving. Using nominal income data $(Y=PQ)$ and real output data (Q), the national income deflator (P) would always equal PQ/Q, and this would be true of its growth rates $(p=y-q)$. However, for the planned economies MIP is not the same as PQ and its growth rate need not be the same. Furthermore, P is not the national income deflator but is the consumer price index. The correlation is across a sample of countries, and I see no reason why it should reflect a definition or be spurious in any other way.

4 The problems of private entrepreneurs in China are well surveyed by Young (1991).

References

Abouchar, Alan (1977) *The Socialist Price Mechanism*, Durham, NC: Duke University Press

Adam, Jan (1979) *Wage Control and Inflation in Soviet Bloc Countries* London: Macmillan

——(ed.) (1982) *Employment Policies in the Soviet Union and Eastern Europe* New York: St. Martin's Press

——(1989) *Economic Reforms in the Soviet Union and Eastern Europe since the 1960s* London: Macmillan Press

Alexeev, Michael (1988) 'Are Soviet consumers forced to save?' *Comparative Economic Studies* vol. 30, no. 4, Winter, pp. 17–23

Alexeev, Nikolai (1990) 'Blizhe k rinku — dal'she ot krizisa (Nearer to the market — further from crisis)' *Nedelya* (The Week) 17–23 September.

Alton, Thad Paul (1955) *Polish Postwar Economy* New York: Columbia University Press

Ames, Edward (1954) 'Soviet bloc currency conversions' *American Economic Review* vol. 44, June, pp. 339–53

——(1965) *Soviet Economic Processes* Homewood, Ill: Irwin

Arnold, Arthur Z. (1937) *Banks, Credit, and Money in Soviet Russia* New York: Columbia University Press

Arouca, L. (1977) On the Balance of Money Incomes and Expenditures in the USSR, unpublished PhD thesis, London University

Aslund, Anders (1989) *Gorbachev's Struggle for Economic Reform: The Soviet Reform Process*, 1985–88 London: Pinter Publishers

Asselain, Jean–Charles (1981) 'Mythe ou réalité de l'epargne forcée dans les pays socialistes' in Lavigne (1981) pp. 115–50

——(1984) *Planning and Profits in Socialist Economies* London: Routledge & Kegan Paul

Atlas, M.S. (1967) *Razvitiye Bankovikh Sistem Stran Sotsializma* (The Development of the Banking Systems of the Socialist Countries) Moscow: Finance Publishers

Bácskai, T. and Várhegyi E. (1983) 'Monetization of the Hungarian economy' *Acta Oeconomica*, vol. 31, nos 1–2, pp. 13–22

Balassa, Bela (1959) *The Hungarian Experience in Economic Planning: A Theoretical and Empirical Study* New Haven: Yale University Press

——(1982) *The Hungarian Economic Reform, 1968–81* World Bank Staff Working Paper no. 506, Washington, DC: World Bank

Barnham, Oliver (1988) 'Banking and financial reform in China' *China News Analysis* no. 1356, 15 March

Batt, Judy (1988) *Economic Reform and Political Change in Eastern Europe: A Comparison of the Czechoslovak and Hungarian Experiences* London: Macmillan Press in association with the Centre for Russian and East European Studies, University of Birmingham

Baylis, Thomas A. (1986) 'Explaining the GDR's economic strategy' in Comisso and Tyson (1986) pp. 205–44

Bennett, Gordon (ed.) (1978) *China's Finance and Trade: A Policy Reader* White Plains, NY: M.E. Sharpe

Berend, I. T. and Ranki G. (1974) *Hungary: A Century of Economic Development* Newton Abbot: David and Charles

——(1985) *The Hungarian Economy in the Twentieth Century* London and Sydney: Croom Helm

Berliner, Joseph S. (1950) 'Monetary planning in the USSR' *The American Slavic and East European Review* vol. 9, pp. 237–54

Berry, L. Yu (ed.) (1977) *Planning a Socialist Economy* 2 vols, Moscow: Progress Publishers

Bertinelli, Roberto (1981) 'Alcune considerazioni sulla moneta nella PRC. (Some thoughts on money in the People's Republic of China)' *Revista Internazionale di Scienze Economiche e Commerciali* (International Review of Economics and Commerce), vol. 28, September, pp. 852–63

Birman, Igor (1980a) 'The financial crisis in the USSR' Soviet Studies, vol. 32, no. 1, January, pp. 84–105

——(1980b) 'A Reply to Professor Pickersgill' *Soviet Studies*, vol. 32, no. 4, October, pp. 586–91

——(1981) *Secret Incomes of the Soviet State Budget*, The Hague: Martinus Nijhoff

——(1983) *Ekonomika Nedostach: The Economy of Shortages*, New York: Chalidze Publications

——(1988) 'Rosefielde and my cumulative disequilibrium hypothesis: a comment' *Soviet Studies* vol. 41, no. 1, January, pp. 141–8

——(1990) 'The budget gap, excess money and reform' *Communist Economies*, vol. 2, no. 1, pp. 25–45

Birman, Igor and Clarke, Roger A. (1985) 'Inflation and the money supply in the Soviet Economy' *Soviet Studies*, vol. 37, no. 4, October, pp. 494–504

Bor, Mikhail (1967) *Aims and Methods of Soviet Planning*, London: Lawrence and Wishart

Bordo, Michael D. (ed.) (1989) *Money, History, and International Finance: Essays in Honor of Anna J. Schwartz*, Chicago and London: University of Chicago Press

Bordo, Michael D. and Jonung, Lars (1987) *The Long-run Behaviour of the Velocity of Circulation* Cambridge: Cambridge University Press

Borisov, V (1966) *Balans Denezhnikh Dokhodov i Raskhodov Naseleniya*, (The Balance of Money Incomes and Expenditures of the Population), Moscow

Bornstein, Morris (1961) 'The reform and revaluation of the ruble' *American Economic Review*, vol. 51, pp. 117–23

——(ed.) (1979) *Comparative Economic Systems: Models and Cases*, 4th edn, Homewood, Ill: Irwin

Bortolani, Sergio and Santorum, Anita (1984) Moneta e Banca in Cina (Money and Banking in China) Milan: Finafrica

Bova, Russell (1988) 'The Soviet military and economic reform' *Soviet Studies*, vol. 40, no. 3, pp. 385–405

Bowles, Paul and White, Gordon (1989) 'Contradiction in China's financial reforms: the relationship between banks and enterprises' *Cambridge Journal of Economics*, vol. 13, no. 4, December, pp. 481–95

Bowring, Philip and Delfs, Robert (1990) 'A puzzling cut' *Far Eastern Economic Review*, 6 December, p. 42

Brabant, Jozef M. van (1980) *Socialist Economic Integration: Aspects of Contemporary Economic Problems in Eastern Europe* Cambridge: Cambridge University Press

——(1987) *Adjustment, Structural Change, and Economic Efficiency: Aspects of Monetary Cooperation in Eastern Europe* Cambridge: Cambridge University Press

——(1989a) *Economic Integration in Eastern Europe: A Handbook* New York: Harvester Wheatsheaf

——(1989b) 'Economic reform and monetary cooperation in the CMEA' in Kessides et al. (1989) pp. 170–95

——(1990) 'Socialist economics: the disequilibrium school and the shortage economy' *Journal of Economic Perspectives*, vol. 4, no. 2, Spring, pp. 157–75

Brada, Josef C. and Dobozi Istvan (eds) (1988) The Hungarian Economy in the 1980s: Reforming the System and Adjusting to External Shocks, Greenwich and London: JAI Press

Brada, J.C. and King, A.E. (1986) 'Taut plans, repressed inflation and the supply of effort in centrally planned Economies' *Economics of Planning*, vol. 20, pp. 162–78

Bresciani–Turroni, Costantino (1937) *The Economics of Inflation: A Study of Currency Depreciation in Post-war Germany* London: George Allen & Unwin

British Broadcasting Corporation (1990) *Summary of World Broadcasts, Soviet Union*, 26 October

Brooks, Karen M. (1990) 'Soviet agriculture's halting reform' *Problems of Communism*, March–April, pp. 29–41

Brus, Wlodzimierz and Laski, Kazimierz (1989) *From Marx to the Market: Socialism in Search of an Economic System* Oxford: Clarendon Press

Buck, Hannsjörg F. (1987) 'The GDR financial system' in Jeffries and Melzer (1987) pp. 149–201

Buck, Trevor and Cole, John (1987) *Modern Soviet Economic Performance*, Oxford: Basil Blackwell

Bukharin, N and Preobrazhensky, E. (1966) *The ABC of Communism: A Popular Explanation of the Program of the Communist Party of Russia* Ann Arbor: University of Michigan Press

Bush, Keith. (1973) 'Soviet inflation' in Laulan (1973) pp. 97–105

Byrd, William (1983) China's Financial System: The Changing Role of Banks, Boulder, Col: Westview Press

Cagan, Philip (1989) 'Money–income causality—a critical review of the literature since *A Monetary History*' Bordo (1989) ch.3

The Cambridge Encyclopedia of Russia and the Soviet Union (1982) Cambridge: Cambridge University Press

Cassel, Dieter (1984) 'Inflation in socialist planning economies: causes, effects and policy options of inflation in Soviet–type command economies' Discussion Paper no. 64, Fachbereich Wirtschaftwissenschaft Univesität Duisburg Gesamthochschule, July

——(1990) 'Phenomenon and effects of inflation in centrally planned socialist economies' *Comparative Economic Studies*, vol. 32, no. 1, Spring, pp. 1–41

Cassou, Pierre–Henri (1974) 'The Chinese monetary system' *China Quarterly*, no. 59, pp. 559–66; also in Bennett (1978) pp. 171–85

Chai, C.H. (1981) 'Money and banking reform in China' *Hong Kong Economic Papers*, no. 14, pp. 37–52

Chang, Valerie (1989) 'The new look of China's banks' *China Business Review*, May–June, pp. 20–2

Charemza, W. (1990) 'Parallel markets, excess demand and virtual prices: an empirical approach' *European Economic Review*, vol. 34, nos 2/3, May, pp. 331–9

Charemza, W. and Gronicki, M. (1988) *Plans and Disequilibrium in Centrally–Planned Economies: Empirical Investigations for Poland*, Amsterdam: North–Holland

Charlesworth, Harold Karl (1956) *The Economics of Repressed Inflation*, London: George Allen and Unwin

Chen Chien–Hsun (1989) 'Monetary aggregates and macroeconomic performance in mainland China' *Journal of Comparative Economics*, vol. 13, no. 2, pp. 314–24

Chen Ni–ruenn and Hou, Chi–ming (1986) 'China's inflation, 1979–1983: measurement and analysis' *Economic Development and Cultural Change*, vol. 34, no. 4, July, pp. 811–35

Chen Wenlin (1984) 'Controversies over the value basis of the Renminbi' *Social Sciences in China*, vol. 5, no. 4, December, pp. 23–44

——(1989) *Zhongguo Huobi Zhengce Gaige Jianlun* (A Short Essay on the Reform of China's Monetary Policy) Peking: China Finance and Economics Publishing House

Cheng Cho–yuan (1954) *Monetary Affairs of Communist China*, Hong Kong: Union Research Institute

Cheng Hang–sheng (1981) 'Money and credit in China' *Federal Reserve Bank of San Fransisco Economic Review*, Fall, pp. 19–36

——(1988a) 'Monetary policy and inflation in China' in Cheng (1988b) pp. 401–29

——(ed.) (1988b) *Monetary Policy in Pacific Basin Countries*, Boston: Kluwer Academic Publishers

Chi Ti (1975) 'Stable prices and the reasons' Peking Review no. 19, 9 May, pp. 17–20

Childs, David; Baylis, Thomas A.; and Rueschemeyer, Marilyn (eds) (1989) *East Germany in Comparative Perspective*, London and New York: Routledge

China: ASEAN Bankers Examine China's Rural Banking System (1984) United Nations, Economic and Social Commission for Asia and the Pacific

China's stock and bond market' *Beijing Review,* No. 44, 30 October–5 November 1989, pp. 20–3

Chow, Gregory (1987) 'Money and price level determination in China' *Journal of Comparative Economics,* vol 11, no. 3, September, pp. 319–33; also in Reynolds (1988) pp. 29–43

Clarke, Roger A. (ed.) (1989a) Poland: *The Economy in the 1980s,* London: Longman

——(ed.) (1989b) *Hungary: The Second Decade of Economic Reform,* London: Longman

Clarke, Roger A. and Matko, Dubravko J. I. (1983) *Soviet Economic Facts, 1917–81,* 2nd edn, London: Macmillan Press

Cochrane, Nancy J. (1988) 'The private sector in East European agriculture' *Problems of Communism,* vol. 37, March–April, pp. 47–53

Cohen, Stephen F. (1980) *Bukharin and the Bolshevik Revolution* Oxford: Oxford University Press

Comecon Data 1981 (1982) edited by the Vienna Institute for Comparative Economic Studies, London: Macmillan Press

Comecon Data 1985 (1986) edited by the Vienna Institute for Comparative Economic Studies, London: Macmillan Press

Comecon Data 1987 (1988) edited by the Vienna Institute for Comparative Economic Studies, London: Macmillan Press

Comisso, Ellen and Tyson, Laura D'Andrea (eds) (1986) *Power, Purpose, and Collective Choice: Economic Strategy in Socialist States* Ithica and London: Cornell University Press

Cowitt, Philip P. (ed.) (1985) *World Currency Yearbook 1984* Brooklyn: International Currency Analysis

——(ed.) (1986) *World Currency Yearbook 1985* Brooklyn: International Currency Analysis

Crump, Thomas (1981) *The Phenomenon of Money,* London: Routledge & Kegan Paul

Csikós-Nagy, Béla (1977) 'A re-evaluation of the theory of repressed inflation in the light of the experience of some socialist countries' in Lundberg (1977) pp. 417–30

Davis, Christopher and Charemza, Wojciech (1989a) 'Introduction to models of disequilibrium and shortage in centrally planned economies', in Davis and Charemza (1989b) ch. 1

——(eds) (1989b) *Models of Disequilibrium and Shortage in Centrally Planned Economies* London: Chapman and Hall

Day, Richard B. (1975) 'Preobrazhensky and the theory of the transition period' *Soviet Studies* vol. 27, no. 2, April, pp. 196–219

——(1988) 'Leon Trotsky on the dialectics of democratic control' in Wiles (1988b) pp. 1–36

De Brunhoff, Suzanne (1976) *Marx on Money* New York: Urizen Books

De Fontenay, Patrick et al. (1982) Hungary: An Economic Survey, Occasional Paper no. 15, International Monetary Fund, December

De Wulf, L. (1985a) 'Economic reform in China' *Finance and Development* March, pp. 8–12

——(1985b) 'Financial reform in China' *Finance and Development*, December, pp. 19–22

De Wulf, L. and Goldsbrough, D. (1986) 'The evolving role of monetary policy in China' *International Monetary Fund Staff Papers*, vol 33, No. 2, June, pp. 209–42

Decision of the Central Committee of the Communist Party of China on Reform of the Economic Structure (1984) Hong Kong: Joint Publishing Co

Delfs, Robert and Bowring, Philip (1990) 'China's credit gamble' *Far Eastern Economic Review* 6 December pp. 40–1

Dembinski, Pawel (1988) 'Quantity versus allocation of money: monetary problems of the centrally planned economies reconsidered' *Kyklos*. vol. 41, fasc. 2, pp. 281–300

Deng Ziji (principal ed.) (1981) *Caizheng yu Xindai* (Finance and Credit) Peking: China Finance and Economics Publishing House

Denton, M. Elizabeth (1979) 'Soviet consumer policy: trends and prospects' in Soviet Economy in a Time of Change, vol. 1, Joint Economic Committee of Congress, Washington, DC: US Government Printer, pp. 759–89

Desai, P. (ed.) (1983) *Marxism, Central Planning, and the Soviet Economy*, Cambridge, Mass: MIT Press

Dirksen, Erik (1981) 'The control of inflation? errors in the interpretation of CPE data' *Economica*, vol. 48, August, pp. 305–8

Dong Fureng (1980) *Shehuizhuyi Zaishengchang he Guomin Shouru Wenti* (Issues of Reproduction and National Income under Socialism) Peking: Sanlian Bookstore

Drewnowski, Jan (ed.) (1982) *Crisis in the East European Economy: the Spread of the Polish Disease* London and Canberra: Croom Helm

Durgin, Frank (1984a) '*The USSR in crisis: the failure of an economic system*, by Marshall I. Goldman: a review article' *ACES Bulletin*, vol. 26, nos. 2–3, Summer–Fall, pp. 99–110

——(1984b) 'A reply to a reply' ACES Bulletin, vol. 26, no. 4, Winter, pp. 55–64

E–Han Jingji Cihui (1982) (A Russian–Chinese Economic Glossary) Peking: China Social Sciences Publishing House

Eatwell, J., Milgate, M. and Newman, P. (eds) (1987) *The New Palgrave: A Dictionary of Economics*, London: Macmillan Press

Eckland, George N. (1973) 'Banking and finance' in Wu (1973) pp. 579–93

Economic Survey of Europe in 1989–1990 (1990) New York: Secretariat of the Economic Commission for Europe, United Nations

Economy (1984) compiled by the China Handbook Editorial Committee, Peking: Foreign Languages Press

Ellman, Michael (1979) *Socialist Planning* Cambridge: Cambridge University Press

——(1982) 'Did Soviet economic growth end in 1978?' in Drewnowski (1982) ch 6

——(1989) *Socialist Planning*, 2nd edn, Cambridge: Cambridge University Press

Engels, Frederick (1884) 'Preface to the first German edition' in Karl Marx *The Poverty of Philosophy* Peking: Foreign Languages Publishing House, 1978, pp. 1–19

Eysymontt, Jerzy (1989) 'Reform in the Polish economy' in Clarke (1989a) ch. 2

Farrell, John P. (1977) 'Some statistical evidence on money and inflation in

Poland' *Jahrbuch der Wirschaft Osteuropas*, band 7, pp. 285–95

——(1989) 'Financial 'crisis' in the CPEs or "vsyo normalno"?' *Comparative Economic Studies* vol. 31, no. 4, Winter, pp. 1–9

Fedorov, Boris (1989) 'Reform of the Soviet banking system' *Communist Economies* vol. 1, no. 4, pp. 455–61

Fekete, János (1982) *Back to the Realities: Reflections of a Hungarian Banker* Budapest, Akadémiai Kiado

Feltenstein, Andrew and Farhadian, Ziba (1987) 'Fiscal policy, monetary targets, and the price level in a centrally planned economy: an application to the case of China' *Journal of Money, Credit, and Banking* vol. 19, no. 2, May, pp. 136–56

Feltenstein, Andrew, Lebow, David and van Wijnbergen, Sweder (1990) 'Savings, commodity market rationing, and the real rate of interest in China' *Journal of Money, Credit and Banking* vol. 22, May, pp. 2325–52

Fengövári, I. (1980) 'On the Hungarian financial system' *Acta Oeconomica* vol. 25, nos 3–4, pp. 277–90

Fenjinde Sishi Nian 1949–1989 (Forty Years of Struggle and Progress) Peking: China Statistical Publishing House

Fogaras, I. (1978) 'The population's savings deposits in the European CMEA countries' *Acta Oeconomica* vol. 21 nos 1–2, pp. 141–50

Friedman, Milton (1959) 'The demand for money: some theoretical and empirical results' *Journal of Political Economy* vol. 67, no. 4, August, pp. 327–51

——(1980) 'Marx on money' *Newsweek* 27 October, p. 49

——(1987) 'The Quantity Theory of Money' in Eatwell, Milgate and Newman (1987) vol. 4, pp. 3–20

Friedman, Milton and Schwartz, Anna J. (1963) *A Monetary History of the United States, 1867–1960* Princeton: Princeton University Press

Gado, O. (1976) The Economic Mechanism in Hungary—How It Works in 1976, Leyden: Sijthoff; Budapest, Akadémiai Kiado

Gaige: Women Mianlinde Tiaozhan yu Xuanze (1986) (Reform: The Challenges and Choices before Us) compiled by the China Economic Reform Research Institute, Comprehensive Survey Group, Peking: China Economics Publishing House

Galbraith, John Kenneth (1975) *Money: Whence it Came, Where it Went*, Harmondsworth: Penguin

Gardner, H. Stephen (1988) *Comparative Economic Systems* New York: Dryden

Garvy, George (1964) 'The role of the state bank in Soviet planning' in Nove and Degras (1964) pp. 46–76

——(1968) 'East European credit and finance in transition' in Grossman (1968) pp. 153–83

——(1972) 'The monetary system and the payments flow' in Nove and Nuti (1972) pp. 275–306

——(1973) 'Policies and mechanics relating to money' in Laulan (1973) pp. 59–73

——(1977) *Money, Financial Flows, and Credit in the Soviet Union* Cambridge, Mass: National Bureau of Economic Research

Gekker, Paul (1972) 'Statistics on prices and money: summary and assessment' in Treml and Hardt (1972) p. 433–45

German Institute for Economic Research (DIW) (1989) *GDR and Eastern Europe — A Handbook* Aldershot: Gower

Gibsci, Lajos (ed.) (1988) *After the Bargain: The Hungarian Reform*, Budapest: publisher unknown

Goldman, Marshall I. (1983) *USSR in Crisis: the Failure of an Economic System* New York and London: W.W. Norton

——(1984a) 'Reply to Frank Durgin' *ACES Bulletin* vol. 26, nos. 2–3, Summer-Fall, pp. 111—-6

——(1984b) 'A reply to a reply to a reply' *ACES Bulletin* vol. 26, no. 4, Winter, pp. 69–71

Gomulka, Stanislaw, Ha, Yong-chool and Kim, Cae-on (eds) (1989) *Economic Reforms in the Socialist World* London: Macmillan

Goodstadt, Leo (1975) 'Peking's firm hold on the money supply' *Far Eastern Economic Review* 13 June, pp. 39–40

——(1976) 'China: debating the role of money' *Far Eastern Economic Review* 2 January, pp. 39–40

Gordon, Robert J. (1987) *Macroeconomics* 4th edn, Boston: Little, Brown

Gowland, David (1984) *Controlling the Money Supply* 2nd edn, London: Croom Helm

Gray, Kenneth R. (1984) 'The USSR in crisis: comment' *ACES Bulletin* vol. 26, no. 4, Winter, pp. 65–68

Greenaway, David (1990) 'The unwinding of central planning in Eastern Europe: an editorial note' *Economic Journal* vol. 100, June, pp. 577–80

Gregory, Paul, R. and Stuart, Robert C. (1981) *Soviet Economic Structure and Performance* 2nd edn, New York: Harper and Row

——(1986) *Soviet Economic Structure and Performance* 3rd edn, New York: Harper and Row

Griffith–Jones, Stephany (1981) *The Role of Finance in the Transition to Socialism* London: Frances Pinter

Grinberg, R. (1990) 'Inflation in socialist countries: regularities and peculiarities' *Problems of Economics* vol. 33, no. 1, May, pp. 42–58

Grossman, Gregory (ed.) (1968) *Money and Plan: Financial Aspects of East European Economic Reforms* Berkeley and Los Angeles: University of California Press

——(1982) 'A note on Soviet inflation' in *Soviet Economy in the 1980s: Problems and Prospects* Vol. 1, Washington, DC: Joint Economic Committee, Congress of the United States, pp. 267–86

——(1986) 'Inflationary, political, and social implications of the current economic slowdown', in Höhmann, Nove and Vogel (1986) ch. 9

——(1989) 'Monetary and financial aspects of Gorbachev's reform' in Kessides et al. (1989) pp. 28–46

Gurley, John G. (1953) 'Excess liquidity and monetary reforms, 1944–1952' *American Economic Review* vol. 43, March, pp. 76–100

Haddad, L. (1977) 'Inflation under socialism' *Australian Economic Papers* June, pp. 44–52

Haitani, Kanji (1986) *Comparative Economic Systems: Organizational and Managerial Perspectives* Englewood Cliffs: Prentice–Hall

Hardt, John P. (1981) 'East European economies in crisis' in *East European Economic Assessment, Part 1- Country Studies 1980* Washington, DC: Joint

Economic Committee, Congress of the United States, pp. 1–14

Hare, Paul (1989) 'The economics of shortage in the centrally planned economies' in Davis and Charemza (1989b) ch. 3

Hare, Paul, Radice, Hugo, and Swan, Nigel (eds) (1981) *Hungary: A Decade of Economic Reform* London: George Allen and Unwin

Harris, C. Alexander (1987) 'Gresham's law' in Eatwell, Milgate and Newman (1987), Vol. 2, p. 565

Harrison, Mark (1986) 'The USSR state budget under late Stalinism (1945–55): capital formation, government borrowing and monetary growth' *Economics of Planning*, vol. 20, no. 3, pp. 179–205

Hartwig, Karl–Hans (1983) 'Involuntary liquid assets in Eastern Europe: some critical remarks' *Soviet Studies* vol. 35, no. 1, January, pp. 103–5

Haulaman, Clyde A. (1987) 'Financial innovation and the Chinese enterprises' *Journal of North East Asian Studies* vol. 6, no. 2, Summer, pp. 67–74

Heathfield, David F. (ed.) (1979) *Perspectives on Inflation: Models and Policies* London and New York: Longman

Hewett, Ed A. (1988) *Reforming the Soviet Economy: Equality versus Efficiency* Washington, DC: Brookings Institution

Hirsch, Fred and Goldthorpe, John P. (eds) (1978) *The Political Economy of Inflation* Oxford: Martin Robertson

A History of Chinese Currency (16th Century BC–20th Century AD) (1983) Hong Kong: Xinhua (New China) Publishing House, N.C.N. Ltd and MAO Management Group Ltd.

Höhmann, Hans–Hermann, Nove, Alec; and Vogel, Heinrich (eds) (1986) *Economics and Politics in the USSR: Problems of Interdependence* Boulder, Col: Westview Press

Horsman, George (1988) *Inflation in the Twentieth Century: Evidence from Europe and North America* New York: St. Martin's Press; Hemel Hempsted: Harvester–Wheatsheaf

Howard, David, H. (1976a) 'A note on hidden inflation in the Soviet Union' *Soviet Studies* vol. 28, no. 4, October, pp. 599–608

——(1976b) 'The disequilibrium model in a controlled economy: an empirical test of the Barro–Grossman model' *American Economic Review* vol. 66, no. 5, December, pp. 871–9

——(1979a) *The Disequilibrium Model in a Controlled Economy* Lexington: D.C. Heath

——(1979b) 'The disequilibrium model in a controlled economy: reply and further results' *American Economic Review* vol. 69, no. 4, September, pp. 733–8

——(1982) 'Hidden inflation in the Soviet Union: a final reply' *Soviet Studies* vol. 34, no. 2, April. pp. 300–3

Hsiao, Katharine H.Y. Huang (1971) *Money and Monetary Policy in Communist China* New York and London: Columbia University Press

——(1982) 'Money and Banking in the People's Republic of China: recent developments' *China Quarterly*, no. 91, September, pp. 462–75

——(1984) *Money and Banking in the Chinese Mainland* Taipei: Chung–hua Institution for Economic Research

——(1987) *The Government Budget and Fiscal Policy in Mainland China* Taipei: Chung–hua Institution for Economic Research

Hsu, John C. (1989) *China's Foreign Trade Reforms: Impact on Growth and Stability* Cambridge: Cambridge University Press

Huang Da; Chen Gong; Hou Mengchan; Zou Shengye; and Han Yingjie (1981) *Shehuizhuyi Caizheng Jinrong Wenti* (Issues of Socialist Public Finance and Banking) 2 vols, Peking: People's University Publishing House

Huang Xu (1988a) 'Woguo huobi gongqiu yu jiage shuiping' (The demand and supply of money and the determination of the price level in China) *Jingji Yanjiu* (Economic Research) February, pp. 35–45

——(1988b) 'Huobi gongqiu fenxi: (An analysis of the supply and demand for money) in Zhang Fengbo (1988) ch.6

Hussain, Athar (1986) 'Money and socialism: a comment', in Smith (1986) ch. 7

Jackson, Marvin (1990) 'Economic conditions in Eastern Europe' *Report on Eastern Europe*, (Radio Free Europe) vol. 1, no. 40, 5 October, pp. 34–7

Jao, Y.C. (1967–68) 'Some notes on repressed inflation: a suggested interpretation of money and prices in Communist China, 1950–57' *Union College Journal* vol. 6, pp. 99–114

——(1986) 'Banking and currency in the Special Economic Zones' in Jao and Leung (1986) pp. 160–83

Jao, Y.C. and C.K. Leung, (eds) (1986) *China's Special Economic Zones: Policies, Problems and Perspectives*, Hong Kong: Oxford University Press

Jeffries, Ian and Melzer, Manfred (eds) (1987) *The East German Economy*, London: Croom Helm Jianming Jiage Cidian (1982) (A Concise Dictionary of Prices)Tianjin: Tianjin People's Publishing House

Jianming Jinrong Cidian (1984) (A Concise Dictionary of Finance) Tianjin: Tianjin People's Publishing House

Józefiak, Cezary (1989) 'Financial aspects of the economic reform in Poland' in Kessides et al. (1989) pp. 56–63

Kagalovsky, Konstantin (1989) 'The pressing problems of state finances in the USSR' *Communist Economies* vol. 1, no. 4, pp. 447–54

Kaser, Michael (1989) 'Soviet Restructuring in relation to the Chinese reform' pp. 97–107 in Gomulka, Ha and Kim (1989) pp. 97–107

——(1990) 'The technology of decontrol: some macroeconomic issues' *Economic Journal*, vol. 11, June, pp. 596–615

Katsenelinboigen, Aron (1977) 'Disguised inflation in the Soviet Union: the relationship between Soviet income growth and price increases in the post–war period' in Abouchar (1977) pp. 170–83

Katz, Barbara (1979) 'The disequilibrium model in a controlled economy: comment' *American Economic Review* vol. 69, no. 4, September, pp. 721–5

Keizer, W. (1971) *The Soviet Quest for Economic Rationality* Rotterdam: Rotterdam University Press

Keller, J. (1977) 'The relationship between the population's savings and income in Hungary' *Acta Oeconomica*, vol. 19, no. 2, pp. 165–75

Kemény, George (1952) *Economic Planning in Hungary*, London and New York: Royal Institute of International Affairs

Kemme, David (1989) 'The chronic excess demand hypothesis' in Davis and Charemza (1989b) ch. 4

Kessides, Christine; King, Timothy; Nuti, Mario; and Sokil, Catherine (eds) (1989) *Financial Reform in Socialist Economies* Washington, D.C: World Bank

Kincade, William H. and Thomson, T. Keith (1990) 'Economic conversion in the USSR: its role in *perestroyka*' *Problems of Communism* vol. 39, January–February pp. 83–92

Klacek, J. and Klaus, V. (1970) 'Inflationary gap on the consumer goods market' *Czechoslovak Economic Papers*, no. 12, pp. 19–31

Klaus, Vaclav (1990) 'Monetary policy in Czechoslovakia in the 1970s and the 1980s and the nature and problems of the current economic reform' *Communist Economies* vol. 2, no. 1, pp. 61–71

Knight, Peter, T. (1983) *Economic Reform in Socialist Countries: The Experiences of China, Hungary, Romania, and Yugoslavia* World Bank Staff Working Paper no. 579, Washington DC: World Bank

Ko, C.T. (Ge Zhida) (1957) *China's Budget During the Transition Period*, Peking: translated and published by CCM Information Corporation, New York, 1970

Kolodko, Grzegorz W. (1989) 'Economic reform and inflation in socialism: determinants, mutual relationships and prospects' *Communist Economies* vol. 1, no. 2, pp. 167–82

Komiya, Ryutaro (1989) 'Macroeconomic development of China: 'Overheating' in 1984–1987 and problems for reform' *Journal of the Japanese and International Economies* vol. 3, March, pp. 64–121

Kornai, János (1971) *Anti-Equilibrium: On Economic Systems Theory and the Tasks of Research* Amsterdam: North-Holland

——(1980) *Economics of Shortage*, 2 vols, Amsterdam: North-Holland

——(1982) *Growth, Shortage and Efficiency*, Oxford: Blackwell

——(1986) 'The soft budget constraint' *Kyklos*, vol. 39, fasc. 1, pp. 3–30

——(1990) *The Road to a Free Economy: Shifting from a Socialist System — the Example of Hungary*, New York and London: Norton

Kushpèta, O. (1978) *The Banking and Credit System of the USSR*, Boston: Martinus Nijhoff

Lacko, M. (1975) 'Consumer savings and the supply situation' *Acta Oeconomica*, vol. 15, nos 3–4, pp. 365–84

Laidler, David E.W. (1985) *The Demand for Money: Theories, Evidence, and Problems* 3rd edn, New York: Harper and Rowe

Lampton, David M. (ed.) (1987) *Policy Implementation in Post-Mao China* Berkeley: University of California Press

Laski, Kazimierz (1979) 'The problem of inflation in socialist countries' *East European Economics* Summer, pp. 3–84

Laulan, Yves (ed.) (1973) *Banking, Money and Credit in Eastern Europe* Brussels: NATO

Lavigne, Marie (1974) *The Socialist Economies of the Soviet Union and Europe* White Plains, NY: International Arts and Sciences Press

——(ed.) (1981) *Travail et Monnaie en Syst me Socialiste* Paris: Economica

——(1986) 'The creation of money by the state bank of the USSR' in Smith (1986) ch.6

Lee, Tim (1985) 'People's Republic of China: problems of monetary control' *Asian Monetary Monitor* vol. 9, no. 4, July–August, pp. 13–21

Li Chengrui (1984) 'Are the 1967–76 statistics on China's economy reliable?' *Beijing Review* no. 12, 19 March, pp. 21–6

——(1986) 'Money supply and macroeconomic controls' *Social Sciences in China*, vol. 7, no. 3, September, pp. 51–62

———(1986–87) 'An important question in macroeconomic management' *Chinese Economic Studies* vol. 20, no. 2, Winter, pp. 3–12

Li Fang (1985) 'Woguo huobi liutong liang daihou wenti tantao' (An enquiry into the monetary lag question in China)' *Shuliang Jingji Jishu Jingji Yanjiu* (Quantitative and Technical Economic Research) no. 6, pp. 41–7

Li Fuchen (1981) 'Yougan shehuizhuyi guojia tonghuo pengzhangde jige wenti' (On several questions of inflation in socialist countries)' *Zhongguo Jinrong* (Chinese Finance) June, pp. 24–5, 4

Li Jun and Xia Xiaoxun (1986) 'Xiaofei pengzhang: gaige yu fazhan mianlinde yanjun tiaozhan' (Consumption expansion: a grave challenge to reform and development)' in *Gaige: Women Mianlinde Tiaozhan yu Xuanze* (1986) ch. 4

Lin Wei and Chao, Arnold (eds) (1982) *China's Economic Reforms* Philadelphia: University of Pennsylvania Press

Li Yunqi (1989) 'China's inflation: causes, effects, and solutions' *Asian Survey* vol. 29, no. 7, July, pp. 655–68

Lipsey, Richard G.; Steiner Peter O.; and Purvis, Douglas D. (1987) *Economics* 8th edn, New York: Harper and Row

Liu Guangdi (1981) 'Lun zhibi he huangjinde lianxi (On the relationship between paper money and gold)' *Zhongguo Shehui Kexue* (Social Sciences in China) no. 3, pp. 67–82

Liu Hongru (1980) *Shehui Huobi yu Yinhang Wenti* (Issues of Socialist Money and Banking) Peking: China Finance and Economics Publishing House

Liu, J.Y.W. (1962) 'Monetary system of Communist China' in Szczepanik (1962) pp. 72–81

Lokshin, R. (1990) 'K razrabotke balansov denezhnikh dokhodov i raskhodov naseleniya' (Towards the elaboration of the balances of the money incomes and expenditures of the population)' *Planovoye Khozyaystvo* (Planned Economy) no. 1, January, pp. 71–8

Lu Baifu; Wang Dashu; and Wang Guangqian (eds) (1989) *Tonghuo Pengzhang Wenti Yanjiu* (Research on the Issue of Inflation) Peking: China Finance and Economics Publishing House

Lundberg, E. (ed.) (1977) *Inflation Theory and Anti-Inflation Policy* London: Macmillan

Lyons, Thomas P. and Wang Yan (1988) 'Planning and finance in China's economic reforms' Cornell University East Asia Paper, no. 46 Ithica, N.Y.

Ma Hong (principal ed.) (1982) *Xiandai Zhongguo Jingji Shidian* (The Contemporary Chinese Economy: A Compendium) Peking: China Social Sciences Publishing House

Marrese, Michael (1990) 'Perestroika and socialist privatization: a comment' *Comparative Economic Studies* vol. 32, no. 3, Fall, pp. 55–61

Marx, Karl (1875) 'Critique of the Gotha programme' in *Karl Marx and Frederick Engels—Selected Works* London: Lawrence and Wishart, 1968 pp. 315–35

McCauley, Martin (1983) *The German Democratic Republic since 1945* London: Macmillan Press

McKinnon, Ronald I. (1990) 'Stabilising the ruble' *Communist Economies* vol. 2, no. 2, pp. 131–42

Melvin, Michael and Chin-Duu Shiau (1990) 'Property rights, development, and velocity in developing countries' *Economic Development and Cultural Change* vol. 38, no. 4, July, pp. 821–32

Melzer Manfred (1989) 'Price formation' in German Institute for Economic Research (DIW) (1989) pp. 49–54

Michal, Jan M. (1960) *Central Planning in Czechoslovakia: Organization for Growth in a Mature Economy* Stanford: Stanford University Press

Miyashita, Tadao (1966) *The Currency and Financial System of Mainland China* Tokyo: Institute of Asian Economic Affairs

Mojzisková, Sona (1987/88) 'Foreign exchange regulations in the socialist countries' *Soviet and East European Foreign Trade* vol. 23, no. 4, pp. 22–66

Montias, John Michael (1962) *Central Planning in Poland* New Haven and London: Yale University Press

——(1968) 'Bank lending and fiscal policy in Eastern Europe' in Grossman (1968) pp. 38–56

Moore, Basil J. (1988) *Horizontalists and Verticalists: The Macroeconomics of Credit Money* Cambridge: Cambridge University Press

Moscow Narodny Bank Press Bulletin 1988–1990 (London) various issues

Mujzel, Jan (1975) 'Changes in price level in the socialist countries' *Jahrbuch der Wirtschaft Osteuropas* band 6, pp. 105–25

Myant, Martin (1989) 'Poland — the permanent crisis?' ch. 1 in Clarke (1989a)

Narodnoye Khozyaystvo SSSR v 1975 godu (1976) (The National Economy of the Soviet Union in 1975) Moscow: *Statistika* Publishing House

Narodnoye Khozyaystvo SSR v 1980 godu (1981) (The National Economy of the Soviet Union in 1980) Moscow: Finance and Statistics Publishing House

Narodnoye Khozyaystvo SSR v 1988 godu (1989) (The National Economy of the Soviet Union in 1988) Moscow: Finance and Statistics Publishing House

Narodnoye Khozyaystvo SSSR Za 70 Let (1987) (The National Economy of the Soviet Union during 70 Years) Moscow: Finance and Statistics Publishing House

Naughton, Barry John (1986) *Saving and Investment in China: A Macroeconomic Analysis*, unpublished PhD dissertation, Yale University, May

——(1987) 'Macroeconomic policy and response in the Chinese economy: the impact of the reform process' *Journal of Comparative Economics* vol. 11, no. 3, September, pp. 334–53; also in Reynolds (1988) pp. 44–63

'The new Germany (Survey)' (1990) *The Economist* 30 June

Nordhaus, William D. (1990) 'Soviet economic reform: the longest road' *Brookings Papers in Economic Activity* no. 1, pp. 287–318, including discussion

Nove, Alec (1979) 'Inflation in Communist Countries' in Heathfield (1979) ch. 8

——(1982) *An Economic History of the USSR* Harmondsworth: Penguin

——(1983) *The Economics of Feasible Socialism* London: George Allen & Unwin

——(1988) 'Rosefielde on Birman — a comment' *Soviet Studies* vol. 34, no. 4, pp. 640–3

Nove, Alec and Degras, Jane (eds) (1964) *Soviet Planning* Oxford: Basil Blackwell

Nove, Alec and Nuti, D.M. (eds) (1972) *Socialist Economics* Harmondsworth: Penguin

Nuti, D.M. (1986) 'Inflation in Soviet-type economies' *Contributions to Political Economy* vol. 5, March, pp. 37–81: also ch. 5 in Davis and Charemza (1989b)

Oi, Jean C. (1989) *State and Peasant in Contemporary China: The Political*

Economy of Village Government Berkeley: University of California Press

Parker, John (1990) 'A survey of the Soviet Union' *The Economist* 20 October

Peebles, Gavin (1981) 'Money incomes and expenditures of the population of the Soviet Union: an East European comparison' *Hong Kong Economic Papers* no. 14, pp. 53–78

——(1983) 'Inflation, money and banking in China: in support of the purchasing power approach' *ACES Bulletin* vol. 25, no. 2, Summer, pp. 81–103

——(1984a) 'Review of J. Adam (ed.) *Employment Policies in the Soviet Union and Eastern Europe*, New York' *ACES Bulletin* vol. 26, no. 4, Winter, pp. 73–6

——(1984b) 'Inflation in the People's Republic of China, 1950–1982' *Three Banks Review* no. 142, June, pp. 37–57

——(1985) 'Soviet–style agricultural bonuses and their effect on prices in China: a search for perversity and its consequences' *Hong Kong Economic Papers* no. 16, pp. 40–53

——(1986a) 'On the importance of establishing the inverse relationship between open inflation and household liquidity growth under socialism: a critique of Jan Winiecki's saving deposit data' *Comparative Economic Studies* vol. 28, no. 4, Winter, pp. 85–91

——(1986b) 'Aggregate retail price changes in socialist countries: identification, theory and evidence for China and the Soviet Union' *Soviet Studies* vol. 38, no. 4, October, pp. 477–507

——(1987) 'Review of *Zhongguo Tongji Nianjian/Statistical Yearbook of China 1986*' *Comparative Economic Studies* vol. 29, no. 2, Summer, pp. 106–9

——(1988) *Hong Kong's Economy: An Introductory Macroeconomic Analysis* Hong Kong and New York: Oxford University Press

——(1990a) *China's Macroeconomy in the 1980s: The Impact of Reform on Structure and Performance* China Working Paper no. 90/5, Canberra: National Centre for Development Studies, Australian National University

——(1990b) 'Explaining macroeconomic imbalances in mainland China under Reform' *Issues and Studies* vol. 26, no. 10, pp. 65–83

——(1991) *Money in the People's Republic of China: A Comparative Perspective* Sydney: Allen & Unwin

Peng Kuang-hsi (Peng Guangxi) (1976) *Why China Has No Inflation* Peking: Foreign Languages Press

Peng Ziqin (1981) 'Shilun wending huobi dui wending jiagede zhongyao yiyi' (On the importance of stabilising money for the stability of prices)' *Zhongguo Jinrong* (Chinese Finance), no. 3, pp. 22–3

Perkins, Dwight H. (1966) *Market Control and Planning in Communist China* Cambridge, Mass: Harvard University Press

——(1988) 'Reforming China's Economic System' *Journal of Economic Literature* vol. 26, June, pp. 601–45

Pesek, Boris (1958) 'Monetary reforms and monetary equilibrium' *Journal of Political Economy* vol. 66, no. 5, October, pp. 375–88

Pickersgill, Joyce (1976) 'Soviet household saving behaviour' *Review of Economics and Statistics* vol. 58, May, pp. 139–47

——(1980a) 'The financial crisis in the USSR — a comment' *Soviet Studies* vol. 32, no. 4, October, pp. 583–5

——(1980b) 'Recent evidence on Soviet household saving behaviour' *Review of*

Economics and Statistics vol. 62, November, pp. 628–33

Pick's Currency Yearbook (various years) New York: Pick Publishing Corporation

Pindak, F. (1976) 'L'inflation en URSS et en europe de l'est' *Revue d'Etudes Comparative Est-Oeust* no. 3, pp. 7–24

——(1983) 'Inflation under central planning' *Jahrbuch der Wirtschaft Osteuropas* vol. 10, no. 2, pp. 93–131

Podkaminer, Leon (1989) 'Macroeconomic disequilibria in centrally planned economies: identifiability of econometric models based on the theory of household behaviour under quantity constraints' *Journal of Comparative Economics* vol. 13, no. 1, March, pp. 47–60

Podolski, T.M. (1973) *Socialist Banking and Monetary Control: The Experience of Poland* Cambridge: Cambridge University Press

Ponamarev, Yu (1989) 'Review of Soviet foreign economic activity and banking restructure' *Moscow Narodny Bank Press Bulletin* no. 1028, 15 November, pp. 16–18

Portes, Richard (1977) 'The control of inflation: lessons from East European experience' *Economica* vol. 44, May, pp. 109–29; slightly revised version in Bornstein (1979, pp. 448–68)

——(1978) 'Inflation under central planning' in Hirsch and Goldthorpe (1978) ch. 3

——(1981a) 'Macroeconomic equilibrium and disequilibrium in centrally planned economies' *Economic Inquiry*, vol. 19, no. 4, pp. 559–78

——(1981b) 'Reply to E. Dirksen "The control of inflation? Errors in the interpretation of CPE data" *Economica* vol. 48, August, pp. 309–11

——(1982) 'Prices' in *The Cambridge Encyclopedia of Russia and the Soviet Union* (1982) pp. 362–4.

——(1983) 'Central planning and monetarism: fellow travellers?' in Desai (1983) ch. 9

——(1989) 'The theory and measurement of macroeconomic disequilibrium in centrally planned economies' in Davis and Charemza (1989b) ch. 2

Portes, Richard and Santorum, Anita (1987) 'Money and the consumption goods market in China' *Journal of Comparative Economics* vol. 11, no 3, September, pp. 354–71; also in Reynolds (1988) pp. 64–81

Portes, Richard, Quandt, Richard E.; Winter, David; and Yeo, Stephen (1987) 'Macroeconomic planning and disequilibrium: estimates for Poland, 1955–1980' *Econometrica* vol. 55, no. 1, January, pp. 19–41

Portes, Richard and Winter, David (1977) 'The supply of consumption goods in centrally planned economies' *Journal of Comparative Economics* vol.1, December, pp. 351–65

——(1978) 'The demand for money and for consumption goods in centrally planned economies' *Review of Economics and Statistics* vol. 60, February, pp. 8–18

——(1980) 'Disequilibrium estimates for consumption goods markets in centrally planned economies' *Review of Economics and Statistics* vol. 47, pp. 137–59

Powell, Eleanor G. (1987) 'Gresham, Thomas' in Eatwell, Milgate and Newman (1987) vol. 2, pp. 564–5

Powell, Raymond P. (1972) 'Monetary statistics' in Treml and Hardt (1972) pp. 397–432

Prybyla, Jan S. (1978) *The Chinese Economy: Problems and Policies* Columbia: University of South Carolina Press

Qian Jiajun and Guo Yangang (1985) *Zhongguo Huobi Shi Gangyao* (An Outline History of Money in China), Shanghai: Shanghai People's Publishing House

Qian Yingyi (1988) 'Urban and rural household saving in China' *International Fund Staff Papers* vol. 35, no. 4, December, pp. 592–627

Révész, Gábor (1990) *Perestroika in Eastern Europe: Hungary's Economic Transformation 1945–1988*, Boulder, Col.: Westview Press

Reynolds, Bruce L. (ed.) (1987) *Reform in China: Challenges and Choices* Armonk, NY, M.E. Sharpe

——(ed.) (1988) *Chinese Economic Reform: How Far, How Fast?* San Diego, Ca: Academic Press

Rosefielde, Steven (1980) 'A comment on David Howard's estimate of hidden inflation in the Soviet Union' *Soviet Studies* vol. 32, no. 3, July, pp. 423–7

——(1981) 'Hidden inflation in the Soviet Union: a rejoinder to David Howard' *Soviet Studies* vol. 33, no. 4, October, pp. 610–5

——(1988) 'The Soviet economy in crisis: Birman's cumulative disequilibrium hypothesis' *Soviet Studies* vol. 40, no. 2, April, pp. 222–44

Rostowski, Jacek (1989) 'Market socialism is not enough: inflation vs unemployment in reformed communist economies' *Communist Economies* vol. 1, no. 3 , pp. 269–85

'The ruble must still earn its title' (1990) *Problems of Economics* vol. 33, no. 3, July, pp. 54–65

Rudcenko, S. (1979) 'Household money income, expenditure and monetary assets in Czechoslovakia, GDR, Hungary, and Poland, 1956–1975' *Jahrbuch der Wirtschaft Osteuropas* vol. 8, pp. 431–50

Rumer, Boris (1990) 'The "Abalkanization" of Soviet economic reform' *Problems of Communism* vol. 39 January–February, pp. 74–82

Samansky, Arthur W. (1981) *China's Banking System: Its Modern History and Development* Research Paper no. 8108, New York: Federal Research Bank of New York, December

Samuelson, Paul A. and Nordhaus, William D. (1985) *Economics* 12th edn, New York: McGraw–Hill

Santorum, Anita (1989) *The Control of Money Supply in Developing Countries: China, 1949–1988* Working Paper no. 29, London: Overseas Development Institute, April

Schroeder, Gertrude, E. (1982) 'Managing labour shortage in the Soviet Union' in Adam (1982) pp. 3–25

Schüller, A. and Hamel, H. (1985) 'On the membership of socialist countries in the International Monetary Fund' *Acta Oeconomica* vol. 34, Nos 1–2, pp. 113–30

Shehuizhuyi Huobi Xinyong Xue (1981) (The Study of Socialist Money and Credit Peking: China Finance and Economics Publishing House

Shelton, Judy (1989) *The Coming Soviet Crash: Gorbachev's Desperate Pursuit of Credit in Western Financial Markets* New York: The Free Press; London: Collier Macmillan

Sherer, John L. (1978–85) *China Facts and Figures Annual* vols 1–8, Gulf Breeze, Fl.: Academic Institutions Press

Shi Lei (1982) 'Jiandingde zhixing wending huobi fangzhen' (Resolutely implement a policy of monetary stability) *Zhongguo Jinrong* (Chinese Finance) no. 2, pp. 2–4

Shubik, Martin (1987) 'Fiat money' in Eatwell, Milgate and Newman (1987) vol. 2 pp. 316–7

Smith, Alan H. (1983) *The Planned Economies of Eastern Europe* London and Canberra: Croom Helm

Smith, Keith (ed.) (1986) *Soviet Industrialization and Soviet Maturity* London and New York: Routledge and Kegan Paul

Socha, Meiczyslaw (1989) 'Wages and incentive problems' in Clarke (1989a) ch. 3

Sokil, Catherine and King, Timothy (1989) 'Financial reform in socialist economies: workshop overview' in Kessides et al. (1989) pp. 1–27

Solinger, Dorothy (1984) *Chinese Business under Socialism: The Politics of Domestic Commerce 1949–1980* Berkeley: University of California Press

——(1987) 'The 1980 inflation and the politics of price control' in Lampton (1987) pp. 81–118

Solntseva, M. (1990) 'Can inflation be beaten?' *Far Eastern Affairs* no. 2, pp. 81–92

Soviet Financial System (1966) Moscow: Progress Publishers

Stalin, Joseph (1930) 'Political report of CC to XVI Congress of CPSU (B)' in *Works* vol. 12, Moscow: Foreign Languages Publishing House, 1955 pp. 242–385

Stevens, John N. (1985) *Czechoslovakia at the Crossroads: The Economic Dilemmas of Communism in Postwar Czechoslovakia* East European Monographs, Boulder, Col., distributed by Columbia University Press, New York

Szczepanik, E. (ed.) (1962) *Symposium on Economic and Social Problems of the Far East* Hong Kong: Hong Kong University Press

Tam On-kit (1986) 'Reform of China's banking system' *World Economy* vol. 9, no. 4, December, pp

——(1987) 'Development of China's financial system' *Australian Journal of Chinese Affairs* no. 17, January, pp. 95–113

Tan Shouding (1984) 'On the demonetization of gold: a reply to Professor Li Chonghuai' *Social Sciences in China* vol. 5, no. 2, June, pp. 83–96

Tarafás, I. (1985) 'The possibility and conditions of anti-inflationary policy in Hungary' *Acta Oeconomica* vol. 34, nos 3–4, pp. 287–97

Tardos, M. (1980) 'The role of money: economic relations between the state and the enterprises in Hungary' *Acta Oeconomica* vol. 25, nos 1–2, pp. 19–35

——(1985) 'Question marks in Hungarian fiscal and monetary policy (1979–1984)' *Acta Oeconomica* vol. 35, nos 1–2, pp. 29–52

——(1988) 'Can Hungary's monetary policy succeed?' *Acta Oeconomica* vol. 39, nos. 1–2, pp. 61–79

Teichova, Alice (1988) *The Czechoslovak Economy 1918–1980* London and New York: Routledge

Thornton, Judith (ed.) (1976) *Economic Analysis of the Soviet-type System* Cambridge: Cambridge University Press

Treml, Vladimir G. (1989) 'Dr. Vanous's "dark side of glasnost" revisited' *Comparative Economic Studies* vol. 31, no. 4, Winter, pp. 95–109

Treml, Vladimir G. and Hardt, John P. (eds) (1972) *Soviet Economic Statistics* Durham, NC: Duke University Press

Tsakok, Isabelle (1979) 'Inflation control in the People's Republic of China, 1949–1974' *World Development* vol. 7, pp. 865–75

Tsang Shu-ki (1990) 'Controlling money during socialist economic reform: the Chinese experience' *Economy and Society* vol. 19, no. 2, May, pp. 217–41

Tseng Ling and Han Lei (1959) *The Circulation of Money in the People's Rupublic of China* Moscow; English translation published by CCm Information Corporation, New York, 1970

Tsiang, S.C. (1976) 'Money and banking in Communist China' in Joint Economic Committee, United States Congress, *An Economic Profile of Mainland China* vol. 1, Washington, DC: Government Printer, pp. 323–39

Van der Lijn, N.J. (Nick) (1990) 'Repressed inflation on the consumption goods market: disequilibrium estimates for the German Democratic Republic, 1957–1985' *Journal of Comparative Economics* vol. 14, no. 1, March, pp. 120–9

Vanous, Jan (1980) 'Private foreign exchange markets in Eastern Europe and the USSR' Discussion Paper no. 80–20, University of British Columbia, Department of Economics, Vancouver, July

Varga, Stefan (1958) 'Money in socialism' *International Economic Papers* no. 8, pp. 201–35

Vengerskaya Narodnaya Respublika (1983) (The Hungarian People's Republic) Academy of Sciences of the Soviet Union, Institute of the Economics of the World Socialist System, Moscow: Nauka Publishing House

Vortmann, Heinz (1989) 'The state budget' in German Institute for Economic Research (DIW) (1989) pp. 145–51

Wang Ping (1975) 'Long-term stability of "Renminbi"' *Peking Review* no. 15, 23 May, pp. 18–21

Wang Tong-eng (1980) *Economic Policies and Price Stability in China* Berkeley: Institute of East Asian Studies, University of California, Berkeley, Centre for Chinese Studies

——(1988) 'Aggregate price changes in China: a comment' *Soviet Studies* vol. 40, no. 1, January, pp. 142–5

Wang Xiyi (1981) 'Yao jixu jianchi huilong huobide fangzhen' (We must continue to adhere to the policy of withdrawing money from circulation)' *Zhongguo Jinrong* (Chinese Finance) no. 7, pp. 22–3

Wanless, P.T. (1985) 'Inflation in the consumer goods market in Poland, 1971–82' *Soviet Studies* vol. XXXVII, no. 3, July, pp. 403–16

Wei Xia (1975) 'No inflation in China: long-term balance in revenue and expenditure' *Peking Review* no. 10, 16 May, pp. 16–7

White, Gordon and Paul Bowles (1988) 'China's banking reforms: aims, methods and problems' *National Westminster Bank Quarterly Review* November, pp. 28–37

Wilczynski, J. (1978) *Comparative Monetary Economics* London: Macmillan

——(1982) The Economics of Socialism, 4th edn, London: George Allen and Unwin

Wiles, Peter (1973) 'Cost inflation and the state of economic theory' *Economic Journal* no. 83, June, pp. 377–98

——(1982) 'The worsening of Soviet economic performance' in Drewnowski (1982) ch. 7

——(1988a) 'Economic policies under Andropov and Chernenko (November

1982 — February 1984 — March 1985)' in Wiles (1988) pp. 217–50

——(ed.) (1988b) *The Soviet Economy on the Brink of Reform: Essays in Honor of Alec Nove* Boston: Unwin Hyman

Wilson, Dick (1986) 'China's bankers learn a new game' *The Banker* vol. 136, no. 726, pp. 14–25

Wimberley, James (1981) 'The Soviet financial crisis: a comment' *Soviet Studies*, vol. 33, no. 3, July, pp. 444–5

Winiecki, Jan (1985) 'Portes ante portas: a critique of the revisionist interpretation of inflation under central planning' *Comparative Economic Studies* vol. 27, no. 2, Summer, pp. 25–51

——(1986) 'Soviet-type economies: considerations for the future' *Soviet Studies* vol. 38, no. 4, October, pp. 543–61

——(1988) *The Distorted World of Soviet-type Economies* London and New York: Routledge

Wolf, Thomas A. (1990) 'Macroeconomic adjustment and reform in planned economies' International Monetary Fund, European Department, Washington Working Paper WP/90/27, April

World Bank (1983) *China: Socialist Economic Development* 3 vols, Washington, DC: World Bank

——(1989) *World Development Report 1988* New York: Oxford University Press for the World Bank

——(1990) *China: Macroeconomic Stability and Industrial Growth under Decentralized Socialism* Washington, DC: World Bank

Wu Cuilan (1989) 'China's reform of the financial and tax systems' in Kessides et al. (1989) pp. 56–63

Wu Yuan-li (1956) *An Economic Survey of Communist China* New York: Bookman Associates

——(ed.) (1973) *China: A Handbook* Encyclopedia Britannica Inc. Australia

Wyczalkowski, Martin R. (1966) 'Communist economies and currency convertibility' *International Monetary Fund Staff Papers* vol. 30, July, pp. 155–97

Xia Xiaoxun and Li Jun (1987) 'Consumption expansion: a grave challenge to reform and development', in Reynolds (1987) ch. 6

Xu Meizheng (1989) 'Structural reform and financial reform in China' in Kessides et. al. (1989) pp. 126–32

Yang Pei-hsin (Yang Peixin (1975) 'Why China has no inflation' *China Reconstructs* no. 4, April, pp. 4–9

Yeh Chang-mei (1985) 'Mainland China's financial reforms: money and banking' *Issues and Studies* vol. 21, no. 6, June, pp. 80–99

Young, Susan (1991) 'Wealth but not security: attitudes towards private business in China in the 1980s' *Australian Journal of Chinese Affairs* no. 25, January, pp. 115–37

Zaichenko, Alexandr (1990) 'Sobstvennost' kazhdomu — ili chto takoye ekonomicheskoye raskayaniye' (Property to everyone — or what economic repentance is)' *Moskovskiye Novosti* (Moscow News) no. 41, 14 October

Zaitsev, A. (1981) 'The personal savings of the working people under developed socialism' *Problems of Economics* vol. 22, no. 10, February, pp. 64–77

Zalai, Ernó (1988) 'Recent changes in the planned central management system of Hungary and their background' in Brada and Dobozi (1988) pp. 53–65

Zeng Qixian (1983) 'Comments on consumption and savings' *Social Sciences in China* vol. 4, no. 4, pp. 137–63

Zhang Fengbo (1988) *Zhongguo Hongguan Jingji Jiegou yu Zhengce* (China's Macroeconomic Structure and Policies) Peking: China Finance and Economics Publishing House

Zhongguo Maoyi Wujia Tongji Ziliao 1952–1983 (1984) (Statistical Materials on Trade and Prices in China) Peking: China Statistics Publishing House

Zhongguo Shangye Waijing Ziliao 1952–1988 (1990) (Statistical Materials on China's Trade and Foreign Economic Relations 1952–1988), Peking: China Statistics Publishing House

Zhongguo Tongji Nianjian 1981 (1982) (Statistical Yearbook of China) overseas Chinese language edn, (1982) Hong Kong: Economic Information and Agency

——1983, 1984, 1985 (various years) Hong Kong: Economic Information and Agency

Zhongguo Tongji Nianjian 1987 (1988) (Statistical Yearbook of China) Peking: China Statistical Publishing House

——1988, 1989, 1990 (various years) Peking: China Statistical Publishing House

Zhou Zhenhua (1987) 'Tonghuo pengzhangde bijiao fenxi' (A comparative analysis of inflation)' *Caimao Jingji* (Finance and Trade Economics) no. 11, pp. 56–60

Zwass, Adam (1979) *Money, Banking, and Credit in the Soviet Union and Eastern Europe* London: Macmillan.

Index